A-level Study Guide

Law

Revised and Updated

Mary Charman

Jacqueline Martin

Chris Turner

Revision Express

Series Consultants: Geoff Black and Stuart Wall

Project Manager: Julia Morris

Pearson Education Limited

Edinburgh Gate, Harlow

Essex CM20 2JE, England

and Associated Companies throughout the world

© Pearson Education Limited 2000, 2004

British Library Cataloguing in Publication Data

A catalogue record for this title is available from the British Library.

ISBN 1-405-82120-5

First published 2000

Reprinted 2001

Updated 2004

10 9 8 7 6 5 4 3 2

09 08 07 06

Set by 35 in Univers, Cheltenham

Printed by Ashford Colour Press, Gosport, Hants

Sources of law

The sources of law refer to where the law comes from and how it is made. They are important areas and you need to understand them not just for the English legal system but to have a better understanding of substantive law areas. The original sources were custom and then case law, and later equity also. More recently, as Parliament has become more significant, legislation has become more important. Since 1 January 1973 when we joined the EC, European law has also become a vital source of many areas of law such as employment and consumer protection.

Exam themes

→ Binding and persuasive precedent

→ Judicial law making, the use of the Practice Statement 1966 and the limitations on the Court of Appeal

→ Advantages/disadvantages of delegated legislation

→ Comparisons between delegated legislation and legislation

→ The literal/purposive debate in statutory interpretation

→ The use of intrinsic aids and the limitations on use of extrinsic aids

→ Comparisons between the EU institutions

→ The effects of EU membership on the sovereignty of Parliament

→ Comparisons between different law reform bodies

→ The extent to which the limitations of the doctrine of precedent prevent judges from reforming or changing the law

Topic checklist

○ AS ● A2	AQA	OCR	WJEC
Common law and precedent	○	○	○
Precedent and appeal courts	○	○	○
Legislation	○	○	○
Statutory interpretation	○	○	○
European law institutions and sources	○	○	○
The effects of EU membership	○	○	○
Law reform	○	○	○

Common law and precedent

English law originally began with local and general customs which gradually became law. As customs became applied generally throughout the country and the common law developed, case law also became very important in establishing individual principles of law. The common law was later added to by equity which brought some basic fairness into a system that was becoming harsh and rigid.

Common law

The phrase 'common law' can often confuse students because it can have different meanings depending on the context in which it is used:

→ It can refer to the law that developed after the Norman Conquest that became 'common' to the whole country.

→ It can be used to distinguish the law that is developed in the courts from that made in Acts of Parliament or other legislation.

→ When referring particularly to remedies it can be used to distinguish rules that developed in the old common law courts from the rules of equity that developed in the courts of Chancery.

→ Finally we may also refer to a 'common law' system rather than a 'civil system' such as that in France, meaning a system based on development through cases rather than being based on a code.

Equity

Equity created a variety of interests that were not otherwise available such as trusts, and the equitable redemption of a mortgage. It also introduced many remedies more suited to claimants' actual needs such as injunctions, specific performance and rescission.

Case law and the doctrine of precedent

Case law and the doctrine of precedent are very important to your study of the law. This is not just because it is one of the oldest sources of law and there are now at least 400 000 reported cases, but also because large areas of law such as **tort** are to be found mainly in cases. **Judicial precedent** is the most important aspect of case law. It is the means by which judges make law for other judges to follow in the future, so it depends on the principles in past cases being followed in present cases where the material facts are similar. This is the doctrine of *stare decisis* (let what has been decided stand). The doctrine is very rigidly applied in English law. It depends also on a strict hierarchy of courts.

→ The part of the judgment that produces precedent for judges to follow in the future is known as the *ratio decidendi*, meaning the reason for the decision. It is not always easy to find the *ratio* in a case, and a case can have more than one *ratio*.

→ Other parts of a judgment are called *obiter dicta* or 'things said by the way'. They may be what the judge thinks the law would be if the facts were different and do not affect the outcome of that case.

Test yourself

Try to write down these different definitions of common law from memory.

Checkpoint 1

Can you describe any of these interests or remedies?

The jargon

Tort is a simple French word meaning 'wrong'.

"... *the principle of law that decides the case in the light of the material facts* ..."

Zander

Binding precedent ●●●

A binding precedent is one that must be followed by the court in a later case even if the judges do not agree with the principle in it. A binding precedent can only come from the *ratio decidendi* of a past case. It can apply in a future case only if the facts of the second case are sufficiently similar to those in the first, and if the precedent was made in a court capable of binding the court hearing the later case.

Persuasive precedent ●●●

Persuasive precedent is not binding on any court but judges may wish to apply it in later cases. It can come from various sources:

→ *obiter dicta* from a decided case, e.g. *obiter* comments in *Rondel v Worsley* (1969) were later applied by the court in *Saif Ali v Sidney Mitchell & Co.* (1980)
→ *dissenting* judgments from senior judges, e.g. the House of Lords in *Hedley Byrne v Heller & Partners* (1964) accepted Lord Denning's dissenting judgment in *Candler v Crane Christmas & Co.* (1951)
→ judgments of the Privy Council and Commonwealth courts

Ways of avoiding precedent ●●●

There are only a limited number of means available to avoid precedent:

→ overruling – the precedent is declared wrong in a later case
→ reversing – on appeal the higher court changes the decision of the court below
→ distinguishing – the precedent is not applied because the material facts are essentially different, e.g. the principle in *Balfour v Balfour* (1919) was not applied in *Merritt v Merritt* (1971)

Advantages and disadvantages of precedent ●●●

Advantages include:

→ certainty and predictability
→ saving time and money
→ consistency and precision in the law
→ flexibility

Disadvantages include:

→ rigidity and complexity
→ slowness to change outdated and obsolete laws
→ the possibility of illogical distinguishing

Exam questions   answers: page 18

1   Distinguish between binding precedent and persuasive precedent. (20 min)

2   Using cases in illustration, consider the extent to which judges have been able to develop the law despite the constraints of the doctrine of precedent. (45 min)

Checkpoint 2

Explain the difference between the *ratio decidendi* and *obiter dicta*.

Test yourself

Try to write down these three and other sources of persuasive precedent from memory, with illustrations if possible.

Checkpoint 3

Can you say what a dissenting judgment is?

Test yourself

From memory, briefly try to explain and illustrate each of these ways of avoiding precedent.

Checkpoint 4

Why is certainty an advantage and complexity a disadvantage?

Examiner's secrets

You can impress the examiner in question 2 by using an example from the area of law you have studied such as the law on intention in murder, or nervous shock in tort.

Precedent and appeal courts

The doctrine of precedent not only depends on the judges following principles of law from past cases, it also depends on the existence of a hierarchy of courts. Each court is bound to follow applicable precedents from higher courts or those of equal status in the hierarchy. The inferior courts do not make precedents so just follow those of higher courts.

The hierarchy of courts

The European Court of Justice

European law does not affect all areas of English law. However, if a point of European law is at issue then since 1973 the European Court of Justice (ECJ) is the highest court. Decisions made in this court are binding on all courts in England and Wales, although not on the ECJ itself.

The House of Lords

This is the highest national court. Its decisions are binding on all of the courts below. Traditionally it was bound by its own past decisions as in *London Street Tramways v London County Council* (1898). Now it can avoid its past decisions because of the 1966 Practice Statement.

The Court of Appeal

The Court of Appeal is split into two divisions: Civil and Criminal. Both are bound to follow decisions of the House of Lords and ECJ. The divisions also bind the respective civil and criminal courts below them. In limited circumstances each court can avoid its own past decisions.

Divisional Courts of the High Court

Divisional Courts are where the three divisions of the High Court (Family, Chancery and Queen's Bench) hear appeals or exercise a supervisory role. They are bound by all the courts above them, and bind those courts below. They are also bound by their own past decisions but have similar flexibility to the Court of Appeal.

The High Court

The High Court is bound by all the higher courts and in turn binds all the courts below. Judges do not have to follow decisions of other High Court judges but will usually do so.

Inferior courts

The Crown Court, the County Court, and the Magistrates' Court must all follow the decisions of the higher courts. They do not, however, create any precedent themselves, although technically a point of law made by a judge in the Crown Court binds the Magistrates' Court.

Test yourself

See whether you can list the inferior courts without reading any further.

Checkpoint 1

What are the circumstances in which the House of Lords could avoid a past decision after *London Street Tramways v LCC*?

Test yourself

Try to remember the cases that say when the Court of Appeal can avoid its own past decisions before you read any further.

Checkpoint 2

Make a list of the civil courts from highest to lowest and a separate one for the criminal courts.

Don't forget

In answers on precedent don't just list how precedent operates in all the different courts unless this is what the question actually calls for.

The House of Lords and the 1966 Practice Statement

In 1966 the Law Lords recognized that, while the doctrine of precedent was important to ensure certainty, too rigid an approach could stifle the development of law. The Lord Chancellor issued the Practice Statement by which they would be able to 'depart from a previous decision when it appears right to do so'. This flexibility was only to be available to the House of Lords and they would only be able to use it:

→ to avoid injustice in the present case
→ to avoid restricting the proper development of the law

So House of Lords judges may *overrule* past decisions they think are wrong or inappropriate. They do so sparingly to maintain certainty. In fact in *Jones v Secretary of State for Social Services* (1972) they would not overrule the decision in *Re Dowling* (1967) even though they all felt this would lead to injustice and some felt the case had been wrongly decided. It was first used in *Conway v Rimmer* (1968) but only on a technical point. The first major use was in *B R Board v Herrington* (1972) overruling *Addie v Dumbreck* (1929) on the duty of care owed to a trespasser. They were less willing to use it in criminal law where *R v Shivpuri* (1986), overruling *Anderton v Ryan* (1985) on impossible attempts, was the first case, and then only to correct their own error.

The Court of Appeal and avoiding its own decisions

While the Court of Appeal is usually bound by its own past precedent there are some exceptions to this basic rule. These are to be found in *Young v Bristol Aeroplane Co.* (1944). These are:

→ where there are two conflicting past decisions of the Court of Appeal, the court may choose one and reject the other
→ where there is a later inconsistent decision of the House of Lords, the court must follow the House of Lords' decision
→ where the decision was made *per incuriam*, or without reference to all the appropriate authorities

Because of the possible loss of liberty, the Criminal Division can also avoid its own decisions if the law has been 'misapplied or misunderstood' as in *R v Taylor* (1950) and *R v Gould* (1968). Lord Denning always argued that the Court of Appeal should have the same power as the House of Lords, as CA hears many more cases. He altered House of Lords' decisions in *Broome v Cassell* (1971) and *Schorsch Meier v Hennin* (1975), and past Court of Appeal decisions in *Davis v Johnson* (1978) but was criticized by the House of Lords.

Exam questions   answers: pages 18–19

1   Critically examine the circumstances in which the Practice Statement has been used. (20 min)

2   To what extent can a judge in the Court of Appeal be a judicial innovator or reformer of law? (20 min)

Checkpoint 3

When does the Practice Statement suggest that judges should be careful to avoid changing the law?

Watch out!

Candidates often confuse overruling and reversing. Make sure that you know the difference between the two.

Action point

Make brief notes on the facts of these cases for your revision.

Test yourself

Write down the three exceptions in *Young* from memory.

The jargon

Per incuriam literally means through lack of care.

Checkpoint 4

Say why Lord Denning was criticized by the House of Lords in these cases.

Examiner's secrets

Many of Lord Denning's cases above may be useful in answering question 2.

Legislation

The jargon

Acts of Parliament are often also referred to as 'statutes'.

The jargon

Subordinate or delegated legislation mean the same: that law is passed by a body other than Parliament but which is usually given the power to do so by Parliament.

Checkpoint 1

Can you think of any law originally introduced by Private Member's Bill?

Watch out!

Private Bills and Private Member's Bills are quite different. Try not to confuse the two.

The jargon

'Green papers' and 'white papers' are so called because of the colour of the paper on which they are printed.

Checkpoint 2

Can you think why the Royal Assent is always given?

Don't forget

In essays on the passage of a Bill remember to refer to the stages in both Houses of Parliament and the Royal Assent.

Test yourself

Try to write down these five stages from memory.

Legislation developed later than common law as a major source of law. However, it is now more important because Parliament is supreme and can make or unmake any law, and Acts cannot be challenged by the courts (although this is different in the case of EC law). Legislation comes in the form of Acts of Parliament which are first introduced as Bills, but there is also subordinate or delegated legislation passed by bodies or individuals given the appropriate authority to do so, which can be scrutinized.

Types of Bills

There are three main types of Bills which may involve different procedures:

→ Public General Bills – the most common, involving the Government's programme affecting the whole country
→ Private Bills – only apply to a particular body or a local authority
→ Private Member's Bills – any MP or Lord may introduce Bills on issues of concern to them

Stages leading to the introduction of legislation

Most parliamentary law comes out of the Government's own programme. However, Bills may eventually be introduced as a result of other pressures which might include Reports from Royal Commissions, Law Commission Reports, or even public pressure. Where the need for legislation is identified, the Government will usually introduce first a *green paper*, which invites the opinions of interested parties. Once evidence has been taken into account a *white paper* is then published. Specific proposals are then drafted in a *Bill* by Parliamentary Counsel and passed to Parliament, usually the House of Commons. 'Lawyer's law' is often introduced first in the House of Lords.

The passage of a Bill

Bills become Acts when they have gone through a number of stages in both the House of Commons and the House of Lords and received approval and gained the *Royal Assent*. In practice, the House of Lords only have a delaying power, and the Queen's approval is never refused.

The stages in both the House of Commons and the House of Lords are:

→ First Reading – the title of the Bill and its main aims are read out; this is the formal introduction of the Bill
→ Second Reading – the main debate on the Bill followed by a vote which needs a majority in favour for the Bill to go any further
→ Committee Stage – a Standing Committee examines the Bill clause by clause and amendments are made
→ Report Stage – the amended Bill is reported back to Parliament for consideration

→ Third Reading – this is the final debate and vote on the Bill and only minor amendments can be added at this stage

Delegated legislation ●●●

Delegated legislation consists of rules and regulations introduced by bodies other than Parliament. The use of this type of law has grown with the development of the welfare state and the introduction of new types of rights.

Reasons for using delegated legislation

1 Parliament does not have time to debate every small detail of law so enabling Acts are passed, e.g. the Social Security Act 1986, and the detail is left to be filled in by the appropriate department.
2 Parliament will not always have the necessary expertise to deal with the particular issue, whereas a government department may have, and local authorities have knowledge of local needs.
3 Delegated legislation can be changed more easily and allows a quicker response to changing circumstances.
4 Parliament cannot always respond quickly enough in emergencies.

The different types of delegated legislation

There are three types, all introduced by different bodies: .

→ **Statutory Instruments** – these are produced by government departments, and will follow '*enabling Acts*'. They are introduced either by '*affirmative resolution*', which includes some debate, or more commonly by '*negative resolution*' which does not.
→ **Orders in Council** – these are introduced by the Privy Council in times of emergency, such as war.
→ **By-laws** – these are introduced by local authorities or sometimes by large bodies authorized to produce such rules, like the railways. They will only involve matters of local concern or appropriate to the regulation of the body introducing them.

The methods of controlling delegated legislation

Delegated legislation is not introduced by democratic methods as Acts of Parliament are so it is important to be able to ensure that it can be more easily scrutinized. There are two principal methods:

→ Parliamentary Scrutiny Committees – which can question the Minister who introduced the Act and the civil servants
→ Judicial Review – in the Queen's Bench Division (QBD) of the High Court where the legislation can be examined to see if it is *ultra vires*

Exam questions answers: page 19

1 Compare the processes by which Acts of Parliament and Statutory Instruments become law. (20 min)

2 Discuss the advantages and disadvantages of delegated legislation. (20 min)

Action point

Try to think of some of the rights that can be found in the form of delegated legislation.

Checkpoint 3

Say which of these reasons apply to the different types of delegated legislation indicated below.

Test yourself

Try to memorize a list of the different bodies that can introduce delegated legislation.

Test yourself

Try to memorize these three different types of delegated legislation.

Checkpoint 4

Briefly explain what is meant by judicial review.

The jargon

Ultra vires means 'beyond the powers'.

Examiner's secrets

'Compare' in question 1 means that you should add some critical comment, not just describe the processes.

Statutory interpretation

Checkpoint 1

See if you can think of a case to illustrate each of these reasons for interpreting a statute.

Action point

Make brief notes on the points of interpretation in the Interpretation Act.

The jargon

The *canons of construction* is merely another name for the three basic rules.

> *"If the words of an Act are clear you must follow them even though they lead to a manifest absurdity."*
>
> Lord Esher

Watch out!

The golden rule is only used by judges who would prefer to use the literal rule.

Don't forget

Few candidates remember to discuss both applications of the golden rule in exam answers but doing so would get you high marks.

Checkpoint 2

What criticisms are made against the use of the mischief rule?

Statutes and delegated legislation may need interpreting because of the use of ambiguous words, or of broad terms, drafting errors, changes in the use of language over time, use of technical words, or unforeseen developments when the Act or instrument was passed. Parliament has provided some help to interpretation with the Interpretation Act 1978, and many Acts have *interpretation sections*. The judges have also developed some non-binding rules and there are other aids. There is a conflict between whether a *literal approach* or a *purposive approach* should be used.

The three rules or 'canons of construction' ●●●

These have been developed through case law. Different judges prefer different rules so that the law may differ according to which judge is interpreting the statute.

Literal rule

This is where a judge gives the words their '*plain, ordinary or literal meaning*' regardless of whether the result is sensible or fair.

→ This can lead to absurd results as in *Whiteley v Chappell* (1868).
→ It can also lead to injustice as in *LNER v Berriman* (1946).
→ It can also punish Parliament by making it pass another Act as in *Fisher v Bell* (1960).

Golden rule

This is an extension of the literal rule and is only used if the literal rule leads to an absurdity, in which case the words are given a more appropriate meaning. There are two ways of using the golden rule:

→ the narrow approach – which would be used when the words have more than one meaning and the better meaning is chosen, *Adler v George* (1964) where 'in the vicinity of' could include 'in'
→ the broader approach – which is when the words actually have only one meaning but the judges do not want to apply it for policy reasons, *Re Sigsworth* (1935) where a son was thus prevented from inheriting from the mother he had murdered

Mischief rule

This is the oldest rule coming from the four-point procedure identified in *Heydon's case* (1584). The court should:

→ look at the law prior to the passing of the Act
→ identify the 'mischief' or thing missing from the previous law
→ identify the way that Parliament proposed to remedy the defect
→ give effect to that remedy

The rule is useful where things have changed since the Act was introduced, *Corkery v Carpenter* (1951).

Language rules

The courts have developed some rules which apply only in certain linguistic situations:

→ *ejusdem generis* – where a list of specific words in an Act is followed by general words, the general words are limited to the same kind as the list, *Powell v Kempton Park Racecourse* (1899)
→ *expressio unius est exclusio alterius* – the express mention of one thing excludes another of a different kind, *Tempest v Kilner* (1846)
→ *noscitur a sociis* – a word is known by the company it keeps, *Inland Revenue Commissioners v Frere* (1965)

Presumptions

Judges also presume certain things to be the case unless the Act says something different, e.g.:

→ that *mens rea* is required in crime, *Sweet v Parsley* (1970)
→ that the Crown is not bound
→ the presumption against change of the common law
→ the presumption against retrospective legislation

Intrinsic and extrinsic aids

Intrinsic (or internal) aids are those aids that can be found within the Act itself. They are generally used by all judges, but may be of limited help. They include long and short titles, preamble, schedules, headings and interpretation sections. The **extrinsic** (or external) aids are things outside the Act. Some of these are more helpful but their use is more controversial. They include dictionaries, the historical context, similar Acts, and more controversially Law Commission Reports, and, since *Pepper v Hart* (1992), Hansard, the record of daily debate in Parliament.

The literal/purposive debate

The purposive approach is a more modern approach and has been influenced by membership of Europe as it is widely used in European law. It is simply giving effect to what the judges see as the purpose of the Act rather than concentrating on the words as in *Royal College of Nursing v DHSS* (1981). Judges favouring the literal rule say that the purposive rule is too creative and ignores the clear words. More judges though are now using the approach.

Exam questions   answers: pages 19–20

1   Using cases in illustration, discuss the difficulties that may arise when applying the literal rule of interpretation. (20 min)

2   Consider the argument that the rules of statutory interpretation are merely an excuse for a judge to do as he wishes. (45 min)

The jargon

Ejusdem generis literally means of the same type.

Test yourself

Try to write down the three language rules and their explanations from memory.

Don't forget

Examiners often want you to use presumptions or language rules in answering problem questions.

The jargon

'*Intrinsic*' and '*extrinsic*' are only different ways of saying inside and outside.

Checkpoint 3

Write down the conditions stated in *Pepper v Hart* for when Hansard can be consulted.

Checkpoint 4

How does this case illustrate the literal/purposive debate?

Action point

Try to write down and explain why judges may not want interpretation to be 'too creative'.

Examiner's secrets

Try to refer to the other rules and aids in statutory interpretation essays rather than just explaining the three rules.

European law institutions and sources

Britain has been a member of the European Union (European Community) since 1973. As a result EC law is our law and can be used in English courts. It affects many social and economic areas such as the regulation of business and of employment and also the protection of consumers. The major institutions affect the making and administration of EC law and the day-to-day running of the Union. The UK is represented in all the institutions, as is each member state.

The member states

The European Community originally formed in 1957 with six countries: France, Italy, Germany, Belgium, The Netherlands and Luxembourg. Since then nine others have joined – the UK, Eire, Denmark, Spain, Portugal, Greece, Sweden, Finland and Austria. There are a number of other countries that also want to become member states. Ten countries are currently being considered for future membership.

European institutions

There are four main institutions that control the Community or Union, as it is now known. But there are other important institutions besides.

The Council of Ministers

This is the real law-making body of the EU. It is not a permanent body as such. The membership depends on what subject is under discussion when it meets, so if it concerns the Common Agriculture Policy it will be a meeting of Agriculture Ministers. Voting is weighted so individual member states have votes proportionate to their population. Some matters require a unanimous vote, e.g. changes to the Treaties. Others require only a 'qualified majority' of 62 out of the 87 votes available.

The Commission

This is made up of 20 Commissioners, two each for the bigger states and one each for the smaller ones, supported by a staff of around 9 000. Commissioners are appointed by their member states for a four-year term, but must act independently of them. They are each given an area of responsibility, e.g. transport, environment. The Commission formulates policy and prepares draft legislation. It is responsible for the budget and day-to-day administration. It is also the 'guardian of the Treaties' and has *locus standi* in the ECJ to bring enforcement actions.

The European Parliament (formerly the Assembly)

The Parliament's main function is to discuss the Commission's draft proposals, so it has a mainly consultative role in legislating. The number of seats is again weighted according to the size of the member state.

The jargon

The Community now refers to the original legal order created by the treaties. *The Union* is a wider concept created by the Maastricht Treaty.

Action point

Try to find the countries that make up this ten.

Take note

Other bodies include COREPER, the Economic and Social Committee, the Court of Auditors and the European Central Bank.

Checkpoint 1

Can you say what the 'European Council' is?

"The Commission proposes and the Council disposes."

Martin

The jargon

Locus standi means standing or right to take action.

The European Court of Justice

The ECJ is comprised of 15 judges, one from each member state, supported by six Advocates-General who prepare reasoned opinions on cases to submit to the court. Its purpose is to 'ensure that in the interpretation and application of the Treaty the law is observed'. The Court hears three different types of case:

→ actions against member states for their failure to honour Treaty obligations under Article 226 (ex Art 169)
→ actions against the institutions for exceeding their powers or for failing to act under Articles 230 and 232 (ex Art 173 and Art 175)
→ references from member state courts for preliminary rulings on interpretations of EC law under Art 234 (ex Art 177)

The Treaty of Nice has now altered and developed the roles of the institutions.

The sources of European law ●●●

There are a number of sources.

Primary sources

The Treaties are the most important source of law. They:

→ define the powers of the institutions
→ define the rights and obligations of the member states
→ state the broad objectives of the Treaties
→ provide some substantive law, e.g. free movement of workers under Art 39 (ex Art 48) or equal pay under Art 141 (ex Art 119)

Secondary sources

The main secondary source is the legislation introduced under Art 249 in the form of:

→ Regulations – these are *directly applicable* so they are automatically law in member states when passed, and apply throughout the Union
→ Directives – these are binding as to the result to be achieved, so member states should implement them within a strict time limit
→ Decisions – these are usually addressed to a particular individual or body and are binding on that body

The case law of the ECJ is another important source of legal principles.

General principles

A judge in the ECJ will always reach a decision after considering certain basic principles. These are *proportionality*, *equality*, *legal certainty*, and the *protection of human rights*.

Exam questions answers: pages 20–1

1 Compare and contrast the roles of the Commission and the Council of Ministers. (20 min)

2 Explain the sources of European law. (20 min)

Checkpoint 2

Can you remember the name of the other court that helps ease the burden of work on the ECJ?

Checkpoint 3

When will a court make a reference to the ECJ for an interpretation of law, and which courts *must* do so?

The jargon

Directly applicable means the rule applies without further implementation.

Test yourself

Try to write down the major differences between regulations and directives and then to memorize them.

Checkpoint 4

Give brief explanations of the general principles.

The effects of EU membership

Membership of the European Community and now the European Union inevitably involved a number of significant changes. All countries, as a result of joining, have 'pooled their national sovereignty' and there have been a number of important changes to the character of English law and the way that it is administered.

The UK and membership

The UK became a member of the EC as a result of signing the original three Treaties but also, because of the nature of the UK constitution, by passing the European Communities Act 1972 to incorporate the Treaties into English law. The most significant section is section 2(1) which says:

→ all EC law made before we joined was automatically incorporated into English law, at the expense of any inconsistent national law
→ all EC law made after we joined would also become part of our law

The UK has also since accepted the other Treaties that have extended the EC including the Single European Act 1986, the Treaty on European Union (Maastricht) 1992, the Amsterdam Treaty 1997, and the Treaty of Nice 1999.

Supranationalism

The EU is based on the idea of **supranationalism**. This simply means that on those issues covered within the Treaties, the European institutions have power to act over all member states. There are two very important consequences without which this could not work:

→ supremacy of EC law – prevails over all inconsistent national law
→ direct effect – EC law is enforceable in member states' courts

Supremacy of EC law

European law is ultimately beyond the challenge of the member states. The European Court of Justice has made this principle plain on a number of occasions.

The point was first established in *van Gend en Loos* (1962) where the Dutch government was prevented from introducing new customs duties. An early explanation of supremacy came in *Costa v ENEL* (1964) where the ECJ said that '*the member states have limited their sovereign rights, and have thus created a body of law which binds both their nationals and themselves*'.

The duty of national courts in relation to supremacy was made quite clear in *Simmenthal* (1977) where the ECJ said that it was '*the duty of national courts to give full effect to Treaty provisions and not to apply conflicting national law*'.

The most dramatic example of supremacy in action was in the *Factortame case* (1991) where the ECJ directed the House of Lords to suspend operation of the Merchant Shipping Act 1988 because it conflicted with the EC Treaty.

Direct effect ●●●

This is the mechanism that actually ensures supremacy of EC law since it means that rights created under EC law are enforceable throughout all 15 member states.

Direct applicability

Treaty Articles and Regulations are directly applicable, that is they need no further implementation and prevail over inconsistent national law. This was shown in *Re Tachographs: Commission v UK* (1979) when the Government unsuccessfully tried to delay introducing tachographs.

Direct effect of Treaty Articles and Regulations

Generally Treaty Articles and Regulations are 'complete' legal instruments so that if they are clear and create rights, a citizen of Europe can enforce them in a national court through direct effect. This was shown in *Van Duyn v Home Office* (1974).

Direct effect and Directives

Directives are problematic as they are not complete legal instruments but are left to member states to implement within a time limit. So they do not create individual rights. If the member state has failed to implement the Directive, the citizen has no national law to enforce. One way of getting round this is **vertical direct effect**. If the action is against the state or an *arm of the state* then the citizen can still enforce the Directive against the member state as in *Marshall v Southampton AHA* (1986) where a woman was able to prove that different retiring ages was discriminatory. The same action failed in the case of a claim against a private company in *Duke v GEC Reliance* (1988). Another possibility is the doctrine of '**indirect effect**'. Under the von Colson principle 'national courts are required to interpret their national law in the light of the wording and purpose of the Directive'. In *Marleasing* (1992) the ECJ took this a step further and said that under Article 10 of the Treaty (ex Art 5) all member states, including their courts, are bound to 'take all necessary steps to ensure the fulfilment of' obligations contained in a Directive.

Subsequently it is also possible for the citizen to claim damages from the state for a failure to implement a Directive. This is the so-called *Francovich* principle. Following *ex parte Factortame/Brasserie du Pecheur* it can be used where the directive confers rights, the state's breach is sufficiently serious, and there is a causal link between the breach and the damage suffered.

The jargon

Direct applicability means that the measure automatically becomes law in the member state.

Action point

Try to think of some directly effective provisions that you know.

Checkpoint 3

Can you say why the claimant lost in this case?

The jargon

Vertical direct effect is the obligation on the state to comply with the Directive.

The jargon

An *arm of the state* is a body that is under the control or pay of the state.

Checkpoint 4

Try to suggest why this principle is called indirect effect.

Action point

Try to produce a flowchart that explains how vertical direct effect, indirect effect and state liability are used for unimplemented or partially implemented directives.

Exam questions   answers: page 21

1   Discuss the effects of membership of the European Union on the English legal system. (45 min)

2   Compare the principles of horizontal direct effect and vertical direct effect. (20 min)

Examiner's secrets

You might like to add some more effects beside supremacy and direct effect in your answer to question 1.

Law reform

As we have seen, the law has developed through a number of sources. The Government has the major influence on what new laws are enacted and will produce legislation that corresponds with its political views. However, for the law to succeed it must be relevant and it needs to be changed and reformed to respond to the changing needs of society. Pressure for reform comes from various sources and reforms can come even through the common law.

Action point

Try to think of a recent Act that has responded to society's changing needs.

The purpose of law reform

By definition, to reform must mean to improve on what existed before. The main purpose of law reform then is to improve the law but there are a number of ways in which this can be achieved:

→ updating the law and making it more relevant, as well as removing outdated and irrelevant law
→ consolidating existing law to make it easier to find
→ making the law simpler to understand and more accessible by improving the language and by codifying it

Checkpoint 1

Can you give an example of a consolidating Act and a codifying Act?

Stimulus to law reform

Stimulus for reform can come from a variety of sources:

→ Party manifestos – all parties in advance of elections state their programmes for legislative reform; governments also produce their annual programme in the Queen's Speech.
→ Pressure groups – these can be of different types, e.g. interest groups (representing the particular interests of that group) such as a trade union, or cause groups, campaigning for specific principles such as LIFE on abortion or SHELTER on homelessness. If they gain a high profile and public support this may lead to reform.
→ Royal Commission Reports – usually these respond to particular crises such as the Taylor Report on football ground safety.
→ Reports from official law reform bodies such as the Law Commission – such bodies are bound to review the law and draft proposals for reform as with the Draft Criminal Code.

Checkpoint 2

Can you think of any recent Royal Commissions?

Agencies of law reform

The Government has set up various bodies, both full time and permanent and some on a more *ad hoc* and part-time basis. These are given the job of reviewing the law in general or specific aspects of it and suggesting proposals for reform.

The jargon

Ad hoc really means as and when needed, so such a body is not permanent and only sits when it is specifically directed to.

The Law Reform Committee
This is a part-time body called on occasions by the Lord Chancellor to consider areas of civil law. Its proposals led to the passing of the Occupiers' Liability Act 1957 and the Latent Damage Act 1986.

The Criminal Law Revision Committee

This was another part-time body that was able to sit and make recommendations for the reform of the criminal law. It was responsible for the codification of principles in theft leading to the Theft Act 1968, although this later had to be supplemented by the Theft Act 1978 because of problems in the first Act.

The Law Commission

This is the only full-time, permanent law reform body. It was created following the Law Commissions Act 1965. It consists of a Chairman and four Commissioners, and has a support staff and also parliamentary draftsmen to prepare draft legislation. The Law Commission's role is set out in section 3 of the Law Commissions Act, and includes keeping under review the whole of English law with a view to achieving certain objectives:

→ the systematic development and reform of the law
→ codification of certain areas – originally including family law, landlord and tenant law, contract law, and the law of evidence, although most of these have since been abandoned
→ the elimination of anomalies in the law
→ the repeal of obsolete law – by the time of the passing of the Statute Repeal Act 1995, which itself repealed 223 Acts and parts of 259 others, 1600 outdated Acts had already been repealed
→ the reduction of the number of separate enactments – which is achieved through regularly introducing consolidating Acts
→ the simplification and modernization of law

The Law Commission also has to research topics referred to it by the Government which can often detract from its own work. It has had some success, particularly in smaller areas of law. It has been responsible for many important Acts such as the Unfair Contract Terms Act 1977 and the Criminal Attempts Act 1981. In the 1980s very few of its proposals became laws and the **Jellicoe procedure** was introduced for areas that are not controversial. It also prepared a Draft Criminal Code in 1989, but this has not been enacted.

The common law and law reform ●●●

Judges have also been responsible for reforming areas of law in need of development or change. Examples are Lord Atkin's '**neighbour principle**' in *Donoghue v Stevenson* (1932) and the recent development of the offence of rape in marriage in *R v R (Marital rape)* (1991).

Action point

The Law Commissions Act was passed at the insistence of the Lord Chancellor, Lord Gardiner, as was the Practice Statement.

Check the net

http://www.lawcom.gov.uk/homepage/htm

Checkpoint 3

In what ways does the Government interfere with the work of the Law Commission?

The jargon

The *Jellicoe procedure* uses the Special Public Bills Committee of the House of Lords to speed up the process.

Checkpoint 4

Can you think of any important reforms introduced by Lord Denning?

Examiner's secrets

There is no need to write on bodies other than the Law Commission in question 1 but you should give some examples of what it has achieved.

Exam questions   answers: page 22

1   In the light of its role, consider to what extent the Law Commission has been successful. (20 min)

2   Distinguish between 'codification' and 'consolidation' and give examples. (20 min)

Answers
Sources of law

Common law and precedent

Checkpoints

1 A mortgage is a means of borrowing money to buy property with the lender being given the property for security. Trusts are a means of transferring property into the legal ownership of a person who will look after the interests of the beneficial owner. Injunctions are orders of the court to prevent someone from doing something. Specific performance is an order to carry out a contract. Rescission is putting parties back to their pre-contractual position.
2 *Ratio decidendi* is the principle of law leading to the decision, *obiter dicta* is legal comment that is not relevant to the decision but may be influential in later cases.
3 One where the judge disagreed with the majority.
4 Certainty allows lawyers to predict the outcome of cases. Complexity means there may be too much law to consider.

Exam questions

1 This is a short question or part of a question. You should first define what precedent is: *stare decisis*, following principles of law from past cases. You might also add the comment that precedent in English law is very strictly applied.

   Define both *binding precedent* and *persuasive precedent*: binding = past precedent that must be followed in future cases; persuasive = other statements of law that need not be followed but can be influential.

   Say where binding precedent comes from: the *ratio decidendi* of a past case (the principle of law that decided the case), and that binding precedent can only come from the *ratio*.

   Say where persuasive precedent comes from: *obiter dicta* (extra comments in judgments), dissenting judgments, Commonwealth courts.

   Add cases in illustration, e.g. *Rondel v Worsley* can be used for *ratio* and *obiter dicta*.
2 This question has three aspects to it: an explanation of the doctrine of precedent, and of the limited areas of flexibility within it, and a discussion of cases that illustrate judicial innovation (so you will almost certainly be discussing Lord Denning).

   First you should define precedent (*stare decisis*), as following the principles of law coming from the judgments of decided cases and being binding on future cases involving similar facts.

   The hierarchy of courts is also important because it identifies what flexibility there is. The House of Lords has the Practice Statement 1966, allowing it to depart from past precedent 'when it is right to do so'; the Court of Appeal has the three exceptions in *Young v Bristol Aeroplane*, two conflicting decisions, inconsistent House of Lords decision, *per incuriam* decision. The Criminal Division has more flexibility because of loss of liberty, *R v Gould*.

   Identify three main ways of avoiding precedent. Overruling, generally only available to HL and it rarely uses Practice Statement, see *Jones v Secretary of State for Social Services*. Reversing, only applies in appeals, *Milliangos v George Frank Textiles*. Distinguishing because material facts are different, *Balfour v Balfour* and *Merritt v Merritt*.

   Use any cases that show the law developing, e.g. *Donoghue v Stevenson* on negligence, *High Trees* on estoppel, *R v R (Marital Rape)* removing doctrine of implied consent, *Schorsch Meier v Hennin* and *Milliangos v George Frank Textiles* on awarding damages in other currency.

   Finally you should conclude on the extent to which judges have been able to develop law despite this constraint.

Precedent and appeal courts

Checkpoints

1 If the case was decided *per incuriam* or if it was inconsistent with a subsequent statute.
2 *Civil*: European Court of Justice (ECJ), House of Lords (HL), Court of Appeal (CA) (Civil Division), Divisional Courts, High Court, County Court, and Magistrates' Court. *Criminal*: ECJ, HL, CA (Criminal Division), Divisional Court of QBD, Crown Court, and Magistrates' Court.
3 Contracts, property, tax law, and criminal law.
4 Because he was in effect overruling HL precedents, which CA cannot do, or CA precedents against the doctrine.

Exam questions

1 This is a short question or one from a data response paper. It still requires some discussion rather than just fact. There are two aspects to it: how the Practice Statement works and an examination of the cases using it.

   Explain the Practice Statement. It applies only to HL. HL can depart from past precedent 'when it is right to do so', which is either to aid the proper development of the law or to avoid injustice in the present case; HL should avoid disturbing contracts, property settlements, tax matters and the criminal law.

   Consider the occasions when HL has used the Practice Statement to change or develop the law. HL was originally quite reluctant to use it even to avoid injustice, *Jones v Secretary of State for Social Services*, and has not used it often. The first time was on a technical point in *Conway v Rimmer*. First major civil use was *Herrington v B R Board* on duty of care owed to trespassers. First major criminal use not till 1986 in *R v Shivpuri* on criminal attempts and then it was to rectify their own mistake in *Anderton v Ryan*.

2 Again this is a short question or part of a question requiring some critical discussion as well as fact.

First you need to give a brief explanation of the doctrine of precedent, following the principles from the *ratio* of past cases where applicable.

Second you need to identify the position of the Court of Appeal within the doctrine. There is a rigid hierarchy, with CA being bound by the decisions in courts above (HL and ECJ). CA binds all courts below. It is usually bound to follow its own past decisions subject to the exceptions in *Young v Bristol Aeroplane*: two conflicting decisions, later inconsistent HL decision, *per incuriam* decision. Criminal Division has greater flexibility because of loss of liberty *Gould*. So CA has little chance to be innovative.

Finally consider cases that show when it has been innovative, mostly under Lord Denning, e.g. *Broome v Cassell, Schorsch Meier v Hennin, Davis v Johnson, Central London Properties Trust v High Trees House*. Note also the reactions of HL in these cases.

Legislation

Checkpoints

1 The Abortion Act 1967, the Computer Misuse Act 1990, the Obscene Publications Act 1959.
2 Because by convention the monarch will not interfere in government.
3 1, 2 and 3 could apply to Statutory Instruments; 4 could apply to Orders in Council; 2 could apply to By-laws.
4 A process whereby the legitimacy of decisions by administrative and judicial bodies can be challenged in the QBD acting as a Divisional Court.

Exam questions

1 This is a short answer with a hidden element of critical appreciation since it asks for comparison of the two processes, so they must also be evaluated.

Describe the process by which Acts are made. A green paper may be circulated for consultation. This may then become a white paper and a Bill is introduced into Parliament. It goes through two readings (debates and votes), a committee stage, a report stage and a third reading in the Commons and the Lords and then receives Royal Assent to become law as an Act.

Statutory Instruments are drafted by individual departments and implement regulations from an 'enabling Act', e.g. the Social Security Act 1986. They are rarely offered out for consultation. They can be introduced by one of two procedures: a 'negative resolution' – here the instrument becomes law after a proscribed period with no debate unless an MP objects to it; an 'affirmative resolution' – where there is some debate.

Some comment should also be made on the method of introducing Acts being a democratic process with Parliamentary scrutiny, and the method of introducing Statutory Instruments being undemocratic. Reasons for using them might also be considered.

2 This is a straightforward short question. It does say discuss so it requires more than a mere list.

First of all it would be a good idea to briefly describe what delegated legislation is and why it is used. Power is given to subordinate bodies to introduce rules within the scope of their authority. It includes Statutory Instruments introduced by government departments, Orders in Council introduced by the Privy Council, and by-laws introduced by local authorities or certain public bodies like the railways.

Advantages include: suitability for wide-ranging schemes, e.g. Social Security law; allows flexibility; saves time, Parliament does not have to debate all of the 'nuts and bolts' of the law; allows consultation with interested parties; allows for local knowledge; saves money on lengthier processes; can be drafted by specialists.

Disadvantages include: undemocratic procedure; danger of arbitrary decision-making; lack of effective scrutiny; lack of debate which usually adds amendment; lack of publicity so that measures become law before anybody realizes.

Some comment might also be added that it would be impossible to do without delegated legislation, as it is vital for modern situations.

Statutory interpretation

Checkpoints

1 Ambiguity, *Adler v George*; broad terms, *R v Allen*; drafting errors and technical words, *Fisher v Bell*; changes in language, *Cheeseman v DPP*; unforeseen developments, *RCN v DHSS*.
2 It does not concentrate on the actual words, and allows judges to be too creative.
3 The legislation is ambiguous, obscure or leads to absurdity; the part to be consulted was written by the Minister introducing the Bill or other promoter; the part to be consulted is clear.
4 The judges in the different courts took different approaches and even HL was split 3:2.

Exam questions

1 This is a short question focusing on the difficulties created when using the literal rule. Cases must be used in illustration for an effective answer.

Briefly explain what statutory interpretation is, i.e. interpreting specific words of an Act which may be ambiguous when applied to practical or modern situations.

Explain that over time judges have created certain rules and will use certain aids to help them in the process of interpretation.

Define the literal rule: if the words are clear giving them their plain, ordinary, literal meaning even if this leads to an absurdity (Lord Esher in *R v Judge of the City Of London Court*).

Discuss any of the apparent problems in using the literal rule. It may lead to absurd results, *Whiteley v Chappell*. It may cause injustice, *London North Eastern Railway v Berriman*. It may ignore the apparent wishes of Parliament, *Magor & St Mellons v Newport Corporation*. It can 'punish' Parliament by making it pass another Act, *Fisher v Bell*. The Law Commission criticized it for demanding 'an unattainable perfection in drafting'. It may rely on dictionary definitions but these often give many meanings.

2 This is an extensive question and requires both a detailed explanation of all the rules and aids used and commentary on how they are used by judges. The rules and aids should be supported by cases, and appropriate critical comments made.

- Three 'canons of construction' – literal rule means giving 'plain, ordinary, literal meaning', i.e. dictionary meaning, but this can lead to absurd results, *Whiteley v Chappell*, injustice, *Berriman*, and thwart Parliament's intention, *Fisher v Bell*, etc. Golden rule means giving better meaning if literal rule fails and can be applied narrowly to overcome ambiguity, *Adler v George*, or broadly for public policy reasons, *Re Sigsworth*, but it is 'an unpredictable safety valve'. Mischief rule from *Heydon's case* with its four stages or purposive approach, giving effect to purpose, *RCN v DHSS*.
- Language rules: *ejusdem generis* for general words after lists of specific words, *Powell v Kempton Park Racecourse*, *expressio unius* for excluding words not mentioned *Tempest v Kilner*, and *noscitur a sociis* keeping to the context of the words, *IRC v Frere*.
- Presumptions, e.g. of *mens rea* in crime, or that the Crown is not bound, or no retrospective law.
- Intrinsic aids – those found in the statute itself such as titles, schedules, interpretation sections. Extrinsic aids – found outside the Act, e.g. dictionaries, other Acts, and more controversially Hansard, Law Commission Reports, etc. The Interpretation Act 1978 can also be mentioned.
- Valid comments can also be made, e.g. that the rules are judge-made not legal rules, that we have no idea when which rule will be used, that judges taking the purposive approach are criticized for being too creative, etc.

European law institutions and sources

Checkpoints

1 The twice-yearly meeting of heads of state.
2 The Court of First Instance.
3 Where an interpretation of EC law is necessary for the national court to be able to resolve the case and there is no existing interpretation. Where the court will give the final ruling in the national process, it must make a reference to the ECJ for an interpretation.
4 *Proportionality*: nothing should be done that is out of proportion to the actual need. *Equality*: there should be no discrimination between nations or individuals. *Legal certainty*: there should be no retrospective measures that would prevent parties from exercising legitimate expectations. *Protection of human rights*: no arbitrary decision-making, basic rights respected.

Exam questions

1 This is a short question but again it is asking you to compare and therefore to evaluate the two institutions.

Although it is only a short question you should still identify the two institutions and say something of their composition.

The Commission is not the real lawmaker of the EU but it does have a powerful role in drafting legislation. It has 20 Commissioners, each with a distinct responsibility (Directorates). They are selected by their member states but should act independently of them. It has a staff of around 9 000. The Commission has three main purposes: drafting legislative proposals for presentation to the Council of Ministers; acting as administrator to the European Union, managing the budget, etc; acting as the 'watchdog' or 'guardian' of the Treaties, ensuring they are honoured by both member states and the institutions.

The Council of Ministers is a fluid concept but has Ministers from member states, the identity of whom depends on the topic being considered. They will represent member states' interests and may thwart the real interests of the Union. They pass legislation prepared by the Commission, usually by a 'qualified majority' voting system.

In comparing the two you should also consider that the Council is the most powerful body despite what is said about the Commission, and that European principles may be sacrificed in order to appease national interests, as was the case at Maastricht. On the other hand the Commission is a fundamentally undemocratic institution enjoying much influence over the direction of the Union as well as being the day-to-day power administratively.

2 This is a short question or part of a question and is straightforward in that it only asks you to explain. There is no requirement for critical discussion, so you should account for the sources methodically and with some illustration if you can.

The primary source of law is the Treaties. Most importantly these set out the objectives of the Treaties such as the 'four freedoms'. They also define the role and powers of the institutions, as well as defining the rights and obligations of the member states. Through Article 249 (ex Art 189) they also provide the mechanisms for legislation and define the different types of legislation. Finally they do provide some substantive law which can often be enforced by European citizens, e.g. equal pay under Art 141 (ex Art 119) and free movement of workers under Art 39 (ex Art 48).

Secondary sources include the three main types of legislation: Regulations which are directly applicable, e.g. 1612/68 on workers' families; Directives which require implementation by member states, e.g. 76/207 on equal access; and Decisions which are directed to an individual or body but are then totally binding on them.

The case law of the ECJ is also a secondary source and you should be able to give examples: *Van Duyn v the Home Office*, *Bulmer v Bollinger*, or *Macarthys v Smith*.

Finally there are the general principles of law such as proportionality, equality, the right to legal certainty, and the protection of human rights.

Examiner's secrets

For question 1 remember that 'compare and contrast' requires some comment as well as factual information on the institutions' roles.

The effects of EU membership

Checkpoints

1 European Coal and Steel Communities Treaty, EURATOM (Atomic energy and research), European Communities Treaty.
2 Spanish fishermen were prevented from fishing in UK waters because of the Merchant Shipping Act 1988 which was inconsistent with EC law.
3 Because the UK could use Article 48(3) to deny her access on the ground of public policy.
4 Because it is being given effect through indirect means.

Exam questions

1 This is a question on the really controversial aspect of EC law. You will be required to say something about membership but also to look at the effects in detail and it is not as simple as loss of sovereignty.

First of all membership should be explained. The UK joined Europe by signing all the Treaties and then by incorporating the process into English law by the European Communities Act 1972. The most important section is section 2(1) which says that all existing EC law at that time automatically became law, and all future EC legislation would also be given force. As part of that membership the UK has also had to sign other Treaties since, though on occasions it has 'dragged its feet'. As a result of membership we have given up certain rights to

legislate contrary to Treaty objectives, and this is the loss of sovereignty often referred to. In fact a 'pooling' of sovereignty is a more accurate description.

EC law works because of supremacy, the principle that European law takes precedence over inconsistent national measures. There are many clear statements of supremacy: *Costa v ENEL*, *Simmenthal*, and particularly *Factortame* where the effect was to allow English judges to suspend operation of an English Act of Parliament in order to grant injunctive relief.

Member state citizens can also enforce European law in national courts through the principle of direct effect. A number of cases illustrate direct effect, *Defrenne v SABENA* on Art 141 (ex Art 119) on equal pay, *Van Duyn v Home Office* on free movement under Art 39 (ex Art 48). Direct effect of Directives has been a problem where the state has not implemented them, but the ECJ has got round this where vertical direct effect can apply, e.g. *Marshall*, and also where indirect effect can apply, because of Art 10 (ex Art 5) *Marleasing*.

It should be remembered that citizens now have a number of rights they did not have formerly. After Maastricht they are also European citizens.

Finally another effect is the move towards purposive interpretation which is common in Europe, e.g. *RCN v DHSS*.

2 This is a short question, probably part of a question and requires some detailed understanding of a quite difficult area.

Direct effect should firstly be defined: it is the principle whereby a provision of European law becomes directly enforceable in a national court. This may be easy with Treaty Articles, e.g. *Van Duyn v Home Office*.

Horizontal direct effect means that the principle of European law is enforceable by one citizen against another citizen. So again this may be easy with provisions that are already part of national law, but it can be a problem with Directives which require implementation.

Vertical direct effect is the obligation on the state to give effect to that provision so an individual employed by the state may still enforce it, e.g. *Marshall*. In comparison, the same Directive was unenforceable against an employee of a private firm in *Duke v GEC Reliance*.

Don't forget

Directives are never horizontally directly effective because they are not complete in themselves but depend on implementation by the member state – candidates often make the mistake that they are.

Examiner's secrets

Question 2 is the ideal example of where you might draw a diagram to illustrate the point and show the examiner your understanding of the concepts.

Law reform

Checkpoints

1 Consolidating: Employment Protection (Consolidation) Act 1978. Codifying: Theft Act 1968.
2 The Runciman Commission on criminal justice.
3 By giving it other things to investigate, and by not introducing draft Bills into Parliament.
4 Promissory estoppel in contract law, divorced wife's equity in family law.

Exam questions

1 There are two aspects here, examining the role of the Law Commission and discussing its success.

   The Law Commission is the only full-time law reform body and has statutory authority from the 1965 Act to review the law. Its objective is 'the systematic development and reform of the law' and its role includes: codifying the law where possible; eliminating anomalies in the law and repealing outdated and obsolete law; reducing the volume and complexity of law and making it simpler by introducing consolidating statutes, making the law more accessible. It also has to research matters sent to it by government.

   It has had much success in simplifying and repealing more than 1 800 Acts. It has had less success in codifying and has abandoned areas like evidence and family. Originally many of its proposals were enacted but this reduced in the 1980s, e.g. the Draft Criminal Code.

2 This is only a short question and you only need to provide good definitions of consolidation and codification. But it does ask for examples so try to give some.

   Consolidation occurs where the existing law is laid out in a number of Acts. It is the process of gathering together these various provisions into a single Act so that it is more accessible. The Law Commission produces about five consolidation Bills each year. The Health and Safety at Work Act 1974 and the Employment Rights Act 1996 are examples.

   Codification is aimed at bringing together all the law on a single area into a single Act and making it much simpler and much easier to follow. The Law Commission has produced a Draft Criminal Code. Critics of codes say that they require too much interpretation so eventually the law builds up with many cases on the area to consult also.

The courts and legal process

It is important to be able to identify civil issues and criminal issues and to be able to distinguish between civil and criminal cases. Do not confuse them, as the type of case, the terminology, the court structure and procedures are all different for civil and criminal cases. There have been problems with both civil justice and criminal justice and reforms of some areas have been made in an effort to improve access to justice.

Exam themes

→ Problems of the system and reforms

→ Scenarios on civil or criminal cases

→ Police powers

→ Miscarriages of justice

→ Aims of sentencing and their application in cases

Topic checklist

○ AS ● A2

	AQA	OCR	WJEC
Civil cases and courts	○	○	○
ADR and tribunals	○●	○	○
Criminal cases and courts	○	○	○○
Criminal appeals: miscarriages of justice	○	○	○●●
Police powers		○	●●
Sentencing aims	○	○	●●
Sanctions: civil and criminal	○	○	●●

Civil cases and courts

The civil justice system is designed to decide disputes between individuals. You need to know the nature of civil cases, the court structure and procedure. You need to be able to identify the problems that have occurred with the system and to discuss the reforms that have been made.

Civil cases

Civil claims will arise when an individual or a business believes that their rights have been infringed in some way. Civil cases cover a wide range of issues, as there are different areas of civil law. These include:

→ contract
→ tort
→ family law
→ employment law
→ company law

The types of dispute that can arise are equally varied. A claim may be for a few pounds or for several million. Money may not be the point at issue: another remedy such as an injunction may be sought or the court may be asked to order the winding up of a company or to grant a decree of divorce.

Civil courts

The party starting a court case is called the claimant and the other party is the defendant. A court where a case is first heard is called a court of first instance. For civil cases these are:

→ the County Court
→ the High Court

In addition the Magistrates' Court hears some civil cases, especially family matters.

Problems of using the courts

→ cost – can be more than the amount of the claim
→ delay – it can take five years from the incident to a trial in the High Court
→ complexity – the procedure is confusing for the ordinary person

As a result of these problems, the procedure for cases was changed in April 1999 by the Woolf reforms. The small claims limit was increased to £5000 and the fast-track procedure introduced. Other reforms included encouraging the use of **ADR**, simpler documents and procedures and giving judges more responsibility for managing cases.

Taking a case to court

For most cases the claimant may start proceedings in any County Court or the High Court *except*:

Checkpoint 1

Give examples of disputes that could arise in
(a) contract law and
(b) tort

Checkpoint 2

Can you name the three divisions of the High Court and briefly explain the types of cases that each deals with?

Check the net

There is up-to-date information on the civil courts at www.lcd.gov.uk

---

Checkpoint 3

Try to explain the reforms recommended by Lord Woolf in more detail.

The jargon

ADR stands for Alternative Dispute Resolution.

→ personal injury cases for less than £50 000 must be started in a County Court

→ claims for less than £15 000 must be started in a County Court

All cases are started by filling in a claim form, taking it to the court office and paying the appropriate fee. The claim is then sent to the defendant.

Allocation of cases

If the defendant puts in a defence to the claim, the case will be allocated to the most suitable method of trial. There are three tracks:

→ small claims for cases under £5 000 (except personal injury cases and housing disrepair cases where the limit is £1 000)

→ fast-track for claims between £5 000 and £15 000

→ multi-track for cases over £15 000 or smaller complex claims

Small claims

Litigants are encouraged to take proceedings without using lawyers and there are simple leaflets setting out all the necessary procedures which are available from the court or from Citizens' Advice Bureaux. The advantages of the small claims procedure are:

→ dealt with in a less formal way than in the main County Court

→ district judge will take an active role by asking questions

→ costs are kept low

→ litigants are encouraged to take their own case since the winner cannot claim the costs of using a lawyer from the losing party

Appeals ●●●

In most cases if either party is not satisfied with the decision it is possible to appeal. The general rules on appeals are:

→ from a decision of the small claims court and for fast-track cases the appeal is to the next level of judge, e.g. from a District judge to a Circuit judge

→ for multi-track cases the appeal is to the Court of Appeal (Civil Division)

→ from a decision of the Court of Appeal there is a further appeal to the House of Lords, but only if they give permission to appeal

→ if a point of European law is involved the case may be referred to the European Court of Justice under Article 234 of the Treaty of Rome (such a referral can be made by any English court)

The jargon

The *allocation fee* is a fee paid when the case is allocated to one of the three tracks.

Test yourself

Write down the details of the three tracks from memory.

Checkpoint 4

Make a list of any disadvantages of the small claims procedure.

Action point

Draw a diagram showing these appeal routes.

Examiner's secrets

Often the examiner wants you to look at the wider issues of taking cases to court, so check you also understand funding and ADR.

Exam questions answers: page 38

1   What problems are there in taking a civil case to court? (30 min)

2   Frank has bought some expensive machinery from XYZ Co Ltd. The machinery does not work properly and Frank has complained several times to XYZ Co, but they have ignored his complaints. Frank has decided to sue XYZ. Explain to him which courts the case could go to and what appeal routes are available if he loses the case at first instance. (30 min)

ADR and tribunals

"ADR is an umbrella term . . . applied to a range of techniques for resolving disputes."

Hazel Genn

Action point

Make a chart of the different methods of dispute resolution.

Checkpoint 1

List the advantages of using mediation or conciliation rather than taking a case to court.

Test yourself

From memory write out the list of different types of ADR.

Check the net

The Centre for Dispute Resolution has a website at www.cedr.co.uk

Checkpoint 2

Can you list three advantages and three disadvantages of using arbitration to resolve a dispute?

In civil matters whenever individuals and/or businesses have a dispute most parties concerned will want that dispute resolved fairly, quickly and cheaply. As the courts are criticized for being too slow and too costly there has been a growth in other methods of dispute resolution.

Alternative Dispute Resolution

This is any method of resolving a dispute without resorting to using the courts. The most common methods of ADR are:

→ **negotiation** where the parties or their lawyers try to resolve the problem themselves
→ **mediation** where a neutral mediator helps the parties to reach a compromise solution
→ **conciliation** where a third person actively puts ideas for compromise between the parties
→ **arbitration** where the parties refer the dispute to an independent third party to decide

The advantages of negotiation, mediation and conciliation are that the decision need not be a strictly legal one. It is more likely to be based on commercial realism and may include agreements about the conduct of future business between the parties. There are many organizations that offer mediation services. One of the main ones is the Centre for Dispute Resolution. Many important companies, including some of the big London law firms, have used the Centre's services to resolve disputes and say that this has saved several thousands of pounds in court costs.

Arbitration

An agreement to go to arbitration can be made at any time, even before a dispute arises, by the inclusion of a *Scott v Avery* clause in a contract. This is a clause where the parties in their original contract agree that in the event of a dispute arising between them, they will have that dispute settled by arbitration.

The arbitrator

The agreement to go to arbitration will either name an arbitrator or provide a method of choosing one. Often in commercial contracts it is provided that the president of the appropriate trade organization will appoint the arbitrator. There is also the Institute of Arbitrators which provides trained arbitrators for major disputes. In many cases the arbitrator will be someone who has expertise in the particular field involved in the dispute, e.g. a surveyor in a building dispute.

The award

The decision made by the arbitrator is called an award and can be enforced through the courts if necessary.

Tribunals

Administrative tribunals are statutory creations designed to help enforce rights that have been granted through social and welfare legislation. There are over 2 000 tribunals covering areas such as social security, rent, immigration, and employment.

Composition and procedure

Most tribunals have a legally qualified chairman and two lay members who have expertise in the particular field of the tribunal.

The procedure for each type of tribunal varies but there are common elements in that the system is designed to encourage individuals to bring their own cases and not use lawyers. There are no formal rules of evidence and procedure but the rules of natural justice apply.

Control of tribunals

The **Council on Tribunals** was set up in 1958 to supervise and keep under review the working of tribunals. The Council receives complaints about tribunals and issues an annual report. The main problem is that the Council has very little power; it can only make recommendations.

The **Queen's Bench Divisional Court** hears applications for judicial review against tribunal decisions and can use its prerogative powers, e.g. where there has been a breach of natural justice.

Finally there is an **appeal system** against the decisions of some tribunals, e.g. to the Employment Appeal Tribunal.

Advantages of tribunals

→ Tribunals are cheaper and quicker than the courts.
→ The procedure is simple, with a more informal hearing than in court and most cases are heard in private.
→ Experts are involved in the decision-making.

Disadvantages of tribunals

Government funding is not available for most tribunals. This may put an applicant at a disadvantage if the other side (often an employer or government department) uses a lawyer. Tribunals do not always give reasons for their decisions; this makes it difficult to appeal against the decision. Tribunals do not always follow precedent, so it is difficult to predict the outcome.

Exam questions   answers: page 39

1   Critically comment on why there has been an increased use of ADR to resolve disputes. (30 min)

2   Explain the role played by tribunals in our legal system. (30 min)

Don't forget

Tribunals have to be used for certain types of cases. There is no right to go to court.

Checkpoint 3

Can you give examples of the types of persons who sit as lay members of a tribunal?

Checkpoint 4

Can you explain what the rules of natural justice are?

Action point

Make a chart of the advantages and disadvantages of tribunals.

Examiner's secrets

The examiner likes you to show that you understand why alternative methods of resolving disputes are needed.

Criminal cases and courts

There are two levels of criminal court, the Magistrates' Court and the Crown Court. The Magistrates' Court deals with summary cases, while the Crown Court hears serious cases, known as indictable offences, such as murder, manslaughter and rape. You also need to understand the prosecution process and the role of the Crown Prosecution Service.

Bail

At any point after being arrested a person can be bailed either by the police pending further inquiries or when charged to appear at court or by a court at any stage during the criminal proceedings. Bail means release from custody on condition that the person returns at a set date to either a police station or a court.

Checkpoint 1

There are two situations when there is a presumption against bail. Do you know what these are?

The Bail Act 1976

This is the key Act and starts with the assumption that an accused person should be granted bail. In most cases there is a right to bail but the court need not grant a defendant bail if there are substantial grounds for believing that the defendant, if released on bail, would:

→ fail to surrender to custody
→ commit an offence while on bail
→ interfere with witnesses or otherwise obstruct the course of justice

Checkpoint 2

What other factors do the courts consider when deciding whether to grant bail?

The court can also refuse bail if it is satisfied that the defendant should be kept in custody for his own protection.

Conditions can be imposed on the grant of bail, such as ordering the accused to reside at a bail hostel, to surrender his passport or to report to a police station each day.

Sureties can be demanded; these are people who are prepared to promise to pay a sum of money if the defendant does not attend court in answer to his bail.

Action point

Make your own notes on the role of the Magistrates' Court.

Magistrates' Court

These have jurisdiction over a variety of matters involving criminal cases in their location, especially:

→ trying summary offences and the majority of triable either way offences; these make up 97% of all criminal trials
→ mode of trial proceedings to decide whether a triable either way case will be tried in the Magistrates' Court or the Crown Court

Checkpoint 3

Can you explain what is meant by summary offences, triable either way offences and indictable offences?

→ sentencing committals where magistrates send defendants to the Crown Court because their sentencing powers are not adequate
→ early administrative hearings in indictable offences to deal with bail and legal aid prior to the case being transferred to the Crown Court
→ youth court cases where the defendant is aged 10–17 inclusive
→ matters connected with criminal cases, such as issuing warrants of arrest or deciding bail applications

Crown Court

The first stage at the Crown Court is a Plea and Directions Hearing when the defendant is asked how he pleads to the charges. If the plea is guilty the judge will sentence the defendant, or, if necessary, adjourn the case for reports before sentencing. If the plea is not guilty then the prosecution and defence must inform the court of the issues in the case and the number of witnesses so that a date for jury trial can be arranged.

Choosing trial by jury

The right to choose trial by jury is seen as an important protection of civil liberties. Up to 20 000 defendants charged with an either way offence elect to be tried at the Crown Court each year. Twice in 2000 the House of Lords rejected bills aimed at abolishing the right to elect jury trial. The Government proposes increasing the sentencing power of magistrates so that fewer cases will need to go to the Crown Court. It is also proposing to allow defendants at the Crown Court to opt for trial by judge alone, if they wish to do so.

Implications of jury trial

→ more expensive, about £17 500 for a Crown Court trial as against £1 700 for the same case to be tried in the Magistrates' Court
→ defendant more likely to get legal aid and be represented by an advocate
→ trial by one's peers at the Crown Court
→ higher chance of acquittal – 60% compared with 25%

Crown Prosecution Service ●●●

The Crown Prosecution Service (CPS) was established by the Prosecution of Offences Act 1985. Previously prosecutions were normally conducted by the police, but it was thought that the investigation of crime should be separated from the prosecution of cases. The CPS is headed by the Director of Public Prosecutions (DPP).

Operation of the CPS

After the police charge a defendant, the papers are sent to the CPS to see whether there is sufficient evidence and whether it is in the public interest to continue the case. There has been criticism that the CPS discontinues too many cases. In 1998 the Glidewell Report was very critical of the CPS and this led to decentralization of the service, with Chief Crown Prosecutors being appointed for each of the 42 new areas. Following the Narey Review (1997), Criminal Justice Units have been set up so that the police and the CPS can work more closely together.

answers: page 39

Exam questions

1 To what extent does the law on bail strike a fair balance between protecting the public and allowing those charged with a crime the right to liberty while awaiting trial? (30 min)

2 Critically comment on the role of the Crown Prosecution Service. (30 min)

Checkpoint 4

Explain the role of the jury in a Crown Court trial.

Watch out!

Watch out for changes being made to the criminal justice system by the proposed Criminal Justice Bill 2002.

Checkpoint 5

Can you list the main differences between trials in the Crown Court and the Magistrates' Court?

"The powers of the CPS to discontinue cases . . . caused frustration on the part of victims."

Davies, Croall and Tyrer

Examiner's secrets

The examiner likes you to show that you are aware of the conflicts that arise in topics such as bail and prosecution of offenders.

Criminal appeals: miscarriages of justice

> *"[The Court of Appeal] shall allow an appeal . . . if they think that the conviction is unsafe."*
>
> Criminal Appeal Act 1995

It is important to have a 'safety net' so that cases can be rechecked to make sure that there has not been a miscarriage of justice. Our legal system provides appeal routes for defendants in all criminal cases. There is also the Criminal Cases Review Commission which looks at cases where there is a doubt about the defendant's guilt.

Appeals from the Magistrates' Court ●●●

There are two quite different appeal routes from a decision in the Magistrates' Court.

→ *An appeal to the Crown Court* This is available only to the defence. An appeal can be made against sentence and/or conviction. The case will be reheard at the Crown Court by a judge and two magistrates. Normally the decision by the Crown Court is final, but it is possible for a further appeal to be made to the Queen's Bench Divisional Court on a point of law as below.

→ *An appeal to the Queen's Bench Divisional Court* This is available to the prosecution or the defence. It is an appeal on a point of law by way of **case stated**. This means that the magistrates set out their findings of fact and these are accepted as accurate so that the appeal concentrates on how the law applies to those facts. Following a decision by the Queen's Bench Divisional Court both the prosecution and the defence may appeal to the House of Lords. It is necessary to have the case certified as involving a point of law of general public importance and to have leave to appeal.

Appeals from the Crown Court ●●●

By the defence
When a defendant has been found guilty, his lawyer should advise him on the possibility of an appeal. Notice of appeal must be filed at the Court of Appeal (Criminal Division) within six weeks of conviction. An appeal can be:

→ against conviction on a point of law, fact or mixed law and fact
→ against sentence

Leave to appeal is necessary in all cases. It is difficult to get leave to appeal as about 75% of applications are refused. Even when a defendant gets leave to appeal that does not mean automatic success.

By the prosecution

→ *Against an acquittal* The prosecution has no right of appeal against a finding of not guilty by a jury, but under section 36 of the Criminal Justice Act 1972, the Attorney-General can refer a point of law for the Court of Appeal to rule on. The decision by the Court of Appeal does not affect the acquittal but it creates a precedent for any future case involving the same point of law.

Checkpoint 1

Can you name a case in which there was an appeal by way of case stated?

Action point

Draw a diagram showing the appeal routes from the Magistrates' Court.

Checkpoint 2

Do you know which judges sit in the Court of Appeal?

Action point

Make a chart showing the differences between the defence rights of appeal and the prosecution rights of appeal in the Crown Court.

→ *Against sentence* The Attorney-General can appeal against an unduly lenient sentence under section 36 of the Criminal Justice Act 1988.

Appeals to the House of Lords

In theory both the prosecution and the defence may appeal from the Court of Appeal to the House of Lords. In practice there are only about five appeals each year. It is necessary to have the case certified as involving a point of law of general public importance and to get leave to appeal, either from the House of Lords or from the Court of Appeal.

Miscarriages of justice ●●●

The functions of an appeal process are to:

→ check that the court of first instance reached the correct result and to put matters right if it did not
→ safeguard the integrity of the criminal justice system
→ provide for the harmonious development of the law

In the 1980s and early 1990s there were a number of miscarriages of justice and the Runciman Commission was set up to consider the whole criminal justice system. The Criminal Appeal Act 1995 makes the grounds for allowing an appeal clearer: the Court of Appeal will allow any appeal where it considers the conviction unsafe and will dismiss it in any other case.

Criminal Cases Review Commission (CCRC) ●●●

This is an independent review body set up to consider possible miscarriages of justice. Previously the Home Secretary had the power to review cases and refer them to the Court of Appeal, but cases such as the Birmingham Six and Judith Ward left people feeling that the Home Secretary was not sufficiently independent of the Government. The Commission has the power to investigate possible miscarriages of justice (including summary offences) and to refer cases back to the courts on the grounds of conviction and/or sentence.

Delays

In the first three years of its operation the CCRC was asked to look at over 3 000 cases. This caused a wait of two years for a full review of cases. By the beginning of 2003, the CCRC had referred 184 cases to the Court of Appeal, but only 124 of these had been heard. Of this 124, the Court of Appeal had quashed the conviction in 82 cases.

Exam questions   answers: page 40

1 Jonas is being tried at Amster Crown Court on a charge of attempted murder.
   (a) If Jonas is convicted, advise him on his rights to appeal.
   (b) If Jonas is acquitted, advise the prosecution on their rights to appeal.
       (30 min)
2 Discuss whether the criminal justice system has adequate safeguards in cases of miscarriage of justice. (30 min)

Checkpoint 3

Can you name a case that went on appeal to the House of Lords?

"An effective criminal justice system needs to strike a balance between punishing the guilty and protecting the innocent."

Elliott and Quinn

Check the net

The CCRC has a website at www.ccrc.gov.uk

Checkpoint 4

Can you name a case in which the Court of Appeal quashed the conviction after the Criminal Cases Review Commission referred the case to the court?

Examiner's secrets

The examiner wants you to show clear knowledge of the appeal system for question 1. Vague answers are not enough.

Police powers

It is necessary to obtain a balance between protecting individual liberty and preventing/detecting crime. Parliament has tried to regulate this area of the law and the main police powers are set out in the Police and Criminal Evidence Act 1984 (PACE), as amended by the Criminal Justice and Public Order Act 1994.

Stop and search

Section 1 of PACE gives the police the right to stop and search people and vehicles in a public place. There must be reasonable grounds for suspecting that the person is in possession of (or the vehicle contains) stolen goods or prohibited articles such as offensive weapons. As the power is very wide there are safeguards in that the police officer must give his name and station and the reason for the search. If the search is in public, only outer clothing of coat, jacket and gloves can be removed. A written report has to be made as soon as possible after the search.

Checkpoint 1

Which Code of Practice sets out rules about the use of stop and search powers?

Searching premises

The police can enter premises without the occupier's permission to make a search if:

→ a warrant has been issued by a magistrate (section 16); the warrant need not be shown on entry, only before the search starts, *R v Longman* (1988)
→ it is necessary in order to arrest a person named in an arrest warrant or to arrest someone for an arrestable offence or to recapture an escaped prisoner (section 17)
→ it is believed that there is evidence relating to an arrest (section 18)

Don't forget

Stop and search powers are different to powers of arrest. Don't mix them up.

Powers of arrest

The police may make an arrest when authorized to do so by a warrant naming the person to be arrested and there is a right of arrest for breach of the peace. Also PACE gives the police general rights of arrest in certain circumstances involving arrestable offences.

Section 24 of PACE allows an arrest without a warrant in the following circumstances:

→ where the suspect has committed or is in the act of committing an arrestable offence
→ where an arrestable offence has been or is being committed and there are reasonable grounds for suspecting the person arrested (even if it turns out later he did not commit the offence)
→ where there are reasonable grounds for suspecting that an arrestable offence has been committed (even if it turns out later that no offence was committed) and there are reasonable grounds for suspecting the person arrested
→ where the suspect is about to commit an arrestable offence
→ where there are reasonable grounds for suspecting that the person arrested was about to commit an arrestable offence

Checkpoint 2

What powers of arrest do private citizens have?

Checkpoint 3

Explain what is meant by an 'arrestable offence'.

Action point

Make a chart of the police powers of arrest.

32

Section 25 of PACE allows the police to arrest for any offence where:

→ the suspect's name and address cannot be discovered
→ there are reasonable grounds for believing that the name and address given by the suspect are false
→ there are reasonable grounds for believing that the suspect will cause injury to himself or others or will cause damage to property
→ the arrest is reasonably believed to be necessary to protect a child or other vulnerable person

Detention at the police station

The detainee must be told his rights by the custody officer. These are:

→ having someone informed of his arrest
→ being told that independent legal advice is available free, and being allowed to consult privately with a solicitor
→ being allowed to consult the Code of Practice

For most offences the police may only detain a person for a maximum of 24 hours (the Criminal Justice Bill going through Parliament in 2003 has provision for this to be changed to 36 hours in all cases). If the person is not then charged with an offence, the police must release them. For serious arrestable offences the police may detain for an initial period of 36 hours and may then apply to the Magistrates' Court for permission to detain the person for up to 96 hours.

Interviews

A detained person may be questioned by the police. Such interviews are tape-recorded. Before the interview starts the detainee should be cautioned, pointing out he does not have to say anything but that he may harm his defence if he does not mention something which he later relies on in court. Although the Runciman Report recommended retaining the right to silence, the Criminal Justice and Public Order Act 1994 allows adverse inferences to be made if the defendant does not mention a fact which he later raises at his trial.

Fingerprints and samples

While a person is detained, the police may take fingerprints and non-intimate body samples such as hair and saliva without the person's consent. Intimate samples can also be taken, but only with the person's consent and the sample must be taken by a registered medical practitioner or a nurse.

Checkpoint 4

Do you know which sections of PACE set out the rights to have someone informed of the detention and to consult a solicitor?

Action point

Make a time-line chart showing how long a person can be detained by the police.

Checkpoint 5

What effect may a breach of PACE have on a confession statement?

The jargon

Intimate samples include blood, semen and body tissue or fluids.

Exam questions   answers: page 40

1   Kelvin was stopped and searched in the street by a police officer. The officer did not tell Kelvin why he was being stopped. During the search the police officer insisted that Kelvin take off his sweatshirt. Explain to Kelvin what his rights are. (20 min)

2   Explain and comment briefly on the police powers in respect of detention and interview at the police station. (30 min)

Examiner's secrets

The examiner will be impressed if you can give accurate section numbers for the relevant police powers.

Sentencing aims

In approaching this topic it is useful to be aware of recent trends and any high profile cases that have appeared in the media, but do not base your answers just on these. A balanced view, showing an understanding of the aims of sentencing, is important.

Aims of sentencing

There are two main themes that judges use when deciding a sentence:

→ retribution – looking back to the crime and punishing for it
→ utilitarian – looking forward, aiming to achieve a useful purpose with the sentence

Retribution

This is based on the idea of punishment because the offender deserves punishment for his or her acts. Retribution is based on three points:

→ Revenge – the idea that society is being avenged for the wrong done.
→ Denunciation – this is making it clear to society that certain behaviour will not be tolerated.
→ Just deserts – this is the idea that the criminal should receive a punishment suitable to the crime. This has led to tariff sentences in some countries where each crime has a set penalty and the court has very little discretion. In our system, the Court of Appeal has laid down guidelines for some offences.

Checkpoint 1

Suggest sentences which could be imposed to show revenge, denunciation and just deserts.

Utilitarian theories

The concept behind these principles of sentencing is that the punishment must serve a useful purpose, either to the offender or for society as a whole. There are four main principles:

Deterrence

This can be aimed at the individual who has committed the offence or at other potential offenders. With individual deterrence the aim is to make sure that the offender does not reoffend through fear of future punishment, usually a prison sentence. The problem is that prison does not appear to deter, as about 65% of adult prisoners reoffend within two years of release.

The value of general deterrence is even more doubtful as potential offenders are rarely deterred by severe sentences passed on others.

Protection of society

This involves removing dangerous offenders from society. In Britain today this is achieved through the use of long prison sentences. The Crime (Sentences) Act 1997 introduced automatic life sentences for a second serious violent or sexual offence.

There is also a move towards using community-based sentences that will protect the public such as curfew orders with electronic tagging.

Checkpoint 2

The Crime (Sentences) Act 1997 also introduced minimum sentences for two other types of crime. What are they?

The jargon

Protection of society can also be referred to as *incapacitation* of the offender.

Reformation

This is where the main aim of the penalty is to reform the offender and rehabilitate him or her into society. This principle of sentence became important in the second half of the 20th century with the development of sentences such as probation and community service orders. The Criminal Justice Bill 2002 proposes reinforcing the use of community-based penalties. Reform is a particularly important aim when dealing with young offenders.

Reparation

This is aimed at compensating the victim of the crime, usually by ordering the offender to pay a sum of money to the victim or to make restitution (i.e. return stolen property to its rightful owner). Reparation can also be to society in the form of a community service order.

Background factors considered by the courts ●●●

Whichever principle of sentencing is used, the court will usually consider both the offence and the background of the offender. In looking at the offence some important points are:

→ how serious was it of its type? e.g. how much was stolen? or what injuries were inflicted?
→ was the crime premeditated? this makes it more serious
→ was the offender in a position of trust? this makes it more serious

So far as the offender is concerned the court will want to know such points as:

→ whether there are previous convictions or the offender was on bail
→ the family background
→ medical or psychiatric problems
→ the age of the offender
→ the financial situation of the offender

Government policies ●●●

During the 1990s sentencing was a key political issue and government policies led to changes, especially in the use of prison sentences. In 1991 there was a move to the use of community based-penalties but this was short-lived. By 1993 the Home Secretary stated that 'prison works'. In 1997 automatic minimum sentences were introduced. The prison population rose from 45 000 in 1991 to 67 000 in 1999. By 2003 the prison population had reached 73 000.

Checkpoint 3

Can you explain why reform is so important for young offenders?

Test yourself

Write out the aims of sentencing from memory.

The jargon

Reparation can also be referred to as *restorative justice*.

Checkpoint 4

Do you know what it is called when the lawyer for a defendant makes a speech asking the court to give the defendant as lenient a sentence as possible?

Exam questions answers: page 41

1   Explain and comment on the aims pursued in the sentencing of offenders. (25 min)

2   Discuss the factors a court will take into account when deciding the most suitable sentence for an individual offender. (35 min)

Examiner's secrets

Look at the wording carefully. If the question says 'aims' then the examiner only wants the aims. Don't waste time on the other factors in sentencing.

Sanctions: civil and criminal

In both civil and criminal cases, the courts have a number of sanctions. In civil matters you should try to relate the sanction to the area of law, such as remedies for breach of contract. You should be able to discuss criminal sanctions with reference to the aims of sentencing.

Remedies in civil cases

These are aimed at putting successful claimants back in the position they would have been in had the defendant not infringed their rights. The main civil remedy is damages, but there are also other orders the court can make.

Damages

This is an order that one party in the case pays a sum of money to the other party. In breach of contract cases this will be the amount needed to put the claimant in the same position as if the contract had not been broken. In tort cases the award is to compensate for the wrong done, e.g. for pain and suffering in a personal injury case or for damage to property or reputation.

Other remedies

Checkpoint 1

The other remedies listed here are known as 'equitable' remedies. Can you explain what this means?

These are remedies that can be used when an award of damages does not adequately compensate the claimant. They include:

→ **injunctions** – an order that the defendant does, or does not, do something, e.g. not to make loud noise during the night
→ **specific performance** – to complete a contract
→ **rescission** – returning the parties to their pre-contractual position

Test yourself

From memory write out the different types of civil remedies and give a brief explanation of each.

Sentences in criminal cases

Adult offenders

There are many sentencing options available to the courts when dealing with offenders over 21 years old. These include:

Checkpoint 2

Apart from the sentences listed here do you know any other sentence which can be given to an adult?

→ an immediate term of imprisonment
→ a suspended prison sentence
→ fines
→ community service orders
→ probation orders
→ curfew orders
→ discharges which may be either conditional or absolute

Test yourself

Write out this list of sentences from memory.

There are special powers for dealing with mentally ill offenders.

Prison sentences

For the crime of murder the only sentence a court can impose is life imprisonment. For other crimes, Parliament has laid down a maximum prison sentence, but it is for the court in each individual case to decide whether imprisonment is necessary and if so what length of time the offender should serve in jail. Prisons are seen as a way of containing violent offenders, but there are problems:

→ too many petty offenders are sent to prison
→ there are variations between different courts in sentencing so the chances of being sent to prison and the length of sentence vary
→ there are insufficient constructive activities to give prisoners skills and so help them on their return to the community
→ the reoffending rate for released prisoners is too high

Community sentences

→ **Probation order** This places the offender under the supervision of a probation officer. Conditions may be included, e.g. requiring the offender to live at a certain address.
→ **Community service order** This requires the offender to work on a suitable project organized by the probation service.
→ **Curfew orders** Under these an offender can be ordered to remain at a fixed address at certain times. This order may be monitored by electronic tagging.

The Criminal Justice Bill 2002 proposes extending the types of order that can be made in a community sentence. It will also allow the defendant to be given a mixture of different community orders in one sentence.

Young offenders

These are offenders aged 10 to 20. Within this range of ages there are different methods of sentencing suitable to the age of the offender and the offence committed.

Custodial sentences

These are served in detention and training units. An offender aged 18 or more but under 21 can be given a custodial sentence up to the maximum available for an adult. For those under 18 the maximum custodial sentence is usually two years. However, for serious offences such as rape and robbery, longer periods of detention can be ordered.

Non-custodial sentences

Offenders aged 16 and over can be given the same non-custodial sentences as adults. Those aged under 16 can be given a supervision order or an action plan order. Both these are aimed at reforming the offender. Young offenders in all age groups can be ordered to go to an attendance centre for two or three hours each week. Discharges and fines are also available.

Action point

Draw a spider diagram showing the problems of using prison as a sentence.

Checkpoint 3

Can you give the maximum lengths of time of probation orders, community service orders and curfews?

Checkpoint 4

Can the courts make any orders affecting the parents of young offenders?

Check the net

The Home Office website often has information on current trends in sentencing. Try www.homeoffice.gov.uk

Exam questions answers: pages 41–2

1 Explain and comment on the sentences that a court can pass on a young offender. (35 min)

2 James, aged 22, has been found guilty at the Eastshire Magistrates' Court of causing criminal damage and stealing cars. What sentencing powers does the court have in his case? (20 min)

Examiner's secrets

Where the examiner gives the age of an offender, you need only comment on sentences appropriate to that age group.

Answers
The courts and legal process

Civil cases and courts

Checkpoints

1 (a) Examples of contract cases include suing for:
- failure to pay for goods
- cost of putting right poor quality building work
- failure to deliver machinery on time

   (b) Examples of tort cases include suing for:
- compensation for injuries caused by negligent driving
- compensation for injuries caused by defective premises (Occupier's Liability)
- suing for defamation

2 Queen's Bench Division – contract and tort cases. Chancery Division – trusts/mortgages/company law. Family Division – decisions about residence and contact for children; nullity of marriage.

3 Extra detail on the Woolf reforms includes:
- Fast-track cases should be heard within 30 weeks of setting the case down for trial and limits on advocacy costs and overall cost.
- Multi-track cases case management includes: identifying the issues, fixing the timetable, and encouraging the parties to use ADR (the judge may 'stay' the case so the parties can try ADR).

4 Disadvantages of small claims include the following:
- daytime hearing – parties have to take time off work to deal with the case
- court fees for claims of £1 000 to £5 000 are more expensive than previously, particularly with the allocation fee of £80
- more people are using lawyers
- difficulty of enforcing the judgment (1 out of 3 successful claimants do not get any money from the defendant)

Exam questions

1 A clear understanding of the problems is needed and this means looking at a variety of points such as:
- difficulty of funding cases – under the Access to Justice Act 1999 the Community Legal Service Fund has a set budget and the criteria for funding are more restrictive than previously
- complexity of proceedings – even after the Woolf reforms people have difficulty taking their own case
- delay – this has improved after the Woolf reforms but there is still a wait of several months for a fast-track case and even longer for a multi-track case
- adversarial process: this encourages tension between the parties
- risk of losing and having to pay other side's costs

2 In this problem-style question you are not told the precise size of the claim so you have to cover the possibilities. You are told the machinery is expensive so it is unlikely to be a small claim. State this and go on to consider the other two tracks: fast-track – £5 000–£15 000; multi-track – over £15 000.

Then deal with the possible courts:
- County Court – whatever the size of the claim, the case could be dealt with in this court
- High Court – this can only be used for claims over £15 000

You are also asked to deal with appeal routes and again you must consider all possibilities:
- fast-track – appeal to next level of judge
- multi-track – appeal to Court of Appeal (Civil Division) with a possible further appeal to House of Lords (or even, though unlikely, a 'leap-frog' appeal direct to the House of Lords)

Examiner's secrets

If a question gives a specific amount for a claim, then the examiner only wants you to deal with the courts and methods relevant to that amount.

ADR and tribunals

Checkpoints

1 Advantages of mediation/conciliation include:
- low cost
- speedy resolution (much quicker than going to court)
- parties in control of the process
- avoids winner/loser situation and keeps business relations viable

2 Advantages of arbitration include:
- arbitrator can be an expert in the particular field
- flexible proceedings – parties agree procedure used
- held in private so business matters do not become public knowledge
- relatively cheap

   Disadvantages of arbitration include:
- not suitable for a point of law
- limited rights of appeal
- in commercial arbitration where a professional arbitrator is used there can be delay and expense

3 Employment tribunal – a worker's representative, e.g. a trade union official and a management representative such as a company director. These people must not have involvement with the case being heard. Industrial injuries tribunal – doctors.

4 The two main rules of natural justice are:
- No one is allowed to act as a judge in his own case. This is to prevent possible bias: in the *Pinochet* case (1999) the House of Lords quashed its own decision that General Pinochet could be extradited to Spain to face charges of torture because a judge, Lord Hoffmann, was involved with the human rights organization, Amnesty International.
- Both sides must be allowed to put their case. It is clearly unfair to decide a case after hearing only one side of the story, *Ridge v Baldwin* (1964).

Exam questions

1 This requires an understanding of the problems of using the courts; the role of ADR organizations and an awareness of the pressures to use ADR brought in by the Woolf reforms.

The main points to be included are:
- cost, delay and complexity of using the courts
- the difficulties of funding (this can include a comment on the new Community Legal Service, but keep it brief)
- the above points leading to the setting up of new ADR bodies (e.g. the Centre for Dispute Resolution and local mediation services)
- the new Civil Procedure Rules which allow a judge to suspend a case while ADR is tried

2 You need to show clear understanding of the fact that tribunals operate separately from the courts and deal with special types of cases assigned to them. Point out that different types of tribunals have been set up but that the common factor is that they give individuals the chance to enforce welfare, individual liberties or employment rights.

Discuss the need to have specialist forums to deal with the different areas of law and also that the courts are already over-burdened and could not deal with these extra cases.

Refer to specific types of tribunals to illustrate your points. Useful ones to use are:
- employment tribunals – wide variety of cases – help enforce employment rights
- social security tribunals – people can challenge decisions which deny them benefits
- immigration – those refused entry to this country can challenge this decision

Criminal cases and courts

Checkpoints

1 Where the defendant was already on bail and is now charged with an indictable or triable either way offence.

Where the defendant is charged with murder, attempted murder, manslaughter, rape or attempted rape and he has already served a sentence for one of these offences.

2 • The nature and seriousness of the offence.
- The defendant's previous record.
- What ties the defendant has in the community; has he a place to live or a family? Both these make it less likely that he will abscond.
- If the defendant has been given bail before, did he keep to the bail conditions? The courts are trying to decide whether the defendant will turn up for the next

hearing if given bail and will not commit any further offences in the meantime.

3 Summary offences can only be tried in the Magistrates' Court, e.g. criminal damage of less than £5 000. Triable either way offences can be tried in the Crown Court or the Magistrates' Court, e.g. theft. Indictable offences can only be tried at the Crown Court, e.g. rape.

4 The jury decides the facts of the case, while the judge decides legal points and directs the jury on the law. The jury decides the verdict of guilty or not guilty.

5 *Crown Court* – tried by a judge and jury; more formal; trial takes longer; more expensive; both prosecution and defence will be represented by lawyers; can sentence up to the maximum for the crime concerned. *Magistrates' Court* – tried by three lay magistrates (or in cities possibly by a district judge (Magistrates' Court); court is local; hearing quicker; cheaper; defendant often not represented; prosecution can use lay representatives for some cases.

Exam questions

1 To discuss this you need to explain the rules on bail first. Start with the presumption of bail (Bail Act 1976). This protects the right to liberty. Then discuss the factors which the courts consider, pointing out that these are aimed at trying to strike a balance, e.g. is the defendant likely to interfere with witnesses?

Next set out some of the limitations: e.g. a court must give reasons when granting bail in a case of murder, manslaughter or rape (Criminal Justice Act 1988); the fact that a defendant charged with a second offence of this nature can be granted bail only in exceptional circumstances (Crime and Disorder Act 1998). Both these are aimed at protecting the public.

Finally comment on the large number of defendants who are refused bail (about 20% of the prison population are awaiting trial). Does this suggest that the balance is not being kept?

2 Describe the role of the CPS. Police send papers to CPS which decide whether the case should continue. If case continues, CPS will conduct the prosecution with their own advocate in the Magistrates' Court and an independent advocate at the Crown Court (or since April 2000 a Crown Prosecutor). CPS are available to advise police while investigations are continuing, if the police ask for such advice.

Comment on points such as the need for the prosecution agency to be independent of the police; the improved co-operation between police and CPS reducing the number of cases which are discontinued; better continuity in a case with a Crown Prosecutor conducting the prosecution.

Criminal appeals: miscarriages of justice

Checkpoints

1 There are many cases but a useful one is *C v DPP* (1996), the case in which the House of Lords decided that the presumption of *doli incapax* still applied to defendants aged 10 to 13.

2 The judges are known as Lords Justices of Appeal. The head of the Court of Appeal (Criminal Division) is the Lord Chief Justice.

3 There are many cases. A useful case to know is *R v Shivpuri* (1986) as the House of Lords used the Practice Statement in this case to overrule the earlier case of *Anderton v Ryan* (1985).

4 The best known case is probably that of Derek Bentley who had been hanged for murder. Forty years later the CCRC referred the case to the Court of Appeal which quashed the conviction.

Exam questions

1 (a) Jonas can appeal to the Court of Appeal (Criminal Division) against his conviction and/or his sentence. He will need leave to appeal. An appeal will only be successful if the Court of Appeal decides the conviction is unsafe (Criminal Appeal Act 1995). From the Court of Appeal he can appeal to the House of Lords against his conviction, but he needs leave to appeal and there must be a point of law of general public importance.

(b) The prosecution cannot appeal against Jonas being acquitted. They can ask the Attorney-General to refer a point of law to the Court of Appeal (Criminal Justice Act 1972) but this reference will not affect Jonas. It merely 'tidies up' the law for future cases. The prosecution can ask the Attorney-General to refer the sentence if it is thought to be too lenient (Criminal Justice Act 1988). If there has been a conviction for 'nobbling' the jury or witnesses in the case, then the prosecution can apply to the High Court for the acquittal to be quashed and Jonas to be retried (Criminal Procedure and Investigations Act 1996).

2 There are several safeguards in criminal cases, all of which are designed to prevent miscarriages of justice. The areas you should be discussing include:
- the fact that the defendant is presumed innocent until his guilt is proved; the prosecution have to prove the case
- the high standard of proof needed in criminal cases – 'beyond reasonable doubt'.
- the availability of an appeal system – is this adequate or is the Court of Appeal too reluctant to interfere with a jury verdict? Is the test used of a conviction being unsafe adequate?
- the role of the Criminal Cases Review Commission

Discussion of cases in which there has been shown to be a miscarriage of justice could also be used.

Examiner's secrets

Examiners like you to illustrate your answers with suitable cases wherever possible.

Police powers

Checkpoints

1 Code of Practice A.

2 Private citizens may arrest:
- anyone who is in the act of committing an arrestable offence
- anyone whom they have reasonable grounds for suspecting to be committing an arrestable offence
- where an arrestable offence has been committed, anyone who is guilty of the offence or anyone whom they have reasonable grounds for suspecting

3 An arrestable offence is an offence where the sentence is fixed by law (e.g. murder because there is a fixed sentence of life imprisonment) *or* any offence for which the maximum sentence that could be given to an adult is at least five years.

4 Section 56 – right to have someone informed.
Section 58 – right to consult with a solicitor.

5 Under section 76 of PACE the court can refuse to allow evidence of a confession obtained by oppression or in circumstances which are likely to make the confession unreliable.

Exam questions

1 You should spot that this is about stop and search powers under section 1 of PACE. Points to include are:
- a street is a public place so the police can stop and search
- an officer should stop only if he has reasonable suspicion that Kelvin is in possession of stolen or prohibited items
- if the police officer does not have reasonable grounds then the search is unlawful
- the officer should give name, object of proposed search and the grounds for suspicion
- Kelvin can only be asked to remove his outer coat, jacket and gloves

2 Set out the powers and then comment on them:
- Time limits on detention – don't forget that there are additional powers if the case involves a serious arrestable offence.
- The role of the custody officer and the need to inform the defendant of his rights. The police can withhold the right to inform someone for up to 36 hours for a serious arrestable offence.
- The need to caution before interview.
- The right of a young offender or vulnerable person to have an appropriate person present at the interview.
- Tape recording of the interview.

Sentencing aims

Checkpoints

1 *Revenge* – the death penalty is an example of this.
Denunciation – long prison sentences show society's disapproval.
Just deserts – there are very precise Court of Appeal guidelines for the length of prison sentence for possession of certain types and amounts of drugs.

2 Drug dealing – (Class A drugs) minimum seven years' imprisonment for third offence; and burglary – minimum three years' imprisonment for third offence.

3 A young offender is still impressionable and can be reformed. His life is ahead of him so it is important both to him and to society that he be reformed and not become a perpetual criminal.

4 This is called a speech in mitigation.

Exam questions

1 Set out the main aims of sentencing. It does not matter which order you take them in, but you must explain each one and comment on it.

Retribution – punishment because a crime has been committed. Leads to tariff sentences and consistency in sentencing. Discuss denunciation as well – society showing its disapproval of crime.

Deterrence – tries to 'put off' people committing crime, but very little evidence that either individual or general deterrence is effective, especially using prison as 65% of prisoners reoffend within two years of release.

Protection of the public/incapacitation of the offender – this must be the main aim where dangerous offenders are concerned, e.g. serial killers.

Reform – trying to rehabilitate the offender so that he will not offend in future (particularly important for young offenders).

Reparation – putting right the wrong; repaying society or the victim – suitable only in certain types of case and for offenders who are not dangerous.

2 Give a brief comment about aims of sentencing and a quick list of them: retribution, denunciation, deterrence, protection of the public, reform and reparation. Then go on to explain that the court will consider both the offence and the offender in deciding which of these aims should be used. Point out that matters such as the following will be looked at:
- nature of the offence; the role the defendant played in it; are there any aggravating factors such as premeditation?
- previous convictions of the defendant

- did the defendant plead guilty? – under the Powers of Criminal Courts (Sentencing) Act 2000 the court can give a shorter sentence than it would otherwise do for an early plea of guilty
- background of the defendant and any reports on him
- medical or psychiatric problems

Sanctions: civil and criminal

Checkpoints

1 Equitable refers to remedies developed under the rules of equity, which support fairness in the law. It also means that the remedies are discretionary and will not automatically be granted even if the claimant wins the case. The court will consider points such as did the claimant behave in a fair way and has the claimant delayed in bringing the matter to court. The court may decide that damages are adequate to compensate the claimant and an equitable remedy will not be given.

2 Other sentences include: combination order of up to 100 hours' Community Service together with a probation order; and disqualification from driving.

3 *Probation order* – maximum 3 years.
Community service order – minimum 40 hours, maximum 240 hours.
Curfew order – for between 2 and 12 hours per day for up to 6 months.

4 Yes, there are several orders the courts can make regarding the parents of young offenders under the age of 16. The main ones are:
- ordering that the parents pay any fine imposed on the young offender
- making a parenting order (Crime and Disorder Act 1998)
- binding parents over for a set amount of money to keep their child under control; breach of this order means that the parents can be ordered to pay that money to the court

Exam questions

1 This question asks specifically about young offenders so make sure that you keep your answer relevant to this. You need to set out the main sentences available for young offenders and don't forget that the question asks for comment as well. The main points are:
- Detention and training order of up to two years (you can also point out that longer sentences can be given for very serious offences). Detention and training units are separate from adult prisons so as not to corrupt the young offenders.

- Community penalties – those aged 16 and over can be given community service, probation and curfew orders.
- Supervision orders and action plan orders for younger offenders – aimed at giving the offender guidance so that his behaviour is reformed.
- Fines – the maximum amount varies according to the age of the offender.
- Discharges – a conditional discharge is a common method of dealing with younger first-time offenders.

2 This question gives a specific age for the offender, so be aware of this in the focus of your answer. Also note that the court is the Magistrates' Court so start by pointing out the sentencing limits of the court: six months' imprisonment for one offence (12 months for two or more offences) and a maximum fine of £5 000. Point out that it is possible for the magistrates to send James to the Crown Court for sentencing if they feel that their sentencing powers are not adequate. Go on to list the types of sentences the court could impose:
- custodial
- community penalties – probation, community service order, curfew – all these are likely to be used in this scenario; explain each one briefly
- fine
- compensation order – this can be ordered in addition to any of the above

Conditional discharge is unlikely since there are several offences involved.

Legal personnel

The people who work in the legal system are divided into the professionals (solicitors, barristers and judges) and lay people (those without legal qualifications). The roles of all these different people are the subject of criticism. The division of lawyers into solicitors and barristers does not happen in most other countries. Lay magistrates have a large role trying cases and sentencing offenders. Ordinary members of the public make the decision of guilt or innocence in the most serious criminal cases.

Exam themes

→ The role of barristers and solicitors

→ The problems of funding cases

→ Government schemes providing free or cheap legal advice and representation

→ The independence of the judges and the role of the Lord Chancellor

→ The use of lay people in the legal system

Topic checklist

○ AS ● A2	AQA	OCR	WJEC
Solicitors and barristers	○	○	○
Funding of legal services	○	○	○
The judiciary	○	○	○
Lay magistrates	○	○	○
The jury	○	○	○

Solicitors and barristers

When we talk about the legal professions we are usually referring to solicitors and barristers which are the main types of lawyer. However, legal executives are increasingly important: professionally qualified lawyers who do almost the same work as solicitors. Many legal practices also employ 'paralegals' who are generally not professionally qualified but may have a legal qualification.

The jargon

We have no definition for a *'paralegal'* here as there is in America, where it is a qualified lawyer who has not passed the bar exams to become an attorney. Here it can include unqualified people.

Test yourself

Before you read on see if you can remember the names of the three stages of training for both solicitors and barristers.

Barristers

There are more than 10 000 barristers working in chambers, or as employed barristers, and around 2 000 non-practising barristers.

Qualification and training

Barristers are required to undergo three levels of education and training:

1 The academic stage – this can be a law degree, but it might also be any degree together with the Common Professional Examination (CPE), a conversion degree in the core areas of law.
2 The vocational stage – this is the Bar Vocational Course, formerly sat at the Inns of Court School of Law in London but now available in a number of regional centres; it tests skills, e.g. advocacy.
3 The professional stage – this is pupillage, shadowing a practising barrister who acts as Pupil Master for two periods of six months.

Checkpoint 1

What exactly does being 'called to the bar' mean?

Organization and role

Barristers are self-employed, usually work out of chambers where they share the services of a clerk, and are members of an Inn of Court, either Grays, Lincolns, Middle Temple or Inner Temple. Most are based in London. Barristers are specialist advocates. Their work is of three types:

→ advocacy, particularly in the Crown Court and higher courts
→ writing 'counsel's opinion' on the strength of cases for solicitors
→ drafting legal documents, particularly claims, but also others

The jargon

An *advocate* is a person who presents a case in court.

Checkpoint 2

Some barristers become QCs. What does this mean?

Discipline and complaints

Barristers are controlled by their Inns and the General Council of the Bar. Complaints can be made to either and there is also a Complaints Commissioner. The Senate of the Inn usually carries out disciplinary proceedings. In extreme cases it is possible to be disbarred.

Solicitors

There are more than 80 000 solicitors in England and Wales. Most practise in solicitors' offices in private practice. About 20% of these are employed solicitors working for companies, for local authorities and in the Crown Prosecution Service and as Magistrates' Clerks.

Action point

Try to identify where most solicitors' offices are in your town to discover something about solicitors.

Qualification and training

Solicitors have three stages of training too:

1. The academic stage – again a law degree or any degree plus CPE
2. The vocational stage – this is the Legal Practice Course (LPC) and again it is a skills-based course including, e.g. client counselling
3. The professional stage – a two-year Training Contract in a solicitors' office required before entry on the roll of solicitors

Organization and role

Solicitors in private practice usually work in partnerships as partners or associates. Solicitors have the first contact with clients. Their work is very varied. They may well be advocates, particularly in lower courts, though with an Advocacy Certificate they may now appear in higher courts. Their work also commonly includes conveyancing, drawing up of wills and probate, registering companies, general advice and litigation.

Discipline and complaints

The Law Society is the body that controls solicitors. Complaints may be made to the Office for the Supervision of Solicitors, which is run by the Law Society. The Law Society can discipline a solicitor and if the issue is serious it is possible to remove a solicitor from the role. The Legal Services Ombudsman can also be approached (as with barristers too).

Legal executives ●●●

These are full-time practising professional lawyers who usually work in solicitors' offices. They normally qualify by a part-time, non-graduate route, taking both Part 1 and Part 2 of the Institute of Legal Executives exams and with qualifying service. They can generally do most things a solicitor can. They can also go on to qualify as solicitors by taking LPC.

The future of the professions ●●●

There have been many changes in recent years, removing restrictive practices such as the bar's monopoly on higher court advocacy and the solicitors' monopoly on conveyancing. Continuing Professional Development is also required in both cases. 'Fusion' of the professions used to be an issue, now other events make this irrelevant. The Access to Justice Act means that the bar can lose work to CPS lawyers. Under the Woolf reforms solicitors are less likely to approach barristers to draft claims. Solicitors have lost work to, e.g. licensed conveyancers. There are now around 25 000 'paralegals', one for every three solicitors, and Training Contracts seem hard to find. Also the Lord Chancellor has introduced procedures for his greater control of the professions.

Test yourself

Try to write down the other skills that are necessary for a solicitor from memory.

Checkpoint 3

How do solicitors probably do more advocacy than barristers?

The jargon

Conveyancing is the buying and selling of houses and land. *Probate* is proving wills of deceased people.

Action point

Make some brief notes on what the Ombudsman does.

Checkpoint 4

What qualification does a qualified legal executive hold?

Test yourself

Try to write down from memory a list of the major recent changes to the restrictive practices of the two professions.

Examiner's secrets

When you are considering the role of solicitors remember also to talk about employed solicitors, not just those in private practice.

Exam questions   answers: page 54

1. Describe and comment on the training and work of solicitors. (30 min)

2. Discuss the role of the Legal Services Ombudsman and the OSS. (15 min)

Funding of legal services

If taking a case to court is too expensive, then ordinary people will not have access to justice. It is important that there is a scheme which allows poorer members of society to have access both to advice and to representation in court. The Access to Justice Act 1999 brought in major changes limiting government funding of cases.

Advice agencies

There is a need for local places where people can get free advice about their legal problems. Citizens' Advice Bureaux play a major role as there is a Bureau in most towns. Some Bureaux will have contracts to deliver advice under the Community Legal Services Fund. There are also Law Centres, which often specialize in welfare law and issues such as housing. There are only about 50 Law Centres nationally and they have difficulty in getting enough funding.

Checkpoint 1

Can you name any schemes run by the legal profession to provide free advice or representation?

Legal Services Commission (LSC)

The LSC took over from the Legal Aid Board in April 2000 and it manages the new Community Legal Service Fund. The Commission's responsibilities are to develop local, regional and national plans to match the delivery of legal services to identified needs and priorities. The LSC can make contracts with all types of providers of legal services. The number of contracts is limited so only about 5 000 solicitors nationally will be able to offer help under the scheme.

The Community Legal Service (CLS)

Action point

Make your own notes on the Community Legal Service and the Fund.

This was set up by the Access to Justice Act 1999 for civil cases. The services included are the provision of:

→ general information about the law and legal system and the availability of legal services
→ legal advice
→ help in preventing or settling or otherwise resolving disputes about legal rights and duties
→ help in enforcing decisions by which such disputes are resolved

The Community Legal Service Fund

There is a set budget for the overall fund for civil cases and the LSC allocates budgets to its regional offices. Very expensive cases are funded on a case-by-case basis through individually negotiated contracts from a central fund.

Checkpoint 2

Do you know what is meant by disposable income and disposable capital?

Financial conditions

These are intended to target the neediest cases by requiring people to pay what they can reasonably afford. Contributions will be on a graduated scale, with those nearest the free limit being asked for a smaller proportion of their income. Disposable capital will be banded, with different proportions payable in each band.

Criteria for funding

In considering whether to fund a case the following are looked at:

→ the likely cost of funding and the benefit which may be obtained
→ the availability of sums in the Community Legal Fund
→ the importance of the matters for the individual
→ the availability of other services
→ the prospects of success
→ the conduct of the individual
→ the public interest

These tests are wider than under the old legal aid scheme and mean that even though a person is poor enough to qualify and has a good case they may still be refused funding.

Conditional fee agreements

Under these the client agrees with a solicitor an amount which would be the normal fee for the case. They also agree an uplift of up to 100% which will be payable in addition if the solicitor wins the case. If the case is lost the agreement may be that the client pays the normal fee or nothing is paid. Conditional fee agreements are permitted in most civil cases, except family matters.

A conditional fee agreement allows the client to know exactly how much they have to pay. The main risk is that if they lose the case they will be ordered to pay the other side's costs. To protect against this they can get insurance and if they win they can claim the cost of the insurance premium and the uplift fee from the defendant.

The Criminal Defence Service (CDS)

Section 12 of the Access to Justice Act 1999 requires the CLS to establish the Criminal Defence Service. This service is aimed at: 'securing that individuals involved in criminal investigations or proceedings have access to such advice, assistance and representation as the interests of justice require.'

Advice is available free of charge to people who are being detained or questioned by the police. There is a duty solicitor available to give such advice, though often this is only by telephone.

Advice is also available free of charge from a duty solicitor at the Magistrates' Court. The duty solicitor can also represent a defendant for emergency hearings such as a bail application.

Representation is available provided it is in the interests of justice and the defendant qualifies under the financial conditions.

Test yourself

Write out this list of criteria from memory.

Checkpoint 3

Which Act first allowed conditional fees and which Act extended their use?

The jargon

Conditional fee agreements are often called 'no win, no fee' agreements.

Checkpoint 4

Can you list the five factors that are taken into account in deciding whether it is 'in the interests of justice' to fund legal help in criminal cases?

Don't forget

The CDS also now employs its own defence lawyers.

Exam questions   answers: page 54

1   Discuss whether the present funding arrangements in civil cases provide an adequate service for people on low incomes. (30 min)

2   Errol has been arrested on a charge of robbery. Explain to him what schemes exist to provide him with legal advice and representation. (30 min)

Examiner's secrets

In a scenario question the examiner wants you to identify the type of help that is relevant.

The judiciary

Check the net

In June 2003 the Government issued a consultation paper about judicial appointment. This is on www.lcd.gov.uk

Checkpoint 1

What is the title for judges in
(a) the High Court
(b) the Court of Appeal
(c) the House of Lords?

Checkpoint 2

Can you give the types of judges who sit in
(a) the Crown Court
(b) the County Court?

Check the net

There is usually information about the current composition of the bench on the Lord Chancellor's Department's website at www.lcd.gov.uk

The judiciary is the collective name for judges. There are different levels of judges with some important distinctions between judges in the High Court, the Court of Appeal and the House of Lords and judges at the lower levels. There is a need for judges to be independent of the Government. Here the position of the Lord Chancellor is important as it conflicts with the concept of the separation of powers.

Appointing judges

The Lord Chancellor plays a central role in appointment. He appoints the judges at the lower levels and nominates people for appointment at the higher levels (for judges in the Court of Appeal and the House of Lords, the Prime Minister officially makes the nomination, but after consultation with the Lord Chancellor). There are now advertisements for application for judicial office up to and including the High Court. However, High Court appointment can still be by invitation. A major criticism of the system is that it is secretive and relies heavily on information compiled in the Lord Chancellor's Department about senior advocates who might be considered for future appointment.

Qualifications
To become a judge at any level it is necessary to have qualified as a barrister or solicitor and the relevant qualifications for each level are set out in the Courts and Legal Services Act 1990. For the High Court and above this means having full advocacy rights.

Training
The Judicial Studies Board is responsible for training judges. The training is through one-day or short courses. Much of it is aimed at keeping the judges up to date with developments of law. A recent initiative in training was to include racial awareness courses. Critics point out that the training is very limited.

Composition of the bench
One of the main criticisms of the bench is that it is dominated by elderly, white, upper-class males. Fewer than 10% of judges are women and less than 1% of judges are from ethnic minorities.

Dismissal and retirement

Superior judges cannot be dismissed by the Lord Chancellor or the Prime Minister. Since the Act of Settlement 1701 they can only be removed by the monarch following a petition presented to her by both Houses of Parliament. This gives superior judges protection from political whims and allows them to be independent in their judgments. The Lord Chancellor has the power to dismiss inferior judges for incapacity or misconduct. All judges now retire at 70.

Independence of the judiciary ●●●

An independent judiciary is seen as important. Our judges can be seen to be independent in the following ways.

→ *Independent from politics* – judges are not allowed to be members of the House of Commons. The Law Lords do sit in the House of Lords but by convention do not take part in political debates.
→ *Independent from the Government* – superior judges cannot be dismissed by the Government. However their appointment is not independent as the Lord Chancellor is involved in the appointment of judges at all levels.
→ *Freedom from pressure* – judges have immunity from being sued for actions taken or decisions made in the course of their judicial duties, *Sirros v Moore* (1975). Judges must not have an interest in the case they are trying (*Pinochet*).

Checkpoint 3

Can you give two cases in which judges gave a judgment that ruled against a government department?

The doctrine of the separation of powers ●●●

This theory was put forward by Montesquieu in the 18th century. It identifies three functions or 'arms' of the state as:

→ **legislative** – making law: in our system this is Parliament
→ **executive** – administering the law: the Cabinet
→ **judicial** – applying the law: the judges

Montesquieu thought these three areas needed to be separate so that each could keep a check on the others. In our system the Lord Chancellor is the only person who is involved in all three arms.

Test yourself

Write out from memory the three arms of the state.

Action point

Draw a spider diagram showing the Lord Chancellor's roles in the three arms of the state.

The Lord Chancellor ●●●

The Lord Chancellor is:

→ the speaker of the House of Lords in its legislative capacity
→ a member of the Cabinet
→ one of the judges in the House of Lords and head of the Chancery division in the High Court and entitled to act as judge there

In addition, the Lord Chancellor plays a major part in the appointment of judges and also has important administrative functions such as controlling the Community Legal Service and being responsible for the work of the Law Commission and the Council on Tribunals.

The Lord Chancellor is also a political appointment as he is appointed by the Prime Minister and can be dismissed by the Prime Minister. He also holds office only while that political party is in power and if there is a change of government there will be a new Lord Chancellor.

Check the net

The Government proposes abolishing the Lord Chancellor's position. Check what is happening on www.lcd.gov.uk

Checkpoint 4

Can you name an Act of Parliament that gives the Lord Chancellor power in an area of the legal system?

Exam questions answers: page 55

1 What criticisms can be made of the appointment and training of judges? (30 min)

2 Discuss whether the Lord Chancellor's role is in conflict with the principle of judicial independence. (30 min)

Examiner's secrets

In both these questions the examiner is directing you to look at two points, so make sure you do this.

Lay magistrates

> *"Lay magistrates are the workhorses of the English legal system."*

Lay magistrates are unqualified, part-time and unpaid (save for expenses), yet they deal with the vast majority of cases in the legal system. They do not hear cases on their own but sit as a bench or panel of two or three magistrates. The use of such unqualified judges is open to criticism.

Appointment of lay magistrates

Lay magistrates must live within 15 miles of the commission area, normally be aged between 27 and 65 on appointment, and sit at least 26 half days per year.

The Lord Chancellor has set out six key qualities they should have. Some people are not eligible; these include people with serious criminal convictions, undischarged bankrupts, and members of the police or traffic wardens.

Checkpoint 1

Can you name the six key qualities required for lay magistrates?

Local Advisory Committees

Names are put forward to Advisory Committees by groups such as the local political parties, trade unions and chambers of commerce, or by individuals themselves. The committees will interview candidates and then submit the names of those they believe are suitable to the Lord Chancellor. The Lord Chancellor has the final decision and will not necessarily appoint all the people whose names are put forward.

Training

New magistrates are given about 40 hours of training spread over the first three years. This consists of:

→ observing court proceedings and learning 'on the job'
→ attending lectures and workshops
→ visiting penal institutions

Checkpoint 2

What are qualified judges in the Magistrates' Court called, what qualifications must they have and what areas are they usually used in?

The training is not meant to make magistrates proficient in the law, but to give them an understanding of their duties. A major part of the training is aimed at sentencing. Magistrates on the Youth panel and the Family panel receive extra training for this.

Composition of the bench

A major criticism is that most magistrates are Conservatives, even in areas where there is a high Labour vote. Women now account for 49% of lay magistrates. Ethnic minorities are slightly under-represented, though appointments are increasing.

> *"... middle-class, middle-aged and middle-minded ..."*

The role of magistrates

Action point

Make your own notes on the role of magistrates.

Lay magistrates are expected to deal with a wide variety of cases. Their main work is trying minor criminal cases, but they also have some civil functions, e.g. hearing applications for licences to sell alcohol and dealing with community debts such as non-payment of the community charge.

The criminal cases they deal with include:

→ trying all summary offences

→ trying either way offences which are suitable for trial by magistrates

→ deciding issues such as whether to grant bail or a warrant of arrest

There is also a Youth Court to hear cases relating to those under 18 years old. In addition magistrates decide family cases ranging from adoption orders to orders to prevent domestic violence, though they cannot deal with divorce cases.

The clerk ●●●

Every bench is assisted by a clerk. The main duty is to guide the magistrates on questions of law, practice and procedure. The clerk should not assist in the decision-making. Clerks have been given increased powers to deal with routine matters at early administrative hearings.

Advantages of using lay magistrates ●●●

→ The system involves members of the community and provides a wider cross-section on the bench than would be possible with the use of professional judges.

→ Lay magistrates have local knowledge.

→ Improved training means that lay magistrates are not complete 'amateurs'.

→ A legally qualified clerk is available to give advice.

→ It is cheap, both for the Government and for the defendant.

→ Cases are dealt with relatively quickly.

→ There are few appeals from magistrates' decisions.

Disadvantages of using lay magistrates ●●●

→ Lay magistrates tend to be 'middle-class, middle-aged and middle-minded' and will have little in common with the young working-class defendants who make up the majority of defendants.

→ Both working-class and ethnic minorities are under-represented.

→ The training is inadequate for the workload.

→ Lay magistrates tend to be prosecution biased, believing the police too readily. They acquit in only about 25% of cases.

→ Some magistrates may rely too heavily on their clerk.

→ There is inconsistency in sentencing and in the granting of bail.

→ The workload is becoming too great and complicated, especially in the family court.

Exam questions answers: page 55

1 (a) Explain the role of lay magistrates.

   (b) Discuss whether the use in the legal system of such 'amateurs' is desirable. (30 min)

2 Explain and comment on the role played by lay people in the English legal system. (40 min)

Checkpoint 3

What is the maximum sentence that magistrates can impose?

Check the net

Look for information on magistrates on www.open.gov.uk/lcd and www.magistrates-association.org.uk

Checkpoint 4

Can you explain where appeals can be made to from a decision by the magistrates?

Action point

Make a list comparing the advantages and disadvantages of using lay magistrates.

Examiner's secrets

If the examiner uses the term 'lay people' you must consider both lay magistrates and juries.

The jury

Juries are mainly used in criminal cases at the Crown Court, but they are used in other courts as well. In criminal cases the jury is seen as an important safeguard of our rights. However, there are criticisms that can be made of juries.

Jury qualifications

The qualifications to be a juror are set out in the Jury Act 1974. To qualify for jury service a person must be:

→ aged between 18 and 70
→ registered to vote on the Register of Electors
→ ordinarily resident in the United Kingdom, the Channel Islands or the Isle of Man for at least five years since their 13th birthday

Disqualified or ineligible

Certain people are not permitted to sit on a jury even though they are within the basic qualifications. Some people are disqualified because of a criminal conviction. Others are ineligible because they are connected to the administration of justice. Also ineligible are ministers of religion and those with certain mental illnesses.

Excusals

Some people are eligible to serve on a jury but may demand to be excused. This is known as 'excusal as of right'. If people have problems that make it very difficult for them to do their jury service, e.g. illness or business commitments, they may ask to be excused or for their service to be put back to a later date. This is a discretionary excusal.

The Criminal Justice Bill 2002 proposes abolishing the categories of ineligible and excusable as of right. This means that almost everyone will have to do jury service.

Selection of a jury

The names are selected at random from the electoral registers for the area which the court covers. There are limited rights to reject jurors.

Vetting

Prospective jurors can be checked prior to a trial. This is called vetting and there are two types: (1) routine police checks on prospective jurors to eliminate those disqualified and (2) political vetting where a wider check is made on a juror's background and political affiliations. This second is used only in terrorist cases or cases involving official secrets.

Challenging

→ **To the array** – this means challenging the whole jury on the basis that it has been chosen in an unrepresentative or biased way.
→ **For cause** – this is a challenge to an individual juror pointing out a valid reason why that juror should not serve on the jury, such as the juror is disqualified or is related to a witness or defendant.

Checkpoint 1

Give details of who is disqualified from jury service.

Checkpoint 2

Give three examples of people who are entitled to be excused from jury service as of right.

Checkpoint 3

What criticisms can be made of the selection of juries?

Action point

Make a spider diagram of the different ways in which a juror can be checked or challenged.

→ **Prosecution right to stand by jurors** – this puts that juror to the end of the list of potential jurors without any reason being given. They will not be used unless there are not enough other jurors.

The jury's role

Criminal cases

In the Crown Court a jury of 12 is used in cases where the defendant pleads not guilty. The judge decides points of law and the jury decides the facts. The jury decides whether the defendant is guilty or not guilty and must try to come to a unanimous verdict. If this is not possible a majority verdict of 10-2 or 11-1 will be allowed.

Civil cases

A jury may be used in the Queen's Bench Division of the High Court (12 jurors) and in the County Court (eight jurors) for cases of fraud, defamation, false imprisonment and malicious prosecution. The jury decides who wins the case and the amount of damages to be awarded.

Advantages of jury trial

→ Public confidence – the idea of trial by jury is very old and people prefer it to having a verdict by a single judge.
→ Upholds democracy and allows ordinary people to show their disapproval of a certain law, *Ponting's Case*.
→ Makes law more open as points have to be explained to the jury and the whole process is public.
→ Random cross-section should mean an impartial jury cancelling out each other's biases.

Disadvantages of jury trials

→ Failure to understand the issues involved.
→ Prejudice as jurors may be biased, e.g. against the police or against ethnic minority defendants, or media coverage may influence them.
→ The compulsory nature of jury service is unpopular.
→ No reasons have to be given for the verdict, so there is no way of knowing whether the jury did understand the case. Also makes it difficult to appeal against a jury verdict.
→ Jury 'nobbling' does occur and in some cases juries have had to be provided with police protection.
→ Slow and expensive as having to explain each point to the jury means that trials take longer and costs rise.
→ Awards of damages in civil cases are unpredictable.

Checkpoint 4

Can you suggest alternative methods to using a jury for criminal trials?

Checkpoint 5

Try to explain *Ponting's Case*.

Test yourself

Try writing out these lists of advantages and disadvantages from memory.

Exam questions answers: page 56

1 In criminal cases the right to jury trial is regarded as important. Explain why this is so. (30 min)

2 Explain and comment on the decline of the use of juries in civil trials. (30 min)

Examiner's secrets

The examiner likes you to support your answers with specific examples, e.g. of cases in which there were problems with media influence.

Answers
Legal personnel

Solicitors and barristers

Checkpoints

1 They have passed both the academic and vocational stages and are now qualified as a barrister.
2 QC means Queen's Counsel. They are appointed by the Lord Chancellor and are barristers or solicitors with at least ten years' advocacy experience.
3 All solicitors have the right to do advocacy in the Magistrates' Court, the County Court and tribunals. As these deal with the vast majority of cases, solicitors are likely to do more cases than barristers.
4 Fellow of the Institute of Legal Executives.

Exam questions

1 Deal with training first, explaining the academic, vocational and professional stages. You could also explain that solicitors are expected to keep their knowledge up to date with continuous professional development (CPD), in one-day or short courses. After describing the training you need to make some comments on it, e.g.:
   - cost of training, especially the LPC, means that poorer students find it difficult to qualify
   - difficulty of getting a training contract
   - the wide spread of training with the three stages means solicitors are fully equipped to practise
   - Access to Justice Act 1999 training to be altered to include training in advocacy

   Go on to describe the work of solicitors: private practice, partnerships, first point of contact for the public, variety of work. Give examples, e.g. drafting contracts, drafting leases, conveyancing, advocacy.

   Finally, comment on the work, e.g.:
   - increasing amount of advocacy
   - variety of work; specialism of solicitors in large firms
   - the loss of the monopoly on conveyancing

2 Again note there are two matters to be discussed. Start with the role of the Legal Services Ombudsman:
   - an independent person set up by the Courts and Legal Services Act 1990 to investigate complaints against all branches of the legal profession
   - only investigates the way the complaint was handled by the legal profession
   - does not reinvestigate the subject of the complaint; this is a source of dissatisfaction for complainants
   - can order compensation to be paid

   The Office for the Supervision of Solicitors investigates complaints against solicitors. It is not independent as it is funded by the Law Society. It has been criticized for delays and inefficiency. Those who are not satisfied can complain to the Legal Services Ombudsman.

Funding of legal services

Checkpoints

1 • ALAS, the Law Society's free Accident Legal Advice Service.
   • FRU, the Free Representation Unit under which barristers will do cases free.
2 *Disposable income* is the amount of income available after payment of essential living expenses. A set amount is allowed for this.
   Disposable capital is assets such as money in the bank or building society, shares, jewellery, and the equity value of your house (i.e. the value of the house after deducting the amount of mortgage still owed).
3 Courts and Legal Services Act 1990 introduced conditional fees. Access to Justice Act 1999 extended their use.
4 The five factors taken into account are whether:
   - the defendant is likely to lose his liberty or livelihood or suffer serious damage to his reputation
   - a substantial point of law is involved
   - the defendant can understand the proceedings
   - tracing, interviewing or expert cross-examination of witnesses is involved
   - it is in the interests of another person that the defendant should be represented

Exam questions

1 This only asks about funding of civil cases.
   Private funding – comment on the cost of paying and the availability of conditional fees; also the risk of paying the other side's costs if the case is lost.
   Public funding – outline the role of the Community Legal Service Fund and explain the limitations on funding. This should include such points as:
   - not available for personal injury cases (except medical negligence)
   - not available for small claims or tribunal hearings
   - set budget which may mean that no funds are left for some cases
   - are the financial limits too low? Should government funding be available to only the very poorest?
2 This is a criminal case, so you need to advise Errol about relevant advice and representation schemes.
   - Free advice from duty solicitor at the police station.
   - Advice at the Magistrates' Court on the first hearing; this is also available free from the duty solicitor.
   - Representation in court – the Criminal Defence Service allows for this if it is in the interests of justice. As robbery is a serious charge and likely to lead to a prison sentence if he is found guilty, Errol is likely to qualify. But point out to Errol that he may have to pay for this if his disposable income and capital are above the free limits.

The judiciary

Checkpoints

1. (a) High Court – High Court judges or 'puisne' judges
   (b) Court of Appeal – Lords Justices of Appeal
   (c) House of Lords – Lords of Appeal in Ordinary
2. (a) Crown Court:
   - High Court judges to try the most serious cases
   - Circuit judges who deal with the majority of cases
   - Recorders who are part-time judges
   (b) County Court:
   - Circuit judges for fast-track and multi-track cases
   - District judges to deal with small claims
3. Well-known cases include:
   - *R v Secretary of State, ex parte Venables and Thompson* (1997) where the House of Lords ruled that the Home Secretary should not have set a minimum period of 15 years' custody for two young offenders.
   - *R v Secretary of State for Foreign Affairs, ex parte World Development Movement Ltd* (1995) where a grant of aid to Malaysia for the Pergau Dam project was held to be beyond the Secretary of State's powers.
4. The Access to Justice Act 1999 is a good example as it gives the Lord Chancellor very wide powers over the Community Legal Service.

Exam questions

1. In order to criticize you must explain first! Start by explaining appointment and training, including:
   - the Lord Chancellor's major role in appointment
   - the increasing use of adverts for judicial posts
   - the appointment by invitation only for Court of Appeal and House of Lords
   - the role of the Judicial Studies Board in training
   Don't forget to include some critical comments, e.g.
   - risk of political influence in appointment (should there be an independent appointments commission?)
   - the fact that there are so few women and ethnic minority judges
   - is the limited training adequate – would a career judiciary be better?
2. Start by explaining the principle of judicial independence. Also include an explanation of the doctrine of the separation of powers as this shows why judges should be independent from the executive. This sets the scene and you can then explain the Lord Chancellor's role, linking what he does to whether there is a conflict. Include:
   - Lord Chancellor is appointed by the Prime Minister
   - Lord Chancellor's role in appointing judges
   - Lord Chancellor can dismiss lower level judges for incapacity or misbehaviour
   - judges' role in judicial review
   Illustrate the latter with cases where decisions of the Lord Chancellor have been the subject of judicial review, e.g. *R v Lord Chancellor ex parte Witham* (1997) on court fees and *R v Legal Aid Board and Lord Chancellor ex parte Duncan* (2000) on the reduction of the number of legal aid contracts offered to solicitors.
   Finally write a brief conclusion which is supported by your arguments.

Lay magistrates

Checkpoints

1. Good character; understanding and communication; social awareness; maturity and sound temperament; sound judgement; commitment and reliability.
2. District judges (Magistrates' Court) formerly called stipendiary magistrates. Must have been qualified as a barrister or solicitor for at least seven years. Used in cities and bigger towns with large workloads.
3. Six months' imprisonment for one offence (12 months for two or more offences) and £5 000 fine.
4. The normal route is to the Crown Court, where the case is retried by a judge and two magistrates. It is also possible to appeal against conviction to the Queen's Bench Divisional Court on a point of law.

Exam questions

1. (a) Explain the role in criminal cases of dealing with all summary offences and also triable either way cases suitable for the Magistrates' Court. Point out the wider role of issuing warrants and deciding bail and civil matters such as licensing. Include the role in the Family Court and the Youth Court.
   (b) This requires a brief discussion of the advantages and disadvantages of lay magistrates. Cover points on both sides of the argument and give a conclusion.
2. This is a wider question. You must include juries as well as lay magistrates and briefly mention others such as lay members of tribunals.
   Magistrates – criminal, administrative (licensing), Youth Court and Family panel.
   Jury – main use in Crown Court trying serious crimes; also some use in civil courts (Queen's Bench Division and County Court, see pages 52–3) and also Coroners' Courts.
   Comments can include: the idea of trial by one's peers; public confidence in juries; can lay people understand legal cases? does it lead to inconsistent decision-making? how could they be replaced?

The jury

Checkpoints

1 Disqualified if:
- currently on bail
- has ever been sentenced to life imprisonment or to a custodial sentence of five years or more
- has in last ten years served a custodial sentence of less than five years or had a suspended sentence or a community service order
- been placed on probation in the last five years

2 Excused as of right includes: Members of Parliament; doctors and nurses; members of the armed forces.

3 Too many people are disqualified, ineligible or excused; this can mean there is not a cross-section of society. Vetting is an invasion of privacy and unconstitutional.

4 Alternatives include: a panel of three judges; two lay members with a judge; a judge sitting alone.

5 Ponting was charged under the old section 2 of the Official Secrets Act 1911 because he leaked information on the sinking of a ship in the Falklands war to an MP. He claimed this was in the public interest and the jury acquitted him.

Exam questions

1 This only asks for juries in criminal cases. Explain the role of a jury in such a case. Go on to consider why the right to jury trial is thought important, e.g.:

- the jury is a cross-section of the general public
- random selection means bias should be avoided
- historically viewed as protector of liberty, *Bushell's case* (1670)
- law is more open
- unpopular laws can be challenged, *Ponting's Case*

2 As you have to explain the decline in use in civil cases start with a brief history of their use:

- Up to 1854 all common law cases were tried by jury, after this parties could agree not to have a jury but to have the case tried by a single judge.
- 1933 the Administration of Justice Act limited the right to use a jury so that they could not be used for breach of contract cases.
- *Ward v James* (1966) which decided that juries were not suitable in personal injury cases.
- Now the Supreme Court Act 1981 gives right to jury trial only for defamation, malicious prosecution and false imprisonment and allegations of fraud.
- Damages awarded by juries can now be changed on appeal by the Court of Appeal.

This shows that the decline is partly due to the change in the law, but also that when a choice exists parties prefer trial by judge. Comment on why this is so: quicker, cheaper, more predictable, etc.

In criminal law it is necessary to understand the key principles of the law and also to be able to put these principles into practice in specific areas of the law. The key principles are *actus reus* and *mens rea*, and the concept of strict liability. The offences which are common to all exam boards are murder, manslaughter and assaults. For all offences you must know the definition and relevant cases. There are also general defences which you need to understand and be able to apply in different situations.

Exam themes

→ The acts/omissions need to prove an offence (*actus reus*)

→ The level of intention needed (*mens rea*)

→ Scenarios where a death has been caused (murder and/or manslaughter)

→ The law on assaults (usually in a scenario-type question)

→ Offences against property (also usually in a scenario-type question)

→ The availability of defences

Topic checklist

○ AS ● A2

	AQA	OCR	WJEC
Actus reus	○●	●	●
Mens rea	○●	●	●
Strict liability	○	●	●
Participation and attempts		●	
Murder	●	●	●
Involuntary manslaughter	●	●	●
Assaults	○●	●	●
Theft, robbery and burglary	●	●	
Other offences against property	●	●*	
Insanity and automatism	●	●	●
Duress, necessity and self-defence	●	●	●
Intoxication and mistake	●	●	●

*criminal damage only

Actus reus

"Actus non facit reum, nisi mens sit rea."

Latin Maxim

Checkpoint 1

Do you know what the Latin maxim quoted above means?

Checkpoint 2

Can you list any other offences in which an Act of Parliament makes an omission the *actus reus* of the offence?

Action point

Make a spider chart of the situations in which there is a duty to act.

Test yourself

From memory write down the five circumstances in which a duty can exist and give a case for each.

Checkpoint 3

Can you explain the case of *Airedale National Health Trust v Bland* in more detail?

Actus reus is often described as the 'guilty act' which has to be done for the offence to be committed. However, this is not a full enough or accurate enough definition. In some cases failing to act (an omission) makes the defendant liable. For some offences there must also be a consequence which occurs as a result of the act.

Omissions as *actus reus*

Some Acts of Parliament create offences of omission, such as failing to report a road traffic accident. In such offences the failure to do something is the *actus reus*.

For **common law crimes**, an omission will only be enough for the *actus reus* if the defendant is under a duty to act. Such a duty can exist in the following circumstances:

→ *Under a contract*, e.g. in a contract of employment where the failure to fulfil a contractual obligation is likely to endanger the lives of others, *R v Pittwood* (1902).

→ *By virtue of relationship* especially the parent/child relationship. Parents are under a duty to care for their child. In *R v Gibbins and Proctor* (1918) a father and the woman he was living with were guilty of murder when they starved his child to death.

→ *Voluntary undertaking of the care of another* where that other is incapable of caring for themselves and relies on the accused. In *R v Stone and Dobinson* (1977) the defendants were found guilty of manslaughter as they were under a legal duty to summon help or to continue to care for Stone's invalid sister themselves.

→ *A duty which exists by virtue of holding some public offices*
A person may be under an obligation to act as a result of his office, *R v Dytham* (1979). But if the duty to act would involve 'greater danger than a man of ordinary firmness and activity may be expected to encounter' a person is not responsible for failing to act.

→ *A duty arising from the accused's conduct*, e.g. *R v Miller* (1983) where Miller accidentally started a fire in a squat, but did nothing to stop the fire from spreading. In *R v Khan* (1998) the Court of Appeal said that new duty situations could occur.

The duty of doctors

A doctor is under a duty to care for a patient unless the patient refuses medical treatment. In this case if the doctor omits to act then that omission cannot form the *actus reus* of any crime. However, where a patient is not in a position to give instructions about treatment, it is a question of what is in the patient's best interests. In *Airedale National Health Service Trust v Bland* (1993) Bland was in a persistent vegetative state. The House of Lords held that it was in his best interests for feeding to be withdrawn to allow him to die.

Causation

The *actus reus* may require a consequence which follows from the act or omission. In these cases the court has to be satisfied that the accused's conduct caused that consequence, e.g. in an assault causing actual bodily harm it must be shown that the accused not only assaulted the victim but that that assault also caused 'actual bodily harm'.

Intervening acts

A main problem with causation is where the defendant sets in motion a chain of events which finally ends with the forbidden consequence, but there has been an intervening act contributing to the causation of that consequence. This can occur where:

→ *the victim takes avoiding action* – e.g. jumps into a river to escape an attacker and then drowns, *R v Pitts* (1842), *R v Corbett* (1996)
→ *a third person reacts reasonably to the defendant's threats* – in *R v Pagett* (1983) police officers shot a girl who was being used as a shield by the defendant while he fired at the police. Pagett was held liable for her manslaughter
→ *poor medical treatment fails to save the victim* – in *R v Cheshire* (1991) the victim was shot. He needed a tracheotomy and died because this had become blocked due to a rare complication. At the time of his death the wounds from the shots were healing well, but it was held that the defendant was still liable for the death

The following have been held *not* to break the chain of causation:

→ switching off a life support machine where the patient is pronounced brain dead, *R v Malcherek* (1981)
→ not giving a blood transfusion that could have saved the victim because the victim refused treatment, *R v Blaue* (1975)

Coincidence of *actus reus* and *mens rea*

Whatever type of *mens rea* is required, there is the rule that both the *mens rea* and the *actus reus* must be present at the same time. But where there is a chain of events the courts take a broad view. If a defendant intended to kill and the victim died as a result of the plan then the defendant would be guilty as both the *actus reus* and the *mens rea* were present at some time during that plan, *Thabo Meli v The Queen* (1954).

Checkpoint 4

Can you list other offences for which a consequence has to be proved?

Test yourself

Write out from memory the situations in which an intervening act has been held not to break the chain of causation.

> "... *if the original wound is an operating and substantial cause, then the death can properly be said to be the result of the wound.*"
>
> *R v Smith* (1975)

Checkpoint 5

Can you name other cases in which there was a decision about the coincidence of *actus reus* and *mens rea*?

Examiner's secrets

The examiner wants comments on the law, not just a list of facts.

Exam questions

answers: page 82

1 Critically analyze the circumstances in which a person may be criminally liable for failing to act. (45 min)

2 Explain what is meant by a break in the chain of causation. Discuss why this concept is important in criminal law. (45 min)

Links

There is also a question on page 69 where you have to apply the concepts of causation to a given set of facts.

Mens rea

To be guilty of a crime the defendant must usually have the necessary *mens rea* or guilty mind. There are different levels of *mens rea* for different crimes. The most important types are specific intention, subjective recklessness and objective recklessness.

Specific intention

In *R v Mohan* (1976) specific intention was explained as 'a decision to bring about, in so far as it lies within the accused's power, [a particular consequence] no matter whether the accused desired that consequence of his act or not'.

Specific intention has to be proved for crimes such as murder and causing grievous bodily harm with intent.

Foresight of consequences

The difficulty is where a defendant does not desire the consequence: his main aim is something else, but his actions have the effect of making the consequence happen. This is known as oblique intent or foresight of consequences.

You need to know several cases for this, as each case builds on what the previous one decided. These cases are:

→ *R v Moloney* (1985) where it was decided that foresight of consequences was only evidence from which intention could be inferred.
→ *R v Hancock and Shankland* (1986) which stressed that the probability of the consequence occurring is important in deciding whether there is evidence from which to infer intention.
→ *R v Nedrick* (1986) in which the Court of Appeal said that the jury should ask themselves two questions:
  1 How probable was the consequence which resulted from the defendant's voluntary act?
  2 Did the defendant foresee that act?
  Then, if the consequence was a virtual certainty and the jury were sure that the defendant foresaw it as being so, there would be evidence from which the jury could infer intention.
→ *R v Woollin* (1998) in which the House of Lords did not like the use of the two questions in Nedrick but agreed that the jury should be told that they are not entitled to find the necessary intention unless they feel sure that the consequence was a virtual certainty as a result of the defendant's actions and that the defendant appreciated that such was the case.

Comment

As you can see the decisions of the courts have made this area of law very complicated. It needs to be reformed. A draft Criminal Code, with a definition of intention, was produced by the Law Commission as long ago as 1989, but Parliament has not yet (2003) made it law.

The jargon

Direct intent is where a defendant intends to make a particular consequence happen.

Checkpoint 1

Make a list of crimes which have specific intent as the *mens rea*.

Checkpoint 2

Write out the facts of the four cases featured under 'Foresight of consequences'.

Test yourself

Write this list of cases out from memory. Include a brief summary of facts and the point of law decided in the case.

Subjective recklessness ●●●

This is a lower level of *mens rea* than specific intention. It was explained in *R v Cunningham* (1957). Here the defendant was charged with 'maliciously administering a noxious thing so as to endanger life' when he tore a gas meter from the wall in an empty house in order to steal money from it, and as a result gas leaked into the next-door house, making the woman who lived there ill. The court decided that the word 'maliciously' meant either:

→ an actual intention to do the particular type of harm that was in fact done or

→ recklessness in the sense that the defendant when acting realized there was some risk of such harm occurring

This second meaning is known as subjective recklessness because the defendant realizes there is a risk. This meant that Cunningham could not be guilty unless he at least realized that there was a risk that escaping gas could injure someone. Subjective recklessness is the level of intention which needs to be proved for offences of common assault, assault causing actual bodily harm and malicious wounding.

Objective recklessness ●●●

This is a lower level of *mens rea* since it includes situations where the defendant has not realized there is a risk although an 'ordinary prudent individual' would have realized the risk, *MPC v Caldwell* (1981). The courts are no longer considering what the defendant realized; they are imposing an external test of what others would have realized. This can make a defendant criminally liable even though he or she was incapable of realizing the risk, *Elliott v C* (1983). Objective recklessness is the *mens rea* for offences of criminal damage. The ordinary prudent individual is always taken as being the ordinary prudent adult even when the defendants are only 11 or 12 years old, *R v R and G* (2002).

Transferred malice ●●●

If the defendant intends to attack a particular person but by mistake attacks another person, the law transfers the intention from the intended victim to the actual victim. This prevents a defendant from trying to argue that there was no *mens rea* so far as the actual victim was concerned, *R v Latimer* (1886). But if the original intention was to carry out a quite different crime then it is not possible to transfer that intention, *R v Pembliton* (1874).

The jargon

Cunningham recklessness is another name for subjective recklessness.

Checkpoint 3

Explain in your own words what is meant by subjective recklessness.

The jargon

Caldwell recklessness is another name for objective recklessness.

Checkpoint 4

Identify the key differences between subjective and objective recklessness.

Examiner's secrets

The examiner will be impressed if you can use cases accurately to support your arguments.

Links

There is also a question on page 67 where you have to apply the concepts of *mens rea* to a given set of facts.

Exam questions   answers: page 82

1   Critically discuss the problems the courts have had in trying to define intention. (45 min)

2   Explain and comment on the differences between subjective and objective recklessness. (45 min)

Strict liability

The normal rules of *mens rea* do not apply to crimes of strict liability; the offence is committed by the defendant doing the *actus reus*. This can appear unfair as a defendant will be guilty even though he did not intend to commit a crime.

Absolute liability ●●●

This is where no intention at all is required, nor need there be a voluntary act. The defendant is guilty because a state of affairs exists. This happened in *Winzar v Chief Constable of Kent* (1983) where a drunken man was asked to leave a hospital. When he remained, the police were called to remove him. They took him to the road outside, placed him in the police car and charged him with being found drunk on the highway, contrary to section 12 of the Licensing Act 1872.

Checkpoint 1

Can you give another case example of absolute liability?

Strict liability ●●●

Normally there is a requirement at least to intend to do the act, as shown by *R v Prince* (1875), where the defendant was charged with taking a girl under the age of sixteen out of the possession of her father (section 55 Offences against the Person Act 1861). Prince knew that the girl was in the custody of her father but mistakenly believed that she was eighteen years old. He was guilty because he intended to remove her from her father's custody; his belief about her age was irrelevant as the offence was held to be one of strict liability.

Checkpoint 2

Can you explain the facts of two other cases that are also examples of strict liability?

Presumption that *mens rea* is required ●●●

The courts start by presuming that *mens rea* is required for any offence. As a result there are only a few **common law offences** that do not require *mens rea*. These are: public nuisance, blasphemous libel, and criminal contempt of court.

Checkpoint 3

Explain what is meant by common law offences and statutory offences.

Statutory offences

Again the courts start with the presumption that *mens rea* is required. *Gammon (Hong Kong) Ltd v AG of Hong Kong* (1985) says:

→ the presumption that *mens rea* is required is particularly strong where the offence is 'truly criminal' in character
→ the presumption can only be displaced if this is clearly stated or implied by the statute creating the offence
→ the presumption can only be displaced where the statute is concerned with an issue of social concern
→ even where there is an issue of social concern involved, *mens rea* will still be required unless it can be shown that making the offence one of strict liability will help to prevent the offence occurring

Action point

To make sure you understand the effect of this list, rewrite it in your own words.

In *B v DPP* (2000), the House of Lords stressed that even if an Act was silent on *mens rea*, there was a presumption that it was required. For strict liability to exist it must be 'compellingly clear' either expressly or by implication that Parliament intended this.

Social concern

Where an offence is likely to affect the public interest as a whole, then the courts are more likely to decide that the offence is one of strict liability. This covers such matters as:

→ pollution
→ public safety
→ laws regulating the sale of food
→ revenue offences

Comparing strict liability with levels of *mens rea* ●●●

There are different levels of *mens rea* which are applied to different crimes. Strict liability is the lowest level in proving a criminal offence. Use this diagram to compare the different levels of *mens rea*.

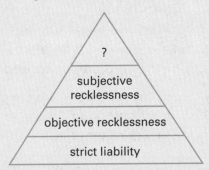

Justification for strict liability ●●●

The main reasons for having strict liability offences are:

→ *the welfare of the community* – it is seen as a way of encouraging high standards of care in areas where there are potential hazards to the community in general
→ *evidential problems* – in many cases it would be impossible to prove *mens rea* – every defendant could say 'I didn't mean to' or 'I didn't know'

However it is argued that it is contrary to the fundamental principles of justice to create offences under which people can be found guilty and may be at risk of losing their liberty, even though they had no blameworthy intent.

Most people argue that there should be a *due diligence* defence so a defendant would not be guilty if he had taken all reasonable steps to avoid committing the offence. A 'no negligence' defence exists for some statutory strict liability offences where the defendant is not guilty provided he was not negligent.

Exam questions
answers: page 83

1 Explain what is meant by 'strict liability' in the criminal law and consider what justifications there are for this concept. (30 min)

2 'The injustices caused by strict liability are often exaggerated: it is needed as it provides important social benefits.' Discuss. (45 min)

"It is of the utmost importance that rivers should not be polluted."

Alphacell Ltd v Woodward (1972)

Checkpoint 4

Explain what this diagram shows about the different levels of *mens rea* and state what should replace the question mark.

Checkpoint 5

Can you give other reasons for and against the use of strict liability offences?

Examiner's secrets

In these questions the examiner wants you to use examples to explain your points.

Participation and attempts

> *"Who so ever shall aid, abet, counsel or procure the commission of any indictable offence . . . shall be liable . . ."*
>
> Section 8 Accessories and Abettors Act 1861

More than one person may be guilty of the same offence. They may not play the same role in the crime but under the law they are all guilty of participating in it. It is also possible for a defendant to be guilty even though he has failed to commit the crime he intended to do. In this case he may be guilty of an attempt to do it.

Principal offenders

The principal offender is the person who is directly responsible for bringing about the *actus reus* of an offence. It it possible for two or more people to be joint principals, for example, one defendant holds the gun while the other grabs the money. A person is also the principal if he uses an innocent agent to carry out the *actus reus*.

Secondary parties

The Attorney-General's Reference (No. 1) of 1975 stresses that each of the words 'aid, abet, counsel or procure' has a distinct meaning.

→ **Aid** – this is any conduct which literally aids the principal to commit the offence, for example being the getaway driver or acting as a lookout or supplying the principal with tools to carry out the offence.

→ **Abet** – this is any conduct which instigates, incites or encourages the principal in the commission of the offence. It includes persuading someone to commit a crime (NB this is also the crime of incitement) or shouting encouragement.

→ **Counsel** – this is where advice is given to the principal before he commits the crime, for example suggesting what type of explosive would be most likely to blow open a safe.

→ **Procure** – setting out to see that something happens and taking the appropriate steps to produce that happening, such as adding alcohol to a driver's drink so he drove while over the limit.

The *mens rea* of secondary parties

A secondary party must have knowledge that the principal is going to commit a crime and must have intended to encourage or assist the commission of that crime.

Knowledge and unforeseen consequences

Knowledge does not mean detailed knowledge. The secondary party need only know the type of offence involved, *R v Bainbridge* (1959), *DPP for Northern Ireland v Maxwell* (1979).

If the principal commits a completely different crime to the one originally envisaged by the secondary party then the secondary party will not be guilty. In *R v Powell*, *R v English* (1997) the House of Lords stated that what was contemplated by the secondary party was the important point. It is for the jury to decide whether the use of a particular weapon went beyond what was contemplated by the secondary party.

Checkpoint 1

Give a case to illustrate each of these four ways of being a secondary participant in a crime.

Test yourself

From memory write out the list of words which set out the ways in which a defendant can be liable as a secondary participant and briefly explain each one.

The jargon

To *procure* means 'to produce by endeavour'. (Attorney-General's Reference (No. 1) of 1975.)

Checkpoint 2

State the facts of the cases of *R v Bainbridge* and *DPP for Northern Ireland v Maxwell.*

Repentance

The secondary party may avoid liability if he withdraws clearly and effectively from the venture before it is committed by the principal. However simply saying 'let's go' and running from the scene is not always enough to avoid guilt, *R v Becerra* (1975).

Attempts ●●●

An attempt is defined in the Criminal Attempts Act 1981 as doing an act which is more than merely preparatory to the commission of an offence with intent to commit that offence.

'More than merely preparatory'

This is the *actus reus* of attempt. What is meant by more than merely preparatory? Here are some useful case examples:

→ Standing on a milk crate looking through a broken window was attempted burglary. The full crime of burglary would be committed once the defendant entered the building, so there was nothing else left to be done, *O'Brien v Anderton* (1984).

→ Running on to a race track to interrupt a race (and so get back a bet) was merely preparatory and not sufficient to convict of attempted theft, *R v Gullefer* (1987).

→ Being outside a post office with an imitation gun in a pocket was merely preparatory and not an attempt to rob, *R v Campbell* (1991).

Mens rea of an attempt ●●●

This has to be the *mens rea* for the completed crime or, in some cases, a higher level of intention, e.g. for a charge of attempted murder, the prosecution must prove an intention to kill as an intention to cause grievous bodily harm is sufficient for the completed crime of murder but not for an attempt. Similarly recklessness is not sufficient for attempted criminal damage, *R v Millward and Vernon* (1987).

> *"He ought to be guilty for harm which he foresaw and which in fact resulted from the crime he encouraged and assisted."*
>
> R v English (1997)

Checkpoint 3

Can you quote the whole of section 1(1) of the Criminal Attempts Act 1981?

Test yourself

Write out this list from memory.

Checkpoint 4

Do you know what was decided by the case of *R v Shivpuri* (1986)?

Exam questions   answers: pages 83–4

1 In the law of attempts, how satisfactory is the test that there must be an act which is 'more than merely preparatory'? (30 min)

2 Andy and Bill decide that they will burgle a local factory. Andy asks Charles for some tools to help break in, but does not tell him where the burglary will be. A week before the planned burglary, Bill tells Andy he does not wish to take part, so Andy asks Don to help him. Andy knows that Don always carries a knife, but thinks there will be no one in the factory. When Andy and Don break into the factory, they are confronted by two guards. Don stabs and kills one of the guards. Don then picks up a chair and batters the other guard to death. Assuming Andy and Don committed burglary and Don murdered the two guards, consider the liability of Andy, Bill and Charles as secondary parties. (45 min)

Examiner's secrets

The examiner tells you to assume Andy and Don committed burglary and that Don is guilty of murder, so the examiner does not want you to waste time discussing these points.

Murder

The definition of murder is an unlawful killing of a human being, under the Queen's peace, with malice aforethought, either express or implied. As well as understanding this definition you need to know the special defences to murder.

Actus reus of murder ●●●

The defendant must do an act or omission which causes the death of another person. You should note that a foetus is not included in the definition of 'person'. However, if the child is born alive and then dies of the injuries inflicted when it was in the womb, this can be murder, Attorney-General's Reference (No. 3 of 1994), 1997.

Checkpoint 1
In the law on causation can you explain the cases of *R v Smith* (1959), *R v Jordan* (1956) and *R v Cheshire* (1991)?

Causation
The rules on causation apply. This means that there must not be an intervening act which breaks the chain of causation (see page 59 for details on causation).

Mens rea of murder ●●●

The *mens rea* of murder lies in the phrase **malice aforethought**. This is the key difference between murder and manslaughter. Murder is a crime of specific intent and the defendant must have the intent either:

→ to kill (express malice) or
→ to cause grievous bodily harm (implied malice)

Comment

Checkpoint 2
Do you know the facts of *R v Vickers* (1957) and *R v Cunningham* (1981)?

Should a defendant who intended to do his victim serious harm, but did not want to kill him, be found guilty of murder if his victim dies? The cases of *R v Vickers* (1957) and *R v Cunningham* (1981) have clearly decided that this lesser intention is sufficient to make the defendant guilty of murder.

Action point
Add notes on the cases in the foresight of consequences section to your notes on murder.

Foresight of consequences
Since murder requires specific intention, the cases on foresight of consequences apply (see page 60). This means that foresight that death or serious injury is virtually certain to result is not intention but can form evidence from which intention can be inferred.

Checkpoint 3
Do you know why it is necessary to allow these special defences to murder?

Special defences to murder ●●●

There are three special defences to murder which reduce the offence to manslaughter. This type of manslaughter is called **voluntary manslaughter**. The defences are:

→ diminished responsibility
→ provocation
→ killing in pursuance of a suicide pact

Remember, these defences apply only to murder.

Examiner's secrets
You must be clear that these special defences apply only to murder and that they only reduce the charge to manslaughter.

Diminished responsibility

This is a defence under section 2 of the Homicide Act 1957 and covers situations where the person killed while suffering from 'an abnormality of mind' which substantially impaired their mental responsibility for acts and omissions in doing or being a party to the killing. The phrase abnormality of mind was explained in the case of *R v Byrne* (1960) as covering the mind in all its aspects, including:

→ the perception of physical acts and matters and the ability to form a rational judgement as to whether an act is right or wrong
→ the ability to exercise will-power to control physical acts

If the defendant is drunk, this must be ignored in deciding whether the diminished responsibility affected his acts, *R v Egan* (1992).

Provocation

Section 3 of the Homicide Act 1957 says that where there is evidence that the defendant was provoked to lose his self-control, then the jury must decide whether the provocation was enough to make a reasonable man do as the defendant did. There must be a sudden loss of self-control. Normally a long time interval between the provocation and the killing will mean the defence will fail. However, in *R v Ahluwalia* (1992) the Court of Appeal accepted that, provided there was a sudden loss of self-control, a delayed reaction did not negate the defence of provocation.

Characteristics of the defendant

There are problems as the jury must decide whether the provocation was enough to make a reasonable man do as the defendant did. In *DPP v Camplin* (1978) it was held that the reasonable man was a person:

'. . . sharing such of the accused's characteristics as they think would affect the gravity of the provocation to him.'

In *R v Morhall* (1995) the fact that the defendant was a glue-sniffer was a relevant characteristic, as the provocation had been about that fact. In *R v Smith* (*Morgan James*) (2000) the House of Lords ruled that a jury could also take into account characteristics, such as depressive illness, which affected the defendant's powers of self-control.

Exam questions

answers: page 84

1 Fiona has often been assaulted by her partner, Gary. As a result of this, she has been suffering from severe depression and has begun to drink a lot. One evening after Gary had hit her several times, Fiona sat in the kitchen and drank several glasses of vodka. She suddenly grabbed a knife and ran into the room where Gary was asleep and stabbed him. Discuss Fiona's liability for Gary's death. (45 min)

2 Herman decides to set fire to a factory he owns in order to claim the insurance money. He waits until after the evening shift have finished work, then he pours petrol through a ventilator, and sets it alight. Ivan, a cleaner, is still in the factory and is killed in the fire. Consider Herman's liability for Ivan's death. (30 min)

". . . a state of mind so different from that of ordinary human beings that a reasonable man would term it abnormal . . ."

R v Byrne (1960)

". . . a sudden and temporary loss of self-control . . ."

R v Duffy (1949)

Checkpoint 4

Do you know the facts in the case of *R v Ahluwalia* (1992)?

Don't forget

Remember to give the section number of the Homicide Act 1957 when mentioning one of the special defences.

Examiner's secrets

Where the examiner wants you to discuss diminished responsibility and/or provocation, the problem will give clear indications about this. Don't miss key words such as 'depressed' or 'teased'.

Involuntary manslaughter

This is committed where a death is unlawfully caused by the defendant, but the defendant did not have the necessary *mens rea* for murder. Involuntary manslaughter can be committed in two ways: by an unlawful and dangerous act (constructive manslaughter) or by gross negligence and, possibly, by reckless manslaughter.

Constructive manslaughter

There are three elements that must be proved:

→ the commission by the defendant of an unlawful act
→ that the act was dangerous in the sense that it was likely to cause harm to another, and
→ that the act was the cause of death

Test yourself

From memory write down the three elements which have to be proved in constructive manslaughter.

Unlawful act

There must be an unlawful act. An omission is not sufficient to make the defendant guilty, *R v Lowe* (1973). The act need not be directed at the victim; the principle of transferred malice applies, *R v Mitchell* (1983). The unlawful act need not even be directed at a person, provided it is dangerous in the sense that it is likely to cause harm to another, *R v Goodfellow* (1986).

Checkpoint 1

Give the facts of the cases of *R v Lowe*, *R v Mitchell* and *R v Goodfellow*.

Dangerous act

The test is an objective one. The defendant does not have to realize it is dangerous. The test is whether the reasonable person would realize the act risked another person being harmed. If the victim dies from a heart attack brought on by the defendant's act the rules are:

→ if a reasonable person would not have realized that any physical harm was likely to happen then the defendant will not be guilty, *R v Dawson* (1985)
→ if a reasonable person would have known that some physical harm was likely to occur, e.g. where a frail and elderly victim was tied up, then the defendant is guilty, *R v Watson* (1991)

The act caused the death

The normal rules of causation apply. If there is an intervening act breaking the chain of causation the defendant is not guilty, as in *R v Dalby* (1982) where the defendant supplied the victim with a class A drug, but the victim prepared the solution and injected it into himself. In *R v Kennedy* (1999) the defendant was guilty because he filled the syringe and handed it to the victim.

Checkpoint 2

Can you name a case in which the defendant was guilty because he injected the drug into the victim?

Mens rea

The only *mens rea* needed by the defendant is an intention to do the unlawful act, *DPP v Newbury and Jones* (1976). The defendant does not have to realize that the act was either unlawful or dangerous.

Gross negligence manslaughter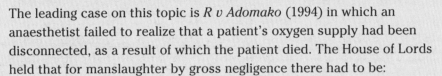

The leading case on this topic is *R v Adomako* (1994) in which an anaesthetist failed to realize that a patient's oxygen supply had been disconnected, as a result of which the patient died. The House of Lords held that for manslaughter by gross negligence there had to be:

→ a duty of care
→ a breach of that duty causing the victim's death, and
→ the breach had to be serious

They approved the statement in *R v Bateman* (1925) that there had to be 'such disregard for life and safety of others as to amount to a crime against the state and conduct deserving of punishment'.

Duty of care
There are many situations in which a duty of care exists. The most obvious ones are the duty owed by a doctor to his patient and the duty owed by a driver to all other road users. However, *R v Khan* (1998) made it clear that a duty can exist in other situations and that the categories of duty are capable of being extended. In *R v Singh* (1999) the defendant owed a duty to take reasonable steps regarding danger from a faulty gas fire.

Seriousness of breach
In considering whether the breach was serious enough to qualify as gross negligence, a jury must look at all the circumstances in which the defendant was placed and 'consider whether the extent to which the defendant's conduct departed from the proper standard of care incumbent upon him, *involving as it must have done a risk of death* to the patient, was such as it should be judged criminal'.

Note that reckless manslaughter may still exist where the defendant realizes the risk of injury, *R v Lidar* (2000).

Exam questions   answers: pages 84–5

1   Jon, in the course of an argument with Ken, picks up a stone and throws it at Ken. It misses Ken, but hits Lucy, who was walking past. Lucy falls to the ground and strikes her head on a concrete slab, causing severe injuries. Lucy is taken to hospital, where she is operated on for head injuries. Four days after the operation, when Lucy's injuries are beginning to heal, antibiotics are prescribed for her. An inexperienced nurse gives the wrong amount and Lucy dies as a result. Discuss Jon's liability for the death of Lucy. (45 min)

2   Mike and Nina are both heroin addicts. Nina buys some heroin from a drug dealer and takes it to Mike where they divide it between them. Mike injects himself with a larger than usual dose and becomes unconscious. Nina sees this and takes a smaller dose herself. Three hours later she realizes that Mike is still unconscious. She telephones for an ambulance but Mike dies before he can be taken to hospital. Discuss Nina's liability for the death of Mike. (30 min)

Checkpoint 3

Explain the House of Lords' judgment in *R v Adomako* in more detail.

Check the net

A short note of the judgments of recent cases can be found at www.lawreports.co.uk. From the menu on the main page choose Daily Notes.

Checkpoint 4

Can you describe the key differences between constructive manslaughter and gross negligence manslaughter?

Test yourself

Name the three different types of involuntary manslaughter and give a case for each one.

Examiner's secrets

The examiner likes you to go through this type of scenario question in a logical manner.

Assaults

Checkpoint 1

Can you give a situation which is an assault and another situation which is a battery?

Test yourself

Check that you remember what is meant by subjective recklessness.

Checkpoint 2

Explain the key differences between section 47 and section 20 offences.

Most of the law of assault comes from the Offences against the Person Act 1861. This law is very old and thought to be in need of reform. One difficulty is the term 'assault' which is often used as a general term, but which also has two very specific legal meanings that you need to know.

Common assault and battery

Assault is the putting of another in fear that unlawful force is about to be used on him. Normally the victim will be able to see the person making the threat, but in *R v Ireland* (1996) it was held that making telephone calls could be an assault if the effect was to put the victim in fear of force.

Battery is the application of unlawful force. So if A raises his fist threatening to punch B in the face, that is an assault; the moment the punch lands on B's face it is a battery. In addition a battery can occur by the application of indirect violence, e.g. setting a booby trap which hits the victim.

Mens rea

Both assault and battery are crimes of basic intent. For assault the defendant must either intend to put the victim in fear of having unlawful force used on him or know there is a risk that his actions might cause the victim that fear. For battery it must be shown that the defendant either intends to use unlawful force or that he knows there is a risk that what he was doing might result in the use of unlawful force. Knowing of the risk makes this subjective recklessness.

Assault causing actual bodily harm

This is an offence under section 47 of the Offences against the Person Act 1861. The offence requires an assault or battery which causes actual bodily harm. Actual bodily harm covers any injury, except those which are very trivial. It also covers psychiatric illness, but not emotional distress.

Mens rea

It is not necessary for the defendant to intend to cause any injury or even to realize there was the risk of injury. If the defendant has the *mens rea* required for assault or battery and uses unlawful force which causes injury, then he is guilty of this offence, *R v Savage* (1991).

Malicious wounding

This is the technical name given to an offence under section 20 of the Offences against the Person Act 1861. It involves the defendant inflicting a wound or grievous bodily harm on the victim. The offence is considered more serious than section 47, even though it carries the same maximum penalty.

Wound or grievous bodily harm

Wound means a cutting of the whole skin. The breaking of a bone is not a wound unless the skin is also broken. An internal injury is not a wound even though there is internal bleeding, *J.C.C. v Eisenhower* (1983). **Grievous bodily harm** straightforwardly means a really serious injury. This includes serious psychiatric illness, *R v Burstow* (1998).

Mens rea

Intention or subjective recklessness that the unlawful act might cause some physical harm is sufficient for the *mens rea*. It is important to note that the defendant does not have to realize that his act might cause serious harm, *R v Mowatt* (1968).

Wounding with intent ●●○

This is the most serious of assault charges. It is defined in section 18 of the Offences against the Person Act 1861 and involves the defendant causing a wound or grievous bodily harm. This is the same level of injury as for section 20 offences.

Mens rea

The difference between section 20 and section 18 lies in the intention. Section 18 is a specific intent crime; it can be committed only if the defendant does the act with the intention of:

→ doing some grievous bodily harm or
→ resisting arrest or
→ preventing the arrest or detaining of another person

Consent as a defence to assaults ●●○

In some situations the consent of the victim will provide a defence to an assault charge. However this defence is limited. It is available if the assault was in course of 'properly conducted games and sports, lawful chastisement, reasonable surgical interference or dangerous exhibitions, etc.' (Attorney-General's reference (No. 6) of 1980). It is *not* available for fights to settle differences, nor for sadomasochistic acts which cause injury, *R v Brown* (1992). The consent must be genuine and not induced by fraud. In *R v Tabassum* (2000) the defendant was guilty when women allowed him to examine their breasts believing he was medically qualified.

Exam questions   answers: page 85

1 How satisfactory is the law on consent as a defence to a charge of assault? (45 min)

2 Pete plays rugby for his local village team. In one match he tackles Reg, a member of the opposing team. Reg falls awkwardly and breaks his wrist. As Reg is being taken off the field, Sam, a team mate of Reg, walks towards Pete, shouting abuse at him. Pete thinks he is going to be attacked and punches Sam in the mouth, causing a split lip. Discuss Pete's criminal liability. (45 min)

> *"There must be a break in the continuity of the whole skin."*
>
> Lord Goff

Checkpoint 3

Can you write out the wording of section 20 and section 18 of the Offences against the Person Act 1861?

Checkpoint 4

Can you explain three ways in which the law in the Offences against the Person Act 1861 is unsatisfactory?

Action point

Write down the different offences listed on these two pages and make notes on the differences between them.

Examiner's secrets

In assault scenarios, it is quite often helpful to start by considering the injury. This identifies the possible range of offences.

Links

See also page 81 for another scenario question.

Theft, robbery and burglary

These three offences are defined in the Theft Act 1968. The definitions are the starting points and you need to know them. You should also know some key cases that explain the offences in more detail.

Theft

Theft is defined by section 1 of the Theft Act 1968 which states that: 'A person is guilty of theft if he dishonestly appropriates property belonging to another with the intention of permanently depriving the other of it.'

Mens rea of theft

The *mens rea* of theft is dishonesty *and* an intention to permanently deprive.

Dishonesty

The Theft Act 1968 does not define dishonesty but *R v Ghosh* (1982) gave a two-stage test for dishonesty. First, was what the defendant did dishonest according to the ordinary standards of reasonable and honest people? Second, did the defendant realize that what he was doing was dishonest by those standards?

Under section 2 of the Theft Act 1978 there are three situations which are *not* to be regarded as dishonest. These are where a person appropriates property in the belief that:

→ he has in law the right to deprive the other of it or
→ he would have the other's consent if the other knew about it or
→ the person to whom the property belongs cannot be discovered by taking reasonable steps

Intention to permanently deprive

If a defendant gives an item back he cannot be guilty of theft. This is clear from the case of *R v Lloyd* (1985) where the defendant was not guilty of theft when he took a film for a few hours, copied and then returned it. But it is theft where a defendant keeps an item 'till all the goodness had gone out of it'.

Actus reus of theft

This is the appropriation of property belonging to another. You need to understand all the words in this phrase.

Appropriation

This is defined in the Theft Act 1968 section 3 as 'any assumption by a person of the rights of an owner'. This is a very wide definition. In *R v Gomez* (1992) the House of Lords said that it included situations where the other person had consented to the appropriation, if that consent had been obtained by deception.

In *R v Hinks* (2001) the House of Lords went further and stated that there could be theft even where there was no deception and appropriation had been consented to. They held it was a neutral term and the important point was whether the defendant was being dishonest.

Test yourself

Write out the definition of theft from memory.

Checkpoint 1

Can you give a situation to explain each of the three exceptions in section 2 of the Theft Act 1968?

Action point

Draw a spider diagram showing all the points which have to be proved for theft.

Checkpoint 2

Explain the facts of the case of *Gomez* and the legal point it decided in more detail.

Property

Section 4 of the Theft Act 1968 defines this as including money and all other property. The following cannot normally be stolen:

→ land
→ mushrooms, flowers, fruit and foliage growing wild unless the defendant picks them for reward, sale or other commercial purpose
→ wild creatures unless they are tamed, in captivity or in the possession of another
→ knowledge, *Oxford v Moss* (1979)

Belonging to another

Section 5 of the Theft Act 1968 extends the meaning of 'belonging' so that property is regarded as belonging to any person having possession or control of it.

Robbery

The essential elements of robbery are (section 8, Theft Act 1968):

→ *theft* – if there is no theft there is no robbery, although there may be an attempt to rob or an assault with intent to steal
→ *force* – but this must be both immediately before or at the time of the theft and in order to steal

Burglary

As defined in section 9(1) of the Theft Act 1968, a person is guilty if:

(a) he enters any building or part of a building as a trespasser with intent to commit theft, inflict grievous bodily harm, rape or do unlawful damage therein or

(b) having entered any building or part of a building as a trespasser he steals or attempts to steal anything in the building, or inflicts or attempts to inflict on any person therein any grievous bodily harm

This means that there are several different ways of committing burglary but the common factors are the defendant must enter a building or part of a building and he must be a trespasser.

Exam questions answers: pages 85–6

Exam questions

1 As Tina leaves works one evening, she takes a video from the shelf to watch at home. She also takes £2 from the till as she realizes she has forgotten to bring money for her bus fare home. Next morning she returns the video and she puts a £2 coin into the till. Discuss whether Tina is liable for theft. (30 min)

2 Victor, while shopping in his local supermarket, sees a storeroom door open. He goes in and takes a bottle of whisky. As he is leaving the room he is challenged by a member of staff. Victor pushes the man aside and runs out of the store. Discuss his criminal liability. (30 min)

Checkpoint 3

List all the elements that have to be proved for theft.

"A person is guilty of robbery if he steals, and immediately before or at the time of doing so, and in order to do so he uses force on any person . . ."

Section 8 Theft Act 1968

Checkpoint 4

Can you explain the differences between the burglary offences in section 9(1)(a) and 9(1)(b)?

Watch out!

Examiners often include both section 9(1)(a) and section 9(1)(b) situations in the same scenario question. Make sure you explain both when relevant.

Examiner's secrets

The examiner wants you to deal with each incident separately.

Other offences against property

There are several offences involving deception. The difference between them lies in what is obtained as a result of the deception. Another important offence against property is criminal damage.

Obtaining property by deception

This is an offence under section 15 of the Theft Act 1968. To be guilty of this offence, the defendant must have obtained property. Property has the same meaning as for the offence of theft. Following the case of *R v Gomez* (1992) there is a large overlap with theft, and almost all situations which could be charged as obtaining property as deception will also be theft.

Checkpoint 1

Can you explain why the case of *Gomez* means that there is a large overlap between section 15 and theft?

Deception

This is defined in section 15(4) of the Theft Act 1968 as 'any deception (whether deliberate or reckless) by words or conduct as to fact, or as to law or as to intention, including a deception as to the present intentions of the person using the deception or any other person'.

This covers many situations including:

→ using someone else's credit card to pay for goods, or
→ the defendant paying with their own cheque when they know the account is overdrawn and the bank will not honour the cheque

The deception must succeed, that is it must be the reason why the property was handed over or the services were supplied, etc. Note that the person deceived need not be the one who suffers the loss. Also a machine cannot be deceived, so that using a fake coin to get cigarettes or chocolate from a machine is not a deception offence but is theft.

Checkpoint 2

Can you give a case example of 'deception' where the defendant used her own credit card?

Obtaining services by deception

Under section 1(1) of the Theft Act 1978 (this is a different Act to the Theft Act 1968), it is set out that: 'A person who by any deception dishonestly obtains services from another shall be guilty of an offence.'

Services covers many things such as a haircut or taxi ride or staying in a hotel room. But note that any food dishonestly obtained by deception while staying in a hotel would be the subject of a section 15 offence of obtaining property. **Deception** has the same meaning as above.

Action point

Make a chart of all the different deception offences.

Watch out!

In scenario questions you may need to consider *both* theft and obtaining by deception.

Evading a liability by deception

Section 2 of the Theft Act 1978 states that there is an offence where any person by deception evades a liability. There are three ways in which a person can commit this offence; where he:

→ Section 2(1)(a) – dishonestly secures the remission of the whole or part of any existing liability to make payments, whether his own liability or another's. This covers situations where someone who owes money tells a false story to the creditor, so that the creditor says the debt need not be repaid.

74

→ Section 2(1)(b) – with intent to make permanent default in whole or in part on any existing liability to make a payment . . . dishonestly induces the creditor to wait for payment or . . . to forgo payment. This is intended to cover situations where such a creditor is persuaded to put off the date for repayment.

→ Section 2(1)(c) – dishonestly obtains any exemption from or an abatement of liability to make payment. This covers situations such as showing an out-of-date season ticket or someone else's season ticket and so evading paying the train fare.

Making off without payment

Section 3 of the Theft Act 1978 makes it an offence to dishonestly make off without paying, when one knows that payment on the spot for any goods supplied or services done is required or expected.

This section was passed to deal with situations where a defendant ran off after a taxi ride without paying or left a restaurant without paying for the meal. However, you should note that *R v Allen* (1985) decided that the prosecution must prove that the defendant never intended to pay in the future (i.e. return later with the money).

Criminal damage

Under the Criminal Damage Act 1971 it is an offence to intentionally or recklessly destroy or damage property belonging to another. Destroying does not mean that the property has to be completely destroyed, but it does have to be made useless for its purpose. Damage includes scratching paintwork on cars and spraying paint on to walls. It can even be non-permanent damage which can be cleaned off such as water-soluble paint or mud, *Roe v Kingerlee* 1986. Recklessly is used in the wider meaning where a defendant is reckless if, either, he realizes that there is a risk of damage, or, if an ordinary careful person would realize there was a risk of damage. This type of recklessness is known as objective or Caldwell recklessness.

Arson

Where the property is damaged or destroyed by fire then the defendant will be charged with arson.

Exam questions answers: page 86

1 While his flatmate, Zack, is on holiday, William takes Zack's football season ticket and uses it to get entry to watch the next match. On the way home he uses Zack's credit card in a shop to buy a pair of jeans. When he gets home he replaces the season ticket and the credit card. Next day William uses Zack's bike. When he returns to the flat with the bike, William lets the bike fall to the ground in order to open the main entrance door. As a result the paint work of the bike is scratched. What offences has William committed? (45 min)

2 Yussef drives to his local garage and fills his car with petrol. He then realizes he has forgotten his purse, so he drives off without paying. Discuss Yussef's criminal liability. (20 min)

Test yourself

Write out from memory the three offences in section 2 of the Theft Act 1978.

Checkpoint 3

Can you explain why it was necessary to create the offence of making off without payment?

Checkpoint 4

Caldwell was charged under the Criminal Damage Act 1971. Can you give the facts of this case?

Examiner's secrets

Where there are several events, the examiner wants you to discuss each one in turn. Also the examiner wants you to remember that there may be an overlap with offences such as theft and criminal damage.

Insanity and automatism

"Every man is to be presumed sane . . . until the contrary is proved."

M'Naghten Rules (1843)

These are two separate defences, both of which give a defendant who was not responsible for his actions a defence. Insanity is a defence to all crimes, but there is a special verdict of 'not guilty by reason of insanity'. Automatism, if successful, is a complete defence and the verdict is 'not guilty'.

Insanity

The definition of insanity in the criminal law comes from the **M'Naghten Rules (1843)**. To prove legal insanity it is necessary to show that:

> 'the accused was, at the time of committing the crime, labouring under such a defect of reason due to disease of the mind, as not to know the nature and quality of his act or, if he did know this, not to know he was doing what was wrong.'

Disease of the mind

The courts have defined this phrase so that it covers physical illnesses which affect the mind as well as mental illnesses. In *R v Sullivan* (1984) the House of Lords said mind meant the faculties of reason, memory and understanding, and if the effect of a disease was to impair these faculties then that was within the M'Naghten definition. As a result, defendants suffering from epilepsy, diabetes and sleepwalking have been brought within the definition of insanity.

Did not know the nature and quality of his act

This means the physical quality of the act. An insane defendant who believes he is killing a gorilla cannot be convicted of murder even though he is actually killing a man. It also covers the situation where the defendant is acting while suffering from an epileptic fit so that he is unaware of what he is doing.

Did not know he was doing what was wrong

This is an alternative to the above test. If a defendant knew the nature and quality of his act, he can still show that he comes within the definition of insanity if he can prove that he did not know he was doing wrong, e.g. a mentally ill person who, as part of their mental illness, believes that they are being attacked and must kill in self-defence. Note that the test does not provide a defence if the accused knows that what they are doing is against the law, *R v Windle* (1952).

Powers of the court

On a verdict of 'not guilty by reason of insanity' the judge can:

→ order admission to a hospital (with or without a restriction order)
→ make a guardianship order
→ impose a supervision order with a condition of treatment
→ give an absolute discharge

Checkpoint 1

Compare insanity with the defence of diminished responsibility (see pages 66 and 67).

Test yourself

Can you write out from memory the M'Naghten definition of insanity?

Checkpoint 2

Can you name relevant cases where the defendant was suffering from
(a) epilepsy
(b) diabetes
(c) sleepwalking?

Checkpoint 3

Make a list of criticisms of the defence of insanity.

Automatism

This is an involuntary act of the body without any control by the mind. The defendant is not guilty because he does not have the *mens rea* for the offence, even though his body may have done the act. There are two categories of automatism:

→ insane automatism
→ non-insane automatism

Insane automatism

This is where the automatism is caused by a disease or an internal factor, as in *R v Sullivan* (1984) where the defendant was acting during an epileptic fit. Sleepwalking used to be regarded as non-insane automatism. However, in *R v Burgess* (1991), the Court of Appeal pointed out that if the sleepwalking was due to a disorder or abnormality which might recur, then it was caused by an internal cause and correctly described as insane automatism. Insane automatism comes within the definition of insanity and the verdict will be 'not guilty by reason of insanity'.

Non-insane automatism

This is where the automatism is caused by an external factor, such as a blow to the head. This is 'pure' automatism which allows the defendant a complete defence to any crime so that the verdict will be not guilty.

Self-induced automatism

In some cases the automatic state has been brought about by the defendant's own actions, e.g. taking alcohol or drugs. In such cases the defendant will not always be able to use automatism as a defence. To decide whether it can be used as a defence it is necessary to consider *what level of intent needs to be proved*. Self-induced automatism is a defence if it means that the defendant did not have the necessary specific intention.

If the crime is one of basic intent (where the prosecution need only prove that the defendant acted recklessly) then a second question must be asked: *did the defendant realize that his actions were likely to cause an automatic state?* If he did not then he has a defence, except where the automatism is caused by voluntary intoxication, *R v Bailey* (1983). If the defendant knows the probable effect (e.g. being warned clearly by a doctor or chemist about the effects of prescribed medication) then he is reckless and so cannot use the defence.

> *"An act done by the muscles without any control by the mind such as a spasm, a reflex action or a convulsion . . ."*
>
> Bratty v Attorney-General for Northern Ireland (1961)

Checkpoint 4

Can you give the two key differences between insane and non-insane automatism?

Action point

Make a chart showing the rules for the different forms of automatism.

Don't forget

When answering a scenario question, you must identify the offences before considering any defences.

Exam questions   answers: page 86

1 Discuss whether the defence of insanity should be reformed. (45 min)

2 Consider to what extent automatism should be allowed as a defence. (30 min)

Examiner's secrets

The examiner likes you to explain the present law and then point out why and what reform is needed.

Duress, necessity and self-defence

Action point

Make a spider diagram of these key features of the defence of duress.

Checkpoint 1

Explain the effect of the two-stage test in duress in your own words.

Checkpoint 2

Can you give a situation which could be duress of circumstances?

The defences of duress and necessity rely on the fact that the defendant has been forced to commit the crime, either through a direct threat by another (duress) or through external circumstances (necessity). Self-defence provides a defence if the force used is reasonable.

Duress

The important factors in this defence are:

→ the threat must be of death or serious injury

→ the threat must be to the defendant himself, or to a close member of his family; there is no authority to say that a threat to kill an unrelated third person will provide a defence

→ duress can be used as a defence to all crimes except murder, *R v Howe* (1987), attempted murder, *R v Gotts* (1991) and some forms of treason, *R v Steane* (1947)

→ duress can only be used as a defence if the defendant is placed in a situation where he has no safe avenue of escape, *R v Gill* (1963)

Subjective and objective tests

The correct approach to deciding whether the defence of duress should succeed was laid down by *R v Graham* (1982) (approved by the House of Lords in *R v Howe* (1987)). This involves a two-stage test:

1 Was the defendant compelled to act as he did because he feared serious injury or death? (the subjective test) and, if so,

2 Would a sober person of reasonable firmness, sharing the characteristics of the accused, have responded in the same way? (the objective test). This means that a defendant who is more vulnerable to threats cannot use the defence, *R v Bowen* (1996).

Self-induced duress

In some cases the defendant has voluntarily joined a criminal gang and then been forced to commit further crimes under duress. If the defendant did not know the gang used violence, the defence of duress is available for the later crimes, *R v Shepherd* (1987). If, however, the defendant knew when he joined the gang that they were likely to use violence, duress will not be available as a defence, *R v Sharp* (1987).

Duress of circumstances

A defendant may be forced to act by the surrounding circumstances. In *R v Martin* (1989) it was decided that duress of circumstances could be available as a defence if, from an objective viewpoint, the accused acted reasonably and proportionately to avoid a threat of death or serious injury and that the same two-stage test put forward in *R v Graham* applied. In *R v Pommell* (1995) the Court of Appeal said that the defence of duress of circumstances was available for all crimes except murder, attempted murder and some forms of treason.

Necessity

The courts did not traditionally recognize a defence under this heading, *R v Dudley and Stephens* (1881). However, in *Re A* (2000), a civil case, the defence of necessity was recognized. Necessity also forms the basis for other defences:

→ *Statutory provisions* – some Acts of Parliament set out defences based on necessity, e.g. allowing emergency vehicles a defence to breaking the speed limit 'if the observation of the limit would be likely to hinder the purpose for which the vehicle is being used'.

→ *Self-defence* – the essence of this defence is that the defendant claims he acted as he did because it was necessary for his protection.

→ *Duress of circumstances* – (see opposite page) this might be considered necessity under a different title and is available for almost all crimes.

Self-defence

This covers actions needed to defend oneself from an attack, and also actions taken to defend another. Section 3 of the Criminal Law Act 1967 also provides a defence of preventing crime or arresting an offender. The defence can be a defence to any crime, including murder as the defendant is justifying the use of force. The main rules are:

→ The force used to defend oneself or another must be reasonable in the circumstances. If excessive force is used the defence will fail, *R v Clegg* (1994).

→ In looking at the circumstances, the defendant must be judged on the facts as he believed them to be, *R v Williams* (1987). However, the amount of force must be reasonable on those facts, *R v Owino* (1996), *R v Armstrong-Braun* (1999).

→ In deciding whether the force used was reasonable, the fact that the defendant had only done what he honestly and instinctively thought was necessary in a moment of unexpected anguish is very strong evidence, *Palmer v R* (1971).

→ If the force is used after all danger from the assailant is over (i.e. as retaliation or revenge), the defence of self-defence is not available.

Exam questions   answers: page 87

1 Consider how and why the courts have limited the availability of the defences of necessity and duress. (45 min)

2 Zara joins an animal rights group. Two other members invite her to come with them to free some dogs being used for research at a laboratory. Zara agrees and the three of them break in and release several dogs. A week later Zara is asked whether she would like to go on another raid. As they are driving to the laboratory, Zara notices that the other two are carrying knives. She tells them she does not approve of violence, asks them to stop the car and let her out. The other two tell her that if she does not help with the raid, they will stab her. She agrees to continue. At the lab the others kill one watchman who tries to stop them and seriously injure a second man. Discuss Zara's criminal liability. (45 min)

Action point

Write out a list of the different cases for duress by threats, duress of circumstances and necessity.

Checkpoint 3

Do you know the facts of *Re A* (2000) and can you give the four tests for necessity quoted in the case?

Checkpoint 4

Can you explain why the judges are so reluctant to recognize necessity as a defence in its own right?

Checkpoint 5

Can you give the facts of the cases of *R v Clegg* and *R v Williams*?

"If the defendant is proved to have been attacking or retaliating or revenging himself, then he was not acting in self-defence."

Lord Lane in *R v Bird* (1985)

Examiner's secrets

In a scenario where there are offences and defences, the examiner wants you to identify offences first and then go on to consider what defences may be used.

Intoxication and mistake

Intoxication covers the effects of alcohol, drugs and other substances such as solvents. It is not a defence as such, but in some cases it will provide a defence because the accused did not have the necessary *mens rea* for the crime. A mistake may also provide a defence where it means that the defendant did not have the necessary *mens rea* or it justifies the action he took.

Voluntary intoxication

This is where the defendant chooses to take a substance that he knows will cause intoxication. This may be a defence in some circumstances depending on what *mens rea* is required for the crime the defendant has been charged with.

Voluntary intoxication and crimes of specific intent

If the offence is one of specific intent then the defendant has a defence if he did not have the *mens rea* for the offence, *R v Beard* (1920). The best way to tackle problems on this area is by considering the following questions:

→ Was the defendant so drunk that he was incapable of forming the *mens rea* required? If so, he is not guilty of the offence.
→ Did the defendant, despite being drunk, have the necessary *mens rea* at the time of the offence? If he did, then he is guilty of the offence. A drunken intent is still an intent as shown in *Attorney-General for Northern Ireland v Gallagher* (1963), where the defendant drank to give himself 'Dutch courage' to kill his wife.

Checkpoint 1

Specific intent and basic intent are important concepts for this area of law. Can you explain them?

Voluntary intoxication and crimes of basic intent

For crimes where recklessness is sufficient to prove the *mens rea*, a defendant who is voluntarily intoxicated cannot use this as a defence. This was stated clearly in *R v Majewski* (1977) where the defendant who had taken drugs and alcohol became involved in a fight. He was guilty of assault causing actual bodily harm and assault on a police officer in the execution of his duty.

Involuntary intoxication

This covers situations where the defendant did not know he was taking an intoxicating substance, e.g. where a soft drink has been 'laced' with alcohol. The test in these cases is:

→ *Did the defendant have the necessary* mens rea *when he committed the offence?* If so he will be guilty, the involuntary intoxication will not provide a defence, *R v Kingston* (1994). Where, however, the defendant did not have the necessary intent he will be not guilty.

Checkpoint 2

Can you explain the legal differences between voluntary and involuntary intoxication in your own words?

Mistake

To be a defence, a mistake must be about a fact, so that if the facts had been as the defendant believed them to be, it would mean either there was no *mens rea* for the offence or that the defendant would have been able to rely on another defence. Simple situations illustrate these ideas:

→ if A picks up an umbrella from a stand as he is leaving a restaurant in the mistaken belief that it is his own umbrella, he does not have the *mens rea* required for theft as he is not dishonest

→ if B, in the mistaken belief that V is pointing a gun at him, throws a stone at V and knocks him out, B can plead he should be judged on the basis that his action was in self-defence

Reasonableness of the mistake

Provided the defendant genuinely makes a mistake, there will be a defence even if the mistake is unreasonable. In *DPP v Morgan* (1976) the House of Lords said that:

'If the words defining an offence provide . . . that a man is not to be found guilty of it if he believes something to be true, then he cannot be found guilty if the jury thinks that he may have believed it to be true, however inadequate were his reasons for doing so.'

This was also applied in *R v Williams* (1987) where the defendant made a mistake over the need for the use of force in the prevention of crime. In *B v DPP* (2000) the House of Lords affirmed that a defendant should be judged according to his genuine mistaken view of the facts, regardless of whether his mistake was reasonable or unreasonable.

Drunken mistakes

Here the rule is more complicated. If the mistake negatives the *mens rea* required for the offence, then the defendant will have a defence. If the mistake is about another aspect, e.g. the amount of force needed in self-defence, the defendant will not have a defence, *R v Lipman* (1970), *R v O'Grady* (1987). The law is trying to balance the needs of the defendant and the protection of victims. However, in *R v Richardson and Irwin* (1999) a drunken mistaken belief that the victim consented was said to be a defence to an assault charge.

"Ignorance of the law is no defence."

Checkpoint 3

Can you give two cases to show how the defence of mistake operated to make the defendant not guilty?

Action point

Make a spider chart showing the legal rules on mistake.

Checkpoint 4

Can you explain why *Jaggard v Dickinson* is an exception to the normal rules on mistake?

Test yourself

Write out from memory all the cases given on these two pages.

Exam questions   answers: pages 87–8

1   Comment on whether the principles governing the law on intoxication can be justified. (45 min)

2   Abel, who has drunk several pints of beer, thinks that he is being attacked by Cain. Abel hits Cain with a wooden post and knocks him unconscious. When Cain comes round, he has a headache and is confused. In his confusion he drinks what he thinks is lemonade, but is actually an alcoholic cocktail. Cain then goes into a shop and takes a packet of biscuits without paying for them. Discuss the criminal liability of Abel and Cain. (45 min)

Examiner's secrets

The examiner always wants you to consider offences first and then look at possible defences.

Answers
Criminal law

Actus reus

Checkpoints

1 An act does not constitute guilt unless there is a guilty mind.
2 Examples include:
   - failure to provide a specimen of breath
   - failure to provide for a child in one's care in terms of food, clothing and medical care
3 Bland had been crushed at the Hillsborough disaster and suffered 'catastrophic and irreversible' brain damage. He had been kept alive for three years by feeding him through a tube. The House of Lords said:
   - there was no absolute rule that a patient's life had to be prolonged and that respect for human dignity had to be considered
   - the wishes of the patient had to be considered and if the patient was incapable of consenting, then treatment should be in the patient's best interests
   - if the treatment is futile then there is no duty on the doctor to continue it if it is not in the patient's best interests
4 Examples include murder and manslaughter for both of which death has to be the consequence.
5 Other case examples include *R v Church* (1966), *Fagan v Metropolitan Police Commissioner* (1969) and *R v Le Brun* (1991).

Exam questions

1 Start with the principle that the law generally does not impose liability for omissions.
   Point out that some offences can never be committed by omission, e.g. burglary, robbery.
   Consider when liability is imposed:
   - by statute (give an example)
   - by the common law
   Analyze these by commenting on decisions in cases such as *Gibbins* (why did the duty arise?), *Stone and Dobinson* (why did the duty arise, when can the carer be released from the duty?) and *Miller* (is this decision justifiable? Isn't this really a case of separation of *actus reus* and *mens rea*?).
2 Explain the idea of a *novus actus interveniens* (new intervening act) which may break the chain of causation. Give examples:
   - unreasonable reaction of the victim, *R v Williams* (1992)
   - overwhelming second cause, *R v Jordan* (1956)
   Discuss why a break in the chain of causation is important. This involves the key fact of the defendant's guilt. If there is a break in the chain the defendant is not guilty.
   Compare cases such as *Jordan and Smith* (1959) to show the dividing line between breaking the chain and not doing so and to discuss whether the decisions in these two cases are compatible.

Mens rea

Checkpoints

1 Specific intent crimes include murder, section 18 of the Offences Against the Person Act 1861, theft and burglary.
2 *Moloney*: Moloney and his stepfather had been drinking and challenged each other to see who could load a shotgun the fastest. Moloney shot his stepfather.
   Hancock and Shankland: in order to scare a striking miner, two miners pushed a concrete block off a bridge on to the road below. This killed the taxi driver.
   Nedrick: Nedrick poured paraffin through the letter box of a house and set fire to it. A child in the house died.
   Woollin: Woollin threw his baby towards the child's pram. The baby's head hit something hard; the child died.
3 The defendant knows there is a chance (or a risk) that his actions will cause a consequence, but he goes ahead and does the action.
4 • *Subjective recklessness* – the defendant realizes there is a risk and takes the risk.
   • *Objective recklessness* – the defendant need not be aware of any risk, but is guilty if an ordinary prudent individual would have realized the risk.

Exam questions

1 Explain that intention can be direct or oblique.
   Point out that it is oblique intention (foresight of consequences) which gives rise to problems.
   Explain and discuss the cases in which the courts have considered foresight of consequences (*Moloney, Hancock and Shankland, Nedrick, Woollin*) and the difficulties the courts have had in these cases.
   Comment on the fact that foresight of consequences is only evidence of intention. Discuss whether the use of the word 'find' instead of 'infer' is helpful (*Woollin*).
   Comment on the need for reform.
2 Explain subjective recklessness (*Cunningham*).
   Explain objective recklessness (*Caldwell*). Use cases to illustrate both these concepts.
   Discuss the subjective/objective differences.
   Identify some of the offences to which the different concepts apply, e.g. subjective – sections 47 and 20 of the Offences Against the Person Act 1861; objective – criminal damage.
   Consider the differences in moral blameworthiness of the two concepts and the harshness of the objective test, *Elliott v C* and *R v R and G*.

Examiner's secrets

In discussion essays always explain what the law is and then go on to discuss problems/possible reforms.

Strict liability

Checkpoints

1 *R v Larsonneur* (1933).
2 Other cases include:

- *Lemon v Gay News* (1979): the defendants were convicted of blasphemous libel even though they did not intend the publication of a poem about Jesus and homosexuality to be blasphemous.
- *Pharmaceutical Society of Great Britain v Storkwain* (1986): a chemist was convicted of selling drugs without a prescription when he sold drugs in the belief that a forged prescription was genuine.

3 Common law offences are those which have been developed by the judges through case law. The offence has never been defined by any Act of Parliament.

   Statutory offences are those which are defined by an Act of Parliament or by delegated legislation.

4 The diagram shows that the lowest level of *mens rea* is strict liability, where the prosecution need only prove the defendant did the act.

   The next level is objective recklessness where the prosecution need only prove that an ordinary prudent person realized the risk.

   The next level is subjective recklessness where the prosecution must prove the defendant realized the risk.

   The missing one is specific intention, which is the highest level of *mens rea*.

5 *Arguments for strict liability*:
- it makes people keep to high standards of care
- protects people from unnecessary hazards
Arguments against:
- people are guilty even though they have taken every care
- there is no evidence it raises standards of care

Exam questions

1 This is a part question and asks only for an explanation. You should explain the most extreme form of strict liability – absolute liability (*Larsonneur* and *Winzar*) where there need be no intention to do any act. The state of affairs makes the person guilty. Then explain the more usual form of strict liability where there is no requirement for *mens rea* in respect of at least one element of the crime (*Prince*).

2 Define strict liability. This will be the same as for question 1. However you must then go on to discuss the quotation by analyzing some of the 'social benefits' of strict liability – promotes high standards of care; protects society from harmful matters such as pollution; the practical benefit of not having to prove *mens rea*.

   Then consider the 'injustices' of convicting those who have taken all possible care; undermining of public respect for the law.

   Finish with a conclusion on whether or not you agree with the quotation.

If there is a quotation in a question, the examiner wants you to use your knowledge to discuss the key points of that quotation.

Participation and attempts

Checkpoints

1
- Aid – *Betts and Ridley* (1930) or to illustrate a situation which was not held to be aiding *R v Clarkson* (1971).
- Abet – *Tuck v Robson* (1970).
- Counsel – *Calhaem* (1985).
- Procure – Attorney-General's Reference (No. 1) of 1975.

2 *Bainbridge*: Bainbridge supplied cutting equipment to another person who used it to break into a bank. Bainbridge did not know where or when the break-in would be, but knew the type of offence which the equipment was going to be used for. Guilty of burglary as a secondary party. *DPP for Northern Ireland v Maxwell*: Maxwell guided members of a terrorist organization to a pub where he knew they were going to carry out some sort of attack, but did not know exactly what. Guilty as a secondary party of doing an act likely to endanger life and of possession of explosives with intent to endanger life.

3 Section 1(1) Criminal Attempts Act 1981: 'If, with intent to commit an offence to which this section applies, a person does an act which is more than merely preparatory to the commission of the offence, he is guilty of attempting to commit the offence.'

4 *R v Shivpuri*: the House of Lords used the Practice Statement (see page 7) to overrule the case of *Anderton v Ryan* (1985): they decided that a defendant could be guilty of attempting to commit a crime even though on the facts of the case it was impossible to commit the full offence.

Exam questions

1 Start with the point that the Criminal Attempts Act 1981 does not give a definition of 'more than merely preparatory'.

   Use cases to show how the words have been interpreted by the courts, *O'Brien v Anderton*, *Gullefer*, *Campbell*. Other useful cases are *R v Jones* (1990), *Widdowson* (1985), and *R v Toothill* (1998).

   Use the cases to discuss whether the test is satisfactory, e.g. at what point does the law intervene to make an act criminal? Is there a need to criminalize attempts to protect the public?

2 Deal with each of the three people separately.
- *Andy* – he has embarked on a joint enterprise of burglary with Don, does this make him liable for the murder? Andy knows Don carries a knife but thinks there will be no one in the factory – is he liable for the death of the guard whom Don battered to death? Could he foresee this might happen? (*R v English*.)
- *Bill* – he agrees to the burglary; does this bring him within 'aid, abet, counsel and procure'? (Attorney-General's Reference (No. 1) of 1975); has he done enough to withdraw from the joint enterprise? (*Becerra*.)
- *Charles* – does supplying the tools make him liable for (1) the burglary, (2) murder? Knowing Andy is going to

'break in' is enough for the burglary (*Bainbridge*), but not for murder.

Examiner's secrets

Where there are several people in a scenario, it is sensible to deal with each one in turn.

Murder

Checkpoints

1 *R v Smith*: Smith stabbed a fellow soldier. The victim was dropped twice when being taken to the medical centre and given treatment which aggravated a stab wound to his lung. Smith was still held to have caused the death.
R v Jordan: Jordan stabbed the victim, who died eight days later in hospital as the result of a drug to which he was allergic. At the time of the death the stab wounds had almost healed. Jordan was found not guilty. The treatment was 'palpably wrong'.
R v Cheshire: Cheshire shot the victim. The victim needed a tracheotomy but died after doctors failed to notice a rare complication following this. Cheshire was still held to have caused the death.

2 *R v Vickers*: Vickers punched and kicked a woman aged 73 when she found him breaking into a shop. She died of her injuries. It was accepted that Vickers did not intend to kill her, but he was guilty of murder because he intended to do her grievous bodily harm.
R v Cunningham: Cunningham hit the victim with a chair. The victim died from his injuries. The House of Lords upheld the decision in *Vickers* and found that Cunningham was guilty of murder. He intended grievous bodily harm and this was sufficient for the *mens rea* of murder.

3 It is necessary to have these special defences to murder to allow the judge discretion in sentencing. If a person is found guilty of murder the judge has no discretion but must give them a sentence of life imprisonment. The special defences mean that the defendant is found not guilty of murder but guilty of manslaughter.

4 *R v Ahluwalia*: Ahluwalia suffered years of violence and abuse by her husband. One night after further threats, she set fire to his bedroom as he slept and he died in the fire.

Exam questions

1 Start by considering whether Fiona had the *mens rea* for murder. On the facts, she possibly had the intention to kill and certainly had the intention to cause grievous bodily harm (*Vickers*).

Next look at possible defences. Three are indicated:
- *Diminished responsibility* Start with the definition in section 2 Homicide Act 1957. Is 'severe depression' enough to bring Fiona within this? Use supporting cases (*Bryne*). What effect does the intoxication have? (*R v Egan*.)
- *Provocation* Start with section 3 Homicide Act 1957. Consider the need for a sudden loss of self-control (*Ahluwalia*). Would a reasonable person have reacted in

the same way? Are there characteristics of the defendant relevant to the provocation (*R v Smith*)?
- *Intoxication* (see page 80) Does this affect the intention of Fiona? A drunken intent is still an intent (*Attorney-General v Gallagher*).

2 The clear issue here is intention and foresight of consequences. Does Herman have the necessary *mens rea* for murder? There is no direct intent, but there may be oblique intent.

Explain the foresight of consequences cases *Moloney, Hancock and Shankland, Nedrick* and *Woollin*. Apply the law to the facts in the question. NB constructive manslaughter should also be considered (see page 68).

Examiner's secrets

Always explain the law and then apply it to the facts given in the question.

Involuntary manslaughter

Checkpoints

1 *Lowe*: Lowe suggested to his partner that she should take their baby to a doctor. She did not do so. Lowe was not guilty of unlawful act manslaughter as he had not done any act, only an omission.
Mitchell: Mitchell punched a man who fell against an elderly woman. She died from the injuries she suffered. Mitchell was guilty of her manslaughter; his intention to hit the man made him liable for her death.
Goodfellow: Goodfellow set fire to furniture in his council home in order to make it necessary for the council to rehouse him. The fire got out of control and his wife, girlfriend and child died. Goodfellow was guilty of their manslaughter. Setting fire to the property was an unlawful act which a prudent person would realize might cause harm to the people in the building.

2 *R v Cato*, 1976.

3 *Adomako*: the House of Lords said that the essence of the matter was a question for the jury – whether, having regard to the risk of death involved, the conduct of the defendant was so bad in all the circumstances as to amount to a criminal act or omission.

4 - *Constructive manslaughter* – must be an unlawful act, objectively dangerous, likely to cause some harm.
- *Gross negligence manslaughter* – can be a lawful act done in a grossly negligent way or an omission; there must be a risk of death.

Exam questions

1 Identify that there is an unlawful act (throwing the stone at Ken). Is that act objectively dangerous? (*Church* test.) Discuss transferred malice (*Mitchell*). Deal with the causation point. Explain the law using cases (*Smith, Jordan, Cheshire*). Apply this to Lucy.

2 Can this be unlawful act manslaughter? Identify the unlawful act of supplying drugs. Does the fact that Mike injects himself affect Nina's liability? (*Cato, Dalby,*

Kennedy.) Which of these cases is the closest to the scenario?

Consider gross negligence manslaughter. Is Nina under a duty to Mike? (*Khan, Singh*.) If there is a duty, has Nina's failure to get medical help earlier caused Mike's death? Is the breach of duty sufficiently serious under the guidelines of *Adomako* to make Nina liable?

Intoxication needs to be considered also (see page 80). Manslaughter is a basic intent offence and so intoxication is not a defence (*Majewski*).

Assaults

Checkpoints

1 *Assault* – waving a knife at someone or throwing a stone, but missing.
  Battery – kicking someone or pulling their hair.
2 Section 47 – only need to prove a minor injury;
  Section 20 – there must be a serious injury or wound;
  Section 47 – intention or recklessness as to an assault;
  Section 20 – must intend or be reckless as to some injury occurring.
3 Section 20
  Whosoever shall unlawfully and maliciously wound or inflict any grievous bodily harm upon any other person, either with or without any weapon or instrument, shall be guilty of an offence.
  Section 18
  Whosoever shall unlawfully and maliciously by any means whatsoever wound or cause any grievous bodily harm to any person with intent to do some grievous bodily harm to any person, or with intent to resist or prevent the lawful apprehension or detainer of any person, shall be guilty of an offence.
4 • Inconsistency in the wording (section 18 cause) (section 20 inflict) (section 47 occasioning).
  • Same *mens rea* for common assault as for section 47.
  • The problem that injury does not include disease (e.g. deliberately risking infecting victim with AIDS).

Exam questions

1 Explain the present law on consent including such points as:
  • available for properly conducted sport
  • available for 'horseplay' situations (*Jones*)
  • not available where serious injury inflicted
  • not available for sadomasochistic acts
  • consent must be genuine, not obtained by fraud
  • belief in consent can be a defence (*Jones, Aitken*)
  Use this knowledge to discuss points such as:
  • the risk of serious injury in sports such as boxing is lawful, but minor injury in sadomasochistic cases is not

  • why is a mistaken belief in consent to rough horseplay allowable, even where it results in serious injuries?
2 Deal with the two incidents separately and in each identify the possible offence(s), before discussing defences.
  • *Pete tackles Reg* this causes a broken wrist. Could it be a serious enough injury for section 20 or section 18? Probably not, so it is a section 47 offence. Does Pete have the intention to use unlawful force on Reg? Probably not, provided the tackle was within the rules. If there is intention, can Pete use consent as a defence? Yes, properly conducted sport.
  • *Pete punches Sam* this causes a split lip. This is a wound (*JCC v Eisenhower*). So, section 20 or section 18 – discuss the *mens rea* – does Pete intend grievous bodily harm? Probably not, so section 20. Can Pete use self-defence as a defence? Is his reaction reasonable in the circumstances? Does it matter if he was mistaken about Sam's intentions? (*Williams*.) (See page 79.)

Theft, robbery and burglary

Checkpoints

1 • Section 2(1)(a) – keeping a football which has smashed a window in the belief that the damage gives a legal right to keep the ball.
  • Section 2(1)(b) – taking a flatmate's car without asking, when your car won't start, in the belief that your flatmate would consent.
  • Section 2(1)(c) – keeping a £10 note found in the street where you do not believe you can find the owner.
2 *Gomez* persuaded the manager of a shop to allow £16 000 of electrical goods to be taken, under the belief that a cheque was genuine. Even though the manager consented to the goods being taken, it was held this was theft as the consent was given as a result of fraud.
3 • dishonesty
  • appropriation
  • property belonging to another
  • intention to permanently deprive that other
4 • Section 9(1)(a) There must be intention to commit one of the four named offences (theft, gbh, rape, criminal damage) at the time of entering the building. There is no need for the defendant to actually commit one of those offences.
  • Section 9(1)(b) There is no need to prove any intention on entering the building, but it must be proved that the defendant stole or caused gbh (or attempted to do one of these) while in the building.

Exam questions

1 Start with the definition of theft, then apply this to Tina. Both the video and the coins are property belonging to another and by taking them, there is an appropriation so

there is no need to discuss these parts of the definition. The key points are:
- dishonesty – does section 2(1)(b) apply?
- intention to permanently deprive – what effect does returning the video have? (*Lloyd*.) What effect does putting back the same value of money have? (*Velumyl*.)

2 Identify that a storeroom is a private part of the shop and that Victor enters as a trespasser. This means that the taking of the whisky is burglary: section 9(1)(a) if Victor intended to steal when he entered; section 9(1)(b) if Victor decided to steal only after he entered. (Don't forget to point out that taking the whisky is also theft.) Pushing the staff member is a common assault, but it is not robbery as the force is not used in order to steal. The examiner will be pleased if you can give accurate definitions from the Theft Act 1968.

Other offences against property

Checkpoints

1 Situations in which a defendant obtains property by deception are offences against section 15 Theft Act 1968, but as a result of the decision in *Gomez* these situations are also theft.

2 *Lambie*, 1982: where the defendant had been asked to return her credit card as she had exceeded the limit allowed. Instead of returning it, she continued to use it to buy goods. Guilty under section 15 Theft Act 1968. The deception was that she had the authority of the bank to use the card.

3 There were many situations in which the defendant was dishonest, but it was not possible to prove theft or a deception offence, e.g. running off without paying a taxi fare. This is not theft as there is no property taken. It is also difficult to prove obtaining services by deception as it is necessary to show that when the defendant started the taxi journey he did not intend to pay.

4 Caldwell had quarrelled with the owner of a hotel. Caldwell got drunk and set fire to the hotel. He was charged under section 1(2) of the Criminal Damage Act 1971 with arson endangering life. He was not aware of the risk to life because of his drunken state, but he was still guilty as the risk would have been obvious to a sober, reasonable person (objective recklessness).

Exam questions

1 Deal with the season ticket situation first. Is using someone else's season ticket a deception? Give the definition of deception and apply it. What has been obtained? Is it services? (Section 1 Theft Act 1978.) Or is it obtaining an exemption from liability to make payment? (Section 2(1)(c) Theft Act 1978.)

   Next deal with the credit card situation. Is using someone else's credit card a deception? What has been obtained? This time it is a pair of jeans, so this is obtaining property by deception (section 15 Theft Act 1968).

   Finally, the bike situation. The paintwork is damaged. Is this criminal damage? What *mens rea* is required for this

offence? Note that as all the items are returned there is no offence of theft.

2 Consider section 3 Theft Act 1978, making off without payment. Define the offence and then apply it to Yussef. The key point is dishonesty and you should consider the case of *Allen* (1985). Note that there is no deception offence on these facts.

Examiner's secrets

Where there are several events in a question, the examiner usually intends you to consider different offences for each.

Insanity and automatism

Checkpoints

1 • *Diminished responsibility*: partial defence for murder only, reduces charge to manslaughter; *Insanity*: full defence for all offences.
   • *Diminished responsibility*: abnormality of the mind, which need only substantially impair the defendant's responsibility for his actions; *insanity* defect of reason due to disease of the mind which must mean that the defendant does not know what he is doing or does not know that it is wrong.

2 (a) Epilepsy – *Sullivan* (1984).
   (b) Diabetes – *Hennessy* (1989).
   (c) Sleepwalking – *Burgess* (1991).

3 The defence of insanity is too narrow. It does not cover many mental illnesses (*Byrne, Windle*).

   The label 'insane' has a stigma attached to it, so that people will not use the defence. Also it wrongly labels epileptics and diabetics as insane.

   The defendant has to prove the defence, rather than raise the presumption of it.

4 • *Insane automatism*: caused by internal factor; *Non-insane automatism*: caused by external factor.
   • *Insane automatism*: special verdict not guilty by reason of insanity; *Non-insane automatism*: verdict not guilty.

Exam questions

1 Start with the M'Naghten Rules and then go on to explain the problems with the definition of insanity. Discuss why the law should be reformed, e.g.
   • wrongly includes physical illnesses (e.g. diabetes)
   • excludes mentally ill people who have some perception that what they are doing is wrong

   You must include cases as it is these that show how much the law is in need of reform. Use cases such as *Sullivan, Hennessy, Quick, Burgess,* and *Windle*. Suggest ways in which the law could be reformed.

2 Start with a definition of automatism (*Bratty*). Point out this is an artificial definition and prone to review, *R v Burgess* (1991). Explain that automatism is a defence because the defendant's actions are involuntary. Explore the need for intention in the criminal law and link this to the reason for allowing the defence of automatism. Expand with reference to cases: *Hill v Baxter*, Attorney-General's Reference (No. 2) of 1992.

Duress, necessity and self-defence

Checkpoints

1 For the first part of the test the defendant must show that he committed the offence because he feared he would be killed or seriously injured if he did not. For the second stage, the defendant must show that a reasonable person of the same age, sex and other relevant characteristics would have done the same.

2 *R v Willer* (1987): where the defendant's car was surrounded by a group of aggressive youths, so that Willer drove on to the pavement to get away from them.

3 The court had to decide whether doctors could be given permission to separate conjoined twins when it was known that the separation would cause one of the twins to die but would save the other one. If the twins were not separated both would die within a few months. The tests were those set out by *Stephens* in the nineteenth century. They are that:
   - the act was done only in order to avoid consequences which could not otherwise be avoided
   - those consequences, if they had happened, would have inflicted inevitable and irreparable evil
   - no more was done than was reasonably necessary
   - the evil inflicted by it was not disproportionate to the evil avoided

4 • Difficult to decide the boundaries of what is 'necessity' in different situations.
   - Fear of 'opening the floodgates' if it is a defence.
   - The fact that allowance can be made in sentencing.

5 *R v Clegg*: a soldier at a checkpoint in Northern Ireland shot at a car which failed to stop and killed a passenger. The shots were fired after the car had gone past. Held: excessive use of force.
   R v Williams: the defendant thought that another man was attacking a third person, so he punched the man. In fact the man was trying to arrest someone. Held: Williams should be judged on his mistaken view of the facts, so he was not guilty of assault.

Exam questions

1 Consider the two defences and take each separately. Explain when duress can be used and the limitations on its use. This should include:
   - not available for murder or attempted murder (*Howe, Gotts*)
   - the threat must be of death or serious injury
   - the subjective/objective test (*Graham*)
   - limitations on self-induced duress (*Sharp*)
   For necessity, point out that it only exists as 'duress of circumstances' and that the same tests apply.
   Consider why these limitations exist.

2 Identify the offences first. Do not jump straight into the defence of duress. So what offences are there?
   - The first 'visit' to the lab involves burglary (section 9(1)(a) Theft Act 1968); theft of the dogs and possibly criminal damage if anything was damaged in the 'break-in'. There is no defence to any of these as necessity cannot be used.
   - The second 'visit': the offences are murder (intention to cause grievous bodily harm is probably there) and section 18 Offences against the Person.
   Now consider whether Zara can use the defence of duress. It is self-induced – did she know at the start that the gang was violent? (*Shepherd, Sharp.*) Duress not available for murder, but could be available for the section 18 offence.

Intoxication and mistake

Checkpoints

1 Specific intent means the defendant must have the relevant intention. Basic intent means that recklessness in getting intoxicated is enough for the *mens rea* of the offence.

2 • *Specific intent offences* If the defendant did not have the necessary *mens rea*, he is not guilty. The rule is the same for voluntary and involuntary intoxication.
   - *Basic intent offences* Voluntary intoxication is never a defence. Involuntary intoxication can be a defence, if the defendant was not reckless.

3 *R v Morgan* (1976): a husband invited other men to have sexual intercourse with his wife, telling them she was willing but liked to pretend she was reluctant. The wife had not agreed, but the other men were not guilty of rape as they believed she was consenting.
   Beckford v R (1987): the defendant was a police officer and believed that a man he had been sent to arrest was in possession of a gun and that his (Beckford's) life was in danger. Beckford shot the man but was not guilty of murder as he had an honest belief which justified using self-defence.

4 There is a special defence under section 5(2)(a) of the Criminal Damage Act 1971, whereby a defendant is not guilty if they believe they have the consent of the owner of the property. In addition section 5(3) states that it is immaterial whether or not a belief is justified provided it is honestly held. This applies even if the defendant is drunk.

Exam questions

1 Explain and comment on the law relating to intoxication. This should include:
   - the specific/basic intention distinction
   - voluntary/involuntary intoxication – should the law be the same for these? Is the decision in *Kingston* 'unfair'?
   - the effect of intoxication on the defence of mistake (including the exception of *Jaggard v Dickinson*)
   Don't forget to use case law to explain your points.

2 Start by identifying the possible offences.

Abel knocks Cain unconscious – this is an assault – is there an injury? Unconsciousness must be at least actual bodily harm (section 47); remember this is a basic intent offence. Can Abel use the defence of self-defence? Not if the mistake was made because he was drunk (*O'Grady, Lipman*).

Cain takes biscuits – theft. Can he use the defence of automatism? Define automatism. Consider involuntary intoxication. Did Cain have the *mens rea* for theft?

The law of contract

The law of contract is about agreements, ranging from a simple purchase of a magazine to a multimillion pound deal between large companies. All contracts have the same basic elements of offer, acceptance, consideration and legal intent, and they can all have problems of vitiating factors. The main aim of the law of contract is to ensure that these agreements are made in a fair way, and to enforce them, whether it is on behalf of the owner of a large company or a consumer buying a bar of chocolate. The rules of contract law are built on fairness and reasonableness, as cases have been decided in court, and on top of these Parliament has formed statutes where issues are of general concern. Much of the law of contract affects us all as consumers, and is knowledge that we need for life, not just for an A-level examination. However, it is useful to know exactly what *is* needed by your own examination board, since some boards form a wider course with less in-depth knowledge.

Exam themes

→ Looking for true agreement in forming a contract
→ Modern methods of communication
→ What kind of material it is possible to bargain over
→ Whether those involved intended to form a legally binding contract
→ Protection of certain people from their inexperience in law, especially minors
→ Protection of consumers
→ Ensuring that any agreements have been formed fairly and not under great pressure
→ Considering fair ways to end a contract, especially where someone cannot meet all of their obligations
→ Looking at individual fairness and commercial reality
→ Examining remedies available to someone with a problem over a contract

Topic checklist

O AS ● A2	AQA	OCR	WJEC
Offer and acceptance	●	●	●
Consideration	●	●	●
Legal intent	●	●	●
Capacity		●	
The terms of a contract	●	●	
Exemption clauses	●	●	
Privity of contract	●	●	
Misrepresentation	●	●	●
Mistake	●	●	
Duress and undue influence		●	●
Restraint of trade		●	
Discharge of a contract	●	●	●
Remedies	●	●	●

Offer and acceptance

The jargon

A *party* is a person who makes a contract (or it could be a group or a company).

Checkpoint 1

Define an offer.

The jargon

An *invitation to treat* is an opportunity to negotiate or form an offer.

Test yourself

Try to list the situations which are treated like a shop window, with the customer making an offer to buy.

Checkpoint 2

Can you remember the situations that are exceptions to the usual shopping situation?

Test yourself

Try to list the ways in which an offer can be terminated.

Agreements are formed by most people every day, many amounting to legally binding contracts. To establish a contract, the courts try to identify an offer from one party and an acceptance by the other. Sometimes it is difficult to identify an offer and acceptance, even though there is a contract: *Brogden v Metropolitan Railway Co.* (1877).

Offer

An offer is an expression of willingness to contract on certain terms, made with the intention that it will become binding on acceptance. There is a difference between an offer and an invitation to treat. A shop window display is generally an invitation to treat, the customer making the offer and the seller being free to accept or reject the offer. This principle upholds the idea of freedom to contract, and also avoids the problem of exhausted stocks. It applies in various situations:

→ shop windows, *Fisher v Bell* (1961)
→ supermarkets, *Pharmaceutical Society of Great Britain v Boots* (1952)
→ small advertisements, *Partridge v Crittenden* (1968)
→ auction sales, *Payne v Cave* (1789), confirmed in Sale of Goods Act 1979 (as amended)
→ sale by tender, *Spencer v Harding* (1870)

Exceptions

1 A general offer may be made to the world at large, *Carlill v Carbolic Smoke Ball Co.* (1893). The advertisement of a reward for a product failing to work was held to be a general offer.
2 This could apply to other promotional campaigns, e.g. an offer that the first five customers to buy a television will receive a free radio.
3 A bus company makes an offer by running the bus along a time-tabled route, *Wilkie v London Passenger Transport Board* (1947).
4 When dealing with a machine the position has to be different, *Thornton v Shoe Lane Parking* (1971). The offer is made by the owners of the machine by holding it in readiness for use, the acceptance being made by the customer operating the machine.
5 In an auction 'without reserve' a collateral contract exists where the auctioneer makes an offer to sell to the highest bidder, *Barry v Davies* (2000).

Termination of an offer

An offer can be terminated by:

→ acceptance or refusal
→ counter offer, *Hyde v Wrench* (1840), *Butler v Ex-Cell-O* (1979), *Stevenson v McClean* (1880)
→ revocation, *Byrne v Van Tienhoven* (1880), *Dickinson v Dodds* (1876), *Shuey v United States* (1875)
→ lapse of time, *Ramsgate Hotel v Montefiore* (1866)
→ death, *Bradbury v Morgan* (1862)
→ failure of a precondition, *Financings v Stimpson* (1962)

Acceptance

Acceptance is the agreement to all the terms of the offer.

Method of acceptance

Acceptance must be communicated, *Felthouse v Bindley* (1862). The general rule is that it is by the same method as the offer, but another method, no less advantageous to the offeror, may be valid, e.g. *Yates v Pulleyn* (1975). Sometimes this may be waived, *Carlill* (above). Acceptance may be over a period of time, *Errington v Errington* (1952).

The postal rule

For acceptance by post, the postal rule generally applies, *Adams v Lindsell* (1818). It does not apply where the method of communicating is more or less instantaneous, e.g. telephone, fax, etc. (see *Entores v Miles Far East Corporation* (1955)). The law needs to develop to cover modern methods of communication, e.g. email, courier deliveries. These can be compared to the post and telephone, e.g. does the communication arrive more or less immediately? Has it been entrusted to a third party for delivery? Is there acknowledgement of receipt?

Distance and electronic trading

The Consumer Protection (Distance Selling) Regulations 2000 apply to situations where parties do not deal face to face, e.g. by telephone, mail order or internet. In addition the Electronic Commerce (EC Directive) Regulations 2002 provide a structure for online trading based on the usual 'rules' of offer and acceptance.

Ignorance of the offer

Where a person performs all that is required for acceptance, but in ignorance of the offer, there will be no contract, as the offeree must act at least partly in response to the offer.

Non-standard situations

A collateral contract is a second contract which may exist within or alongside another, and is dependent on it, *Esso v Commissioners of Customs and Excise* (1970). Multipartite agreement is when several people make a similar agreement with one person, and are deemed to have contracted with each other, *Clarke v Dunraven* (1897).

Exam questions   answers: page 116

1   Explain the difference between an offer and an invitation to treat, using examples from cases. (15 min)

2   Critically discuss the ways in which an offer may be terminated. (45 min)

3   To what extent has the law of acceptance developed to cover modern means of communication? (45 min)

4   'In most agreements it is the customer who makes the offer.' Is this an accurate picture of offer and acceptance? (45 min)

Checkpoint 3

Define acceptance in your own words.

Action point

Make a note of what was said by the uncle in *Felthouse v Bindley* – acceptance cannot be assumed in this way.

Checkpoint 4

List some features that can be used to compare telephone and post with other methods of communicating.

Action point

Find out more about electronic trading on the internet at www.dti.gov.uk

Checkpoint 5

In relation to ignorance of the offer, compare the cases of *R v Clarke* 1927 and *Williams v Carwardine*, 1833. How do they differ?

Test yourself

Can you explain collateral contracts and multipartite agreements?

Examiner's secrets

Always use cases to back up the points you make. The examiner will be pleased to see a very brief summary of the facts of the cases you use.

Consideration

Consideration is the 'thing' exchanged in a contract, and may take many forms. It is often money for goods or services, but may be less obvious and less tangible. An important aspect is that consideration can be a promise, so if a promise is made to pay for goods on delivery, the contract is binding at the moment of agreement, not at the point of payment. This is called executory consideration. Where goods are handed over, consideration is said to be executed.

Definition of consideration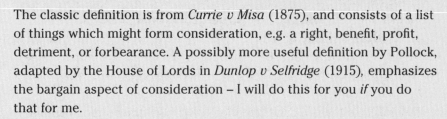

The classic definition is from *Currie v Misa* (1875), and consists of a list of things which might form consideration, e.g. a right, benefit, profit, detriment, or forbearance. A possibly more useful definition by Pollock, adapted by the House of Lords in *Dunlop v Selfridge* (1915), emphasizes the bargain aspect of consideration – I will do this for you *if* you do that for me.

The jargon

Executed consideration is already carried out.
Executory consideration is a promise to do something.

Checkpoint 1

Define consideration in your own words.

Some rules of consideration

Consideration must be sufficient

The jargon

Sufficient means recognizable.
Adequate means a fair bargain (or market price).

It must be recognizable in some way to the court, and usually of some economic value. However it does not need to be adequate, or a fair monetary bargain. So in *Thomas v Thomas* (1842), a woman was allowed to live in a house for £1 per year. This was obviously not adequate, but was sufficient to form a binding contract. Other examples of consideration which are sufficient, even if not adequate, include worthless chocolate wrappers, *Chappell v Nestle* (1960), and the benefit of weighing someone's boilers, *Bainbridge v Furmstone* (1838).

Test yourself

Try to remember some examples from cases of consideration which are sufficient, even though not adequate.

Consideration must not be past

It must be given at the time of the promise of the other party, not an action already done in the past. In *Re McArdle* (1951) work already done on a house was held not to be good consideration for a later promise to contribute to the cost. However, if something is done at the request of the other party, and it is understood by all that payment would be made at the end, then apparently past consideration may be valid. This was so in *Lampleigh v Braithwaite* (1615), and also in *Re Casey's Patents* (1892), where work was done at the other party's request. It could be understood in these situations that some kind of payment would be made if a person is asked to work, especially if that person normally works for the employer who is requesting the work.

Checkpoint 2

Explain why apparently past consideration was valid in *Re Casey's Patents*.

Consideration must not be illegal

In *Foster v Driscoll* (1929) smuggling goods into the USA was held not to be good consideration.

Consideration must not be an existing duty

The performance of an existing duty will not generally buy good consideration, whether this arises under the law of the land or in an existing contract.

→ In *Collins v Godefroy* (1831) a lawyer's promise to appear in court, when he was already obliged to do this as a witness, was held not to be consideration.

→ In *Stylk v Myrick* (1809) the promise of some sailors to a captain to sail a ship home short-handed was not consideration, as they were obliged to do this anyway.

However, something 'extra' may be good consideration, such as doing more than the law of the land or the contract stipulates, e.g.:

→ providing a larger police patrol than usual, *Glasbrook v Glamorgan* (1925)
→ sailing a ship home very short-handed, *Hartley v Ponsonby* (1857)
→ keeping a child well looked after/happy, *Ward v Byham* (1956)
→ performing the same duty to another party, and thus running the risk of being sued twice, *Scotson v Pegg* (1861)

In *Williams v Roffey* (1990) the court held that where performance of an existing duty enabled the other party to obtain some practical advantage or avoid a disadvantage, this would be good consideration. In the case, a firm of builders avoided the disadvantage of late completion, and did not have to look for new carpenters.

Part payment of a debt

Merely repaying part of a debt, even with the agreement of the creditor, does not end the debt. However, if with the creditor's agreement something 'extra' is added to the part payment this may then discharge the whole debt – see *Pinnel's Case* (1602). The debate has reopened, following *Williams v Roffey*, with the case of *Re Selectmove* (1994).

Promissory estoppel

If one party promises to excuse the other party from their duties, but then goes back on this promise in an unfair way, the court may not allow this following the equitable doctrine of promissory estoppel, established in the case of *Central London Property Trust v High Trees House* (1949).

Checkpoint 3

Make two lists, one of cases involving existing duty owed under the law of the land, and the other of cases involving existing duty owed under a contract.

Test yourself

Which cases involve going beyond existing duty?

Checkpoint 4

Explain carefully the facts of *Williams v Roffey*.

Examiner's secrets

Try to explain the reasoning for the decisions in the cases you use, e.g. in *Ward v Byham* the court would no doubt wish to ensure that provision was made for a single mother and child.

Exam questions   answers: pages 116–17

1 Critically consider the rules emerging from cases concerning what may amount to valid consideration. (45 min)

2 Discuss the circumstances in which the performance of an existing duty may amount to valid consideration. (45 min)

Legal intent

> *"The court . . . asks itself: Would reasonable people regard this agreement as intended to be legally binding?"*
>
> Lord Denning

The jargon

A *presumption* is assumed to be true. *Rebuttal* shows that the presumption is not true on this occasion.

> *"There are agreements between parties which do not result in contracts within the meaning of that term in our law."*
>
> Lord Atkin

Checkpoint 1

Can you explain the presumption in social and domestic arrangements?

Test yourself

List six cases concerning social and domestic arrangements, and say what the relationship was, and whether the presumption was established or rebutted.

Checkpoint 2

Explain the presumption regarding commercial agreements.

This is another formation requirement, and is often referred to as the *intention to form legal relations*. Apart from the basic requirements of offer, acceptance and consideration when making a contract, the law requires a general intention to be legally bound. The reason for the requirement is that two people may easily make some arrangement, but not really intend it to be a legal contract for which they could be taken to court. On the other hand, when an agreement is clearly made in a commercial context, those who make it should be bound by it.

Social and domestic arrangements

It is important that the courts enquire into legal intent, in order to prevent the absurd situation of trivial domestic or social agreements unnecessarily turning into contracts (unless there is clear evidence to the contrary). For example, an offer to provide food in return for transport home would have the elements of offer, acceptance and consideration, but the parties almost certainly would not expect to be bound legally. It is therefore *presumed* that there is no legal intent in social and domestic situations, as in *Balfour v Balfour* (1919), but the presumption can be *rebutted* if there is evidence, as in *Merritt v Merritt* (1970) where unlike the couple in Balfour, the husband and wife were legally separated. So it is up to the party wishing to claim that there was legal intent to prove it, and thus rebut the presumption.

Balfour v Balfour and *Merritt v Merritt* both concern husband and wife, but many other relationships have now become the subject of case law:

→ *Jones v Padvatton* (1969) – mother and daughter
→ *Simpkin v Pays* (1955) – grandmother, granddaughter and lodger
→ *Parker v Clark* (1960) – two elderly related couples
→ *Buckpitt v Oates* (1968) – two friends

Commercial agreements

In commercial situations it is *presumed* that legal intent exists. This seems totally reasonable, as most people make agreements in the context of commerce with a view to earning money, so require some kind of investment, either financial or in labour. They therefore expect to enforce payment or provision of goods or services, and should equally be bound to carry out their obligations. The presumption provides some protection for the consumer, especially in promotional campaigns – see the cases of *Carlill v Carbolic Smoke Ball Co.* (1893), and *Esso v Commissioners of Customs and Excise* (1970). In both cases contracts were enforced in favour of the consumer. It can be seen from *Esso* that the value of the subject matter is of little importance in the issue of legal intent.

This presumption of legal intent can be rebutted, but evidence of the intention not to be bound must be made very clear. A written clause containing such a rebuttal is known as an honourable pledge clause.

It arose in the case of *Rose and Frank v Crompton* (1925), and was confirmed in the more recent case of *Kleinwort Benson v Malaysia Mining Corporation* (1989). These two cases both involved two parties who were in business, but the argument for not allowing such clauses must be even stronger when dealing with a consumer situation. An everyday example of this rebuttal is found in football pools coupons. These, of course, are usually consumer contracts, and the consumer is usually unaware of the existence of such a clause. The case of *Jones v Vernons Pools* (1938) is one example. This means that a consumer who forms a contract, pays an entry fee and chooses a winning combination of teams may not enforce payment. Of course the pools company will usually not wish to receive bad press and will make the payment due, but it is not legally obliged to do so. It is questionable now whether such clauses would stand in court under the recent Unfair Terms in Consumer Contract Regulations, and they are certainly against the spirit of the European Directive that initiated the regulations.

Collective bargaining ●●●

To allow negotiations to take place between employers, employees and trade unions, it is presumed that any agreements formed in the course of the negotiations are not intended to be legally binding. When a point is reached where the parties wish their agreement to be binding, they must clearly state this in writing, and this statement would then rebut the initial presumption. An example is *Ford Motors v AUEFW* (1969).

The need for legal intent ●●●

The existence of legal intent is therefore an important element in the formation of a contract. There are three major formation requirements: offer and acceptance, consideration and legal intent. It has been argued by academics, notably Attiyah, that consideration is not strictly necessary, and there have also been changes to the strict doctrine of privity. In light of these, legal intent will play an even greater role.

"A moral obligation only . . ."

Checkpoint 3

Can you explain what an honourable pledge clause is?

Checkpoint 4

Why is an honourable pledge clause unfair towards a consumer?

Checkpoint 5

Why are agreements made during collective bargaining presumed not to have legal intent?

Action point

Make brief notes on facts of the cases on these two pages.

Examiner's secrets

In question 4 remember that marks will be given for explaining *why* the presumptions and rebuttals apply to cases, not just for relating the facts.

Exam questions   answers: page 117

1   Why do the courts require the intention to be legally bound in the formation of a contract? (15 min)

2   How does the court decide whether there is legal intent in social and domestic arrangements? (20 min)

3   How does the court decide whether there is legal intent in commercial agreements? (20 min)

4   Consider whether it is necessary to prove that legal intent exists in the formation of a contract. (45 min)

Capacity

"Necessaries are . . . goods suitable to the condition in life of the minor, and actually required at the time of sale."

An agreement may exist between any two parties, but in order to be able to enforce it in law, the makers of the agreement must have full capacity. Most adults have this contractual capacity, and are therefore competent or able to contract. However, there are limitations to the contractual capacity of: corporations (organizations, such as universities and companies), diplomats and sovereigns, those who are drunk or of unsound mind, and minors.

Checkpoint 1

List those who have limited capacity in forming contracts.

Minors

Minors have limited capacity, and are defined under the Family Law Reform Act 1969 as those who are under 18 years of age. There are three types of contracts where minors may be liable.

Necessaries

A minor will be liable for a contract for the sale of necessaries. If all contracts with minors were unenforceable, retailers would be reluctant to sell to them under any circumstances. So, to enable a minor to obtain basic essentials for ordinary living, the law regards a minor as being bound under a contract for the sale of necessaries sold and delivered to him. The term '**necessaries**' covers more than just items needed to stay alive, such as shelter, food and clothing, but those things which are essential to a young person *and* suited to their position in life: Sale of Goods Act 1979. Some more valuable items with utility value may be regarded as necessaries, the minor therefore having to pay for them, *Chapple v Cooper* (1844).

The jargon

Necessaries are basic things needed for reasonable existence, which are suited to a person's way of life, and not duplicates of goods already owned (do not confuse with necessities).

→ In *Nash v Inman* (1908) it was held that 'eleven fancy waistcoats' from a Saville Row tailor could have been necessaries, but were not because the student's father had already supplied him with plenty.

→ *Chapple v Cooper* (above) shows that services can also be necessaries (here it was payment for funeral services).

"... articles of mere luxury are always excluded, though luxury items of utility are sometimes allowed."

B. Alderson

Contracts of education, training and employment

The courts will uphold such a contract if it is, on the whole, for the benefit of the minor, but will allow *repudiation* of an oppressive one. In *de Francesco v Barnum* (1889), a 14-year-old agreed to train as a stage dancer, but the contract was held to be oppressive because of the unreasonable restrictions imposed on her, so she was no longer bound by the agreement. On the other hand in *Doyle v White City Stadium* (1935) a contract to train as a boxer was held enforceable, even though prize money was not paid, as the training agreement was, on the whole, beneficial to him as it was training him in a career. Similarly, in *Clements v London & NW Rail Co.* (1894) a young porter was bound by his contract of employment, despite a clause removing some rights to insurance benefits, since the contract was on the whole for his benefit.

Checkpoint 2

Why *could* the waistcoats in *Nash v Inman* have been necessaries?

The jargon

Repudiation means to reject a contract.

Checkpoint 3

Can you explain one case involving a training contract that was beneficial and one that was oppressive?

Voidable contracts

A third type of contract with a minor is one of continuing obligation. This usually concerns regular payment, such as the renting of accommodation. The contract will be valid, unless the minor repudiates it on or before reaching 18. This leaves a workable arrangement, but gives the minor an opportunity to 'escape' if he later regrets forming the agreement (see the case of *Edwards v Carter* (1893)).

If the contract does not fall within one of these categories, the minor will not be liable. Section 3 of the Minors' Contracts Act may then apply, the minor being ordered to hand back goods.

The Minors' Contracts Act 1987

Two new measures were enacted to help to balance the protection of minors with fairness towards those adults who contract with them.

→ Section 2 makes a guarantee enforceable against an adult if the minor defaults.
→ Section 3 gives the court the power to order restitution of property, or any property representing it, acquired by a minor without payment.

Exam questions   answers: pages 117–18

1   Who does the law of contractual capacity aim to protect? (5 min)

2   How does a court decide whether a contract of employment with a minor is binding? (10 min)

3   What minors' contracts are voidable? (10 min)

4   How did the Minors' Contracts Act 1987 change the law? (10 min)

5   Critically examine how the law protects a minor who enters into a contract with an adult. (45 min)

6   Nadine and Olivia, both aged 17, decide to pursue a career in dancing and theatre. Nadine gains a place at stage school, and begins her course with enthusiasm. She soon becomes annoyed at a term in her agreement which prevents her from taking part in any professional productions during the school vacation without permission from the school, and another which obliges her to hand over 30% of any earnings from such productions. Nadine would now like to avoid these restrictions in order to take part in a play during the summer. Olivia's career takes a different course. She borrows money from Countrywide Bank to set up her own small but successful business selling dance and stage clothing and equipment, the proceeds of which pay for singing and dancing lessons. After a few months Olivia's main supplier finds out that she is only 17 and refuses to trade further with her. This leaves Olivia unable to pay for this month's lessons and her teacher is pressing her for money. She is also behind with her mobile telephone account and has received a demand for payment. Advise both Nadine and Olivia. (45 min)

The jargon

A *voidable* contract is one where the contract *may* be ended.

Test yourself

List the three types of contracts for which minors may be liable, and outline a case involving each one.

The jargon

Restitution means the handing back of property.

Checkpoint 4

What problems could arise with restitution? (Hint – what if the goods have been sold or consumed?)

Examiner's secrets

The examiner is impressed when you discuss whether the result in a particular case is fair, e.g. the decision in *Nash v Inman* was rather harsh on the tailor.

In question 6 the examiner will look for an understanding that the Minors' Contracts Act 1987 was passed to give discretion to the courts over whether to order restitution.

Always bear in mind that the law should be protecting the minor, while not being too unfair to the adult.

The terms of a contract

> "Detached objectivity
> . . . asking what the
> reasonable third party
> would have taken the
> parties to have intended."
>
> Stone

Checkpoint 1

Can you list four points that the court will use to decide whether a statement is a term or a representation?

Action point

Read the case of *O'Brien v Mirror Group* (2001).

Checkpoint 2

State three ways in which a term can be implied into a contract.

Test yourself

What is the Parol Evidence Rule?
What is the rule in *L'Estrange v Graucob*?

A contract may contain terms that have not been noticed by a party, for example when a contract is partly written and partly oral, and difficulties then arise in determining exactly what the terms of the agreement are.

Terms and representations

Generally a statement made before a contract is formed will be a representation, and one made during a contract will be a term. However, points to consider include:

→ How soon before the contract was the statement made? *Routledge v McKay* (1954).
→ Does the representor have special knowledge? *Oscar Chess v Williams* (1957), *Dick Bentley v Harold Smith* (1965).
→ Is special importance placed on an issue? *Bannerman v White* (1861).
→ How persuasive is the statement? *Ecay v Godfrey* (1914).

Incorporation of terms into a contract

A term will be incorporated into a contract if the affected party is aware of the term, or reasonable steps are taken to bring the term to the party's attention. Again various factors have arisen through cases, including:

→ The degree of notice (how effectively was the term brought to the other party's attention?). This often arises when a ticket is issued, *Chapelton v Barry* (1940), *Parker v S E Railway* (1877).
→ Whether there was a 'course of dealings'. If so, the party suing may be deemed to have had the chance to read the notice, *Hollier v Rambler Motors* (1972), *British Crane Hire*.
→ The time at which notice was given – must be at or before the point of contract, not after the acceptance is made, *Olley v Marlborough Court* (1949), *Thornton v Shoe Lane Parking* (1971).

Written contracts

The Parol Evidence Rule will normally apply to contracts in writing. The rule is that oral or other evidence will not be admitted to contradict or amend a written contract. In addition, the rule in *L'Estrange v Graucob* says that if a person signs a contract he is bound by it, even though he may not have read the terms. However, there are exceptions, and terms can be implied into a contract in three main ways:

→ by custom, especially within a particular trade, as in *British Crane Hire v Ipswich Plant Hire* (1975)
→ by statute, e.g. by the Sale of Goods Act 1979 and the Sale and Supply of Goods Act 1994 goods must be of satisfactory quality
→ by the courts, *Samuels v Davis* (1943) – see the officious bystander test; *Shirlaw v Southern Foundries* (1939) and the business efficacy test; *The Moorcock* (1889) and *Liverpool City Council v Irwin* (1976)

Types of terms within a contract ●●●

Conditions and warranties

Not all terms in a contract are of the same importance. The more important terms are called *conditions*. The less important ones are called *warranties*. The difference is important when a term is breached.

→ Breach of condition: the innocent party can choose whether to affirm (or continue with) the contract and claim damages, or to repudiate (or end) the contract, *Poussard v Spiers and Pond* (1876).

→ Breach of warranty: the innocent party can only claim damages, *Bettini v Gye* (1876).

When a type of term is specified within the contract

The parties may label a term in the contract as a condition, but this is not necessarily conclusive. A party may not be aware of the legal significance of an ordinary English word used in this way, and the courts will need to be sure that the legal consequence was intended.

Terms specified by statute

Some terms are implied into contracts by statute. Where a statute says that a term will be a condition then this is conclusive.

Terms decided by courts

The importance of some terms is not apparent until they are breached. These are known as *innominate* terms. They arose in *Hong Kong Fir v Kawasaki Kishen Kaisha* (1962). It was stated that a ship would be 'in every way fitted for ordinary cargo service', and this term was clearly breached. But the court looked at the effect of the breach, and found that the goods could still be carried, and the delay compensated by appropriate damages. It was considered that this type of term did not lend itself to traditional analysis, and L. J. Diplock said that the breach would be considered serious enough to justify repudiation if the effect was to *deprive the party not in default of substantially the whole benefit of the contract*. This differs from the approach traditionally taken by the courts, looking at the consequences of the breach before deciding whether to treat the term as a warranty or as a condition.

The jargon

A *condition* is a major term of a contract. A *warranty* is a less important term.

Checkpoint 3

What remedy is available when (a) a warranty is breached, or (b) a condition is breached?

Checkpoint 4

Use these two cases to explain the difference between conditions and warranties.

Example

See *Schuler v Wickman Machine Tool Sales* (1973).

Checkpoint 5

Can you remember some of the terms implied into a consumer contract by statute?

The jargon

An *innominate* term is a term that can be breached in many ways, and cannot easily be labelled a condition or a warranty.

Action point

Make brief notes on *Hong Kong Fir* and these cases which followed it: *The Hansa Nord* (1975), *Reardon Smith v Hansen Tangen* (1976), *The Mihalis Angelos* (1970), *The Chikuma* (1981).

Examiner's secrets

In answering all these questions use plenty of cases, with a brief account of the facts on each one, to show the court's reasoning.

Exam questions   answers: page 118

1   Critically consider how a court will decide exactly which terms have been incorporated into a contract. (45 min)

2   Explain the distinction between different types of terms found within a contract. (20 min)

3   To what extent has the introduction of the innominate term led to uncertainty in contracts? (45 min)

99

Exemption clauses

An exemption clause in a contract is one that attempts to exclude or limit one party's liability towards the other. Sometimes these clauses have been used in an oppressive way, where a person in a weak bargaining position has little say in the formation of a fair contract. The courts have therefore sought to limit the use of such clauses, and in addition Parliament has made substantial changes to the common law position through the Unfair Contract Terms Act 1977 and the Unfair Terms in Consumer Contracts Regulations 1994.

Is the exemption clause valid?

An exemption clause can be of two kinds:

→ a limitation clause – where a party tries to restrict liability
→ an exclusion clause – where a party tries to exclude liability

A justified use of an exemption clause may arise in business, such as where a buyer of a product agrees to late delivery in exchange for a lower price, and the courts will not interfere with this. They will, however, be much less willing to enforce an exemption clause that has been imposed on a consumer without free negotiation. The courts use a three-stage process to decide whether an exemption clause is valid.

Incorporation

An exemption clause, just like any other term of a contract, must be incorporated as part of the contract. The main points are:

→ the term must not be too late, *Olley v Marlborough Court* (1949)
→ it must be brought to the notice of the other party, *Thornton v Shoe Lane Parking* (1971)
→ there may be a *course of dealing*, *Hollier v Rambler Motors* (1972)

Construction

In construction the courts will examine whether the clause can be interpreted to cover the damage which has arisen. Two rules are used:

→ The main purpose rule states that the courts will not allow an individual term to defeat the main purpose of the contract. In *Glynn v Margetson* (1893) a clause which allowed a ship to call at any port in Europe or North Africa would have defeated the purpose of a contract to ship oranges in good condition from Spain to Liverpool.
→ The *contra proferentem* rule states that any doubt or ambiguity in an exemption clause will be interpreted against the person seeking to rely on it (or proffering it). In *Houghton v Trafalgar Insurance* (1954) the word 'load' in a car insurance policy was held not to extend to an excess of passengers.

Legislation

The Unfair Contract Terms Act 1977 uses two important concepts:

The jargon

An *exemption clause* is one where a party tries to escape from some, or all, of the duties under the contract.

Checkpoint 1

Can you explain why the courts may be reluctant to uphold exemption clauses?

The jargon

Incorporation of a term means including it in the contract.

Checkpoint 2

Write down three points used to establish incorporation of a term, illustrating each one with a case.

The jargon

Construction in this context means interpretation.

Checkpoint 3

Can you use cases to explain the two main rules of construction?

→ business liability – section 1(3); liability will generally arise from things done in the course of business or from business premises
→ a consumer – section 12; a person 'deals as a consumer' if he is not acting in the course of business and the other party is doing so

The two main provisions regarding exemption clauses are as follows:

→ a contract term cannot now exclude or restrict liability for death or personal injury resulting from negligence, section 2(1)
→ a contract term can exclude or restrict other liability resulting from negligence only if it is reasonable to do so, section 2(2)

Reasonableness

Reasonableness usually means fair given the circumstances known to the parties at the time, and given the resources to meet the liability. Other factors that the court may take into account include:

→ the bargaining power of the parties, and available supplies
→ any inducement to agree to the term, e.g. a favourable price
→ trade custom and previous dealings
→ the difficulty of the task

See *Green v Cade* (1978), *George Mitchell v Finney Lock Seeds* (1983), *St Albans City and DC v International Computers* (1994) and *Overland-shoes v Schenkers* (1998). The Unfair Terms in Consumer Contracts Regulations 1994 state that if a term in a consumer contract is not individually negotiated, then it is unfair if it causes a 'significant imbalance' in the rights and duties under the contract, to the detriment of the consumer, 'contrary to the requirement of good faith'. This requirement is in line with the European nature of the Regulations.

Checkpoint 4

Who does the legislation on exemption clauses aim to protect?

Test yourself

Can you remember the main relevant provisions of the Unfair Contract Terms Act 1977?

Checkpoint 5

List points that the court will take into account when examining reasonableness.

Exam questions   answers: page 119

1   Briefly describe the steps taken by the courts in deciding whether an exemption clause is valid. (30 min)

2   'Exemption clauses have been outlawed.' Discuss. (45 min)

3   As a hobby, Anneliese produces costumes for drama productions. She orders material from a wholesaler, *Clothcut*, which offers her the choice of: (a) supply of the goods by a guaranteed delivery date at a price of £170, or (b) supply of the goods at a price of £120 with the following clause included in the contract, 'We exclude liability for late delivery of goods.' Anneliese chooses option (b), but when the material is over six weeks late, she blames *Clothcut* and says that she will sue. Anneliese also buys a machine for attaching buckles from a supplier called *Banglers*. The machine malfunctions, firing a staple into Anneliese's hand, resulting in pain and absence from work. The contract for the sale of the machine includes a clause that reads: 'The company will not be responsible for any loss or injury, however caused.' Advise Anneliese as to any rights she may have against both *Clothcut* and *Banglers*. (45 min)

Examiner's secrets

In question 3 the examiner will expect you to know about the main provisions of the Act and the Regulations.

Privity of contract

Privity is the relationship between the parties to a contract, and in English law it is very closely connected with the requirement of providing consideration. Changes in the rights of third parties have recently taken place by statute, but the basic rule remains.

The rule of privity

The basic rule, found in *Dunlop v Selfridge* (1915), is as follows: only a person who is party to a contract can sue on it.

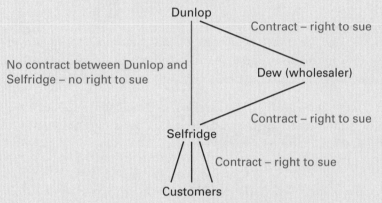

Dunlop, who made tyres and sold them to a wholesaler, Dew, could not sue Selfridge, a customer of Dew, for breaking a price agreement, as they had not contracted with Selfridge.

The rule seems very reasonable when considering the imposition of a duty on a third party. A person would not generally wish to be subject to a duty to which they had not freely agreed.

However, when considering giving a benefit to a third party the rule seems less fair. In *Tweddle v Atkinson* (1861) a man was not able to enforce payment due to him under a contract, even though the contract was formed specifically for this purpose. The Contracts (Rights of Third Parties) Act 1999 has now made changes in this area (see below).

The kind of problems caused by the doctrine can be seen in the case of *Jackson v Horizon Holidays* (1975). Mr Jackson claimed compensation for himself and his wife when their holiday was not as expected. Only Mr Jackson was party to the contract, but on this occasion the Court of Appeal allowed damages for the other family members.

Established exceptions

There are a number of established exceptions to the doctrine of privity.

→ Statute: this overrides the common law, e.g. Law of Property Act 1925, regarding assignments.
→ Agency: a person acts on behalf of another, *The Eurymedon* (1975).
→ Collateral contracts: a way of getting around the doctrine, *Shanklin Pier v Detel* (1951).
→ Covenants which 'run with the land', both restrictive, *Tulk v Moxhay* (1848), and positive, *Smith and Snipes Hall Farm v River Douglas Catchment Board* (1949), in limited circumstances.
→ Price restrictions: where allowed (currently only for medicaments).

Checkpoint 1

Use the *Dunlop v Selfridge* case to explain the rule of privity.

"Principle certainly requires that a burden should not be imposed on a third party without his consent."

L. J. Steyn

Checkpoint 2

What problems did the doctrine cause in *Jackson v Horizon*?

Test yourself

Make sure you can list the established exceptions.

Attempts to avoid the doctrine

Various attempts have been made to avoid the strict doctrine of privity.

→ Applying the rule in *Tulk v Moxhay* (see above) to allow covenants to run with chattels (things other than land). Allowed in *Lord Strathcona SS Co. v Dominion Coal Co.* (1926). Later restricted to charter parties in *Clore v Theatrical Properties* (1936), then held to be wrongly decided in *Port Line v Ben Line Steamers* (1958).

→ Attempting to show that rights under a contract were held on trust, and enforceable by the third party as a beneficiary of the trust. Allowed in *Les Affreteurs Reunis v Walford* (1919), restricted or disapproved in *Re Schebsman* (1943), and *Green v Russell* (1959).

→ Applying section 56 of the Law of Property Act 1925, allowing a person who was not party to a contract to acquire rights in property which formed part of the contract. This has not found favour in the courts, and was not allowed in *Beswick v Beswick* (1968). Mrs Beswick tried to enforce payment of a weekly sum of money owed to her under an agreement between a nephew and her late husband. She was not allowed to receive the money by implying a trust, nor by use of section 56, but as administratrix of her late husband's estate.

Checkpoint 3

Explain the attempts to avoid the doctrine of privity.

Reform of the doctrine

It was unfair that somebody like Mrs Beswick was unable in contract law to claim the benefit that was intended for her. Following long-standing calls for reform, the Contracts (Rights of Third Parties) Act 1999 provides that:

'A person who is not a party to a contract may enforce a term of the contract in his own right if the contract expressly provides that he may, or if it purports to confer a benefit on him. The Act also requires that this party is expressly identified in the contract by name, or as a member of a class, or answering a particular description.'

Note that this only changes the law regarding benefits to third parties, not burdens.

This method of reform was thought to be preferable to extending the exceptions as issues arose, and should go a fair way to providing justice while leaving the basic law of privity intact.

Checkpoint 4

State the main provisions of the Contracts (Rights of Third Parties) Act 1999.

"The autonomy of the will of the parties should be respected . . . they rely on the contract."

L. J. Steyn

Exam questions   answers: page 119

1   State the doctrine of privity and its established exceptions. (15 min)

2   'Reform of the doctrine of privity to allow a third party to claim what was rightfully theirs was long overdue.' Discuss this view of the doctrine of privity. (45 min)

Examiner's secrets

The examiner will be pleased if you have a good working knowledge of privity, and show that you are up to date by knowing the details of the Act.

Misrepresentation

Many statements made before forming a contract are not terms but representations. These do not form part of the contract, but may still be important in helping a party to decide whether to go ahead and form the contract. In many cases such statements will persuade, or induce, a party to enter into a contract. It could then be very unfair if these precontractual statements turned out to be untrue. Where someone has been misled into forming a contract in this way by facts that prove to be untrue, a remedy may be available for misrepresentation.

What will amount to a misrepresentation? ●●●

A misrepresentation is an untrue statement of fact, made by one party to a contract to another, which, while not forming a term of a contract, has an inducing effect on it.

To be actionable there must be a misstatement of fact, and not:

→ a mere commendation (or advertising 'puff'), *Dimmock v Hallett* (1866)
→ an opinion, *Bisset v Wilkinson* (1927), *Esso v Mardon* (1976)
→ a statement of future intentions, *Edgington v Fitzmaurice* (1885)
→ a statement of law, *Solle v Butcher* (1950)

Silence and misrepresentation

Generally, just remaining silent is not a misrepresentation, *Fletcher v Krell* (1873). However many exceptions have arisen in case law:

→ misleading conduct, *Walters v Morgan* (1861)
→ concealing a defect, *Scheider v Heath* (1813)
→ half-true statement, *Dimmock v Hallett* (1866)
→ changed circumstances, *With v O'Flanagan* (1936), *Esso v Mardon* (1976)
→ fiduciary relationship, *Hedley Byrne v Heller* (1964)
→ contracts *uberrimae fidei*, *Seaman v Fonerau* (1743), *Bufe v Turner* (1815)

Inducement

Inducement is persuasion to enter a contract. The untrue statement must have persuaded the other party to enter into the contract, *Attwood v Small* (1838); *Redgrave v Hurd* (1881).

Types of misrepresentation ●●●

Fraudulent misrepresentation is deliberately dishonest – according to *Derry v Peek* (1889) it is made (i) knowingly, or (ii) without belief in its truth, or (iii) recklessly as to whether it be true or false. This is often difficult to prove, since it involves looking into a person's mind.

Negligent misrepresentation is careless – it could have been prevented.

Innocent misrepresentation is where the misrepresentor is not at fault, and could not have known about the statement made not being true.

Checkpoint 1

Explain why a doctrine of misrepresentation is needed.

Checkpoint 2

Define misrepresentation in your own words.

Test yourself

List four kinds of statement that will not amount to misrepresentation.

"Misrepresentation may be in the form of a single word, or . . . a nod or wink, or a shake of the head or a smile."

Lord Campbell

Checkpoint 3

Can you list some exceptions to the principle that silence does not amount to misrepresentation?

Test yourself

Can you explain the three different types of misrepresentation?

Remedies for misrepresentation ●●●

Rescission

For any type of misrepresentation there is the possibility of rescinding the contract, although this could be barred, or not allowed, for various reasons. Recognized bars to rescission are as follows:

→ affirmation – the misrepresentee indicates willingness to continue with the contract, *Long v Lloyd* (1958)
→ lapse of time – an unreasonable delay before bringing an action, *Leaf v International Galleries* (1950)
→ restitution impossible – the goods cannot be handed back in their original state, *Vigers v Pike* (1842)
→ supervening third party rights – a third party now has the goods, *White v Garden* (1851)
→ some other circumstance where the court decide to award damages in lieu under the Misrepresentation Act 1967 Section 2(2)

Damages

For fraudulent misrepresentation a claim may be made for damages in the tort of deceit, or a claim may be made if a special relationship exists, following *Hedley Byrne v Heller*. However it is now much easier to sue under the Misrepresentation Act 1967, and this is now the normal route.

→ Section 2(1) provides a remedy for a misrepresentee without proving fraud. A remedy would have been available, had fraud been proved, unless the misrepresentor can show that he believed in his statements and that this was reasonable. This is unusual, in that once an untrue statement is shown to exist, the burden lies on the misrepresentor to prove his innocence. Damages are assessed on a tort basis, following the decision in *Roycott v Rogerson* (1991), and lost profits may be claimed in some circumstances, following *East v Maurer* (1991).
→ Section 2(2) of the Act allows the court to award damages, at their discretion, in lieu of rescission.

> **The jargon**
>
> *Rescission* means to end a contract.

> **Checkpoint 4**
>
> List the bars to rescission (with appropriate cases or statute).

> **Test yourself**
>
> Which statute provides a remedy of damages for misrepresentation?

> **Checkpoint 5**
>
> (a) Can you explain the remedy of damages given in section 2(1)?
> (b) How are damages assessed? What does section 2(2) provide?

Exam questions   answers: pages 119–20

1 Critically examine the kinds of precontractual statements that will amount to a misrepresentation. (45 min)

2 Are the remedies for misrepresentation satisfactory? Discuss. (45 min)

3 Sam is thinking of selling his car and tells Tom that it is in superb condition, has been serviced regularly and has four new tyres. Tom is impressed and a fortnight later buys the car. A week after the sale, the car develops engine trouble, and Tom finds that the servicing had been done at home by Sam. He also finds that only two tyres are new, and the other two need replacing. Consider what remedies may be available to Tom. (45 min)

> **Examiner's secrets**
>
> Only write about the relevant parts of your knowledge of misrepresentation. In question 1 you do not need the material on remedies, but in question 2 you should only write about material on types of misrepresentation and remedies, not on precontractual statements.

Mistake

"A fundamental false assumption."

Mistakes, or false assumptions, may be made by either party before or during the formation of a contract which, though inconvenient, do not affect the validity of the contract. However some mistakes are fundamental, and make the contract void. Cases on mistake can be categorized in various ways. Here they are referred to in four groups.

Common mistake ●●●

This is where the parties are in agreement, but their contract is based on a common assumption which is false. The cases can be subdivided into contracts where there is mistake over:

The jargon

Subject matter is the thing that a contract is about (often an item to be bought).

Res extincta means that the subject matter does not exist.

Res sua means that the thing to be bought already belongs to the buyer.

→ the existence of subject matter
→ the quality of subject matter

Mistake over the existence of subject matter

Where the subject of a contract no longer exists, unknown to both parties, it can obviously not be passed on, e.g. if a car is sold, but unknown to both buyer and seller it has been destroyed by a bomb, the contract can no longer proceed. This is often referred to as *res extincta* (the thing is destroyed). See the following cases: *Couturier v Hastie* (1856) – a non-existent cargo of corn; *Galloway v Galloway* (1914) – a non-existent marriage. See also section 6 of the Sale of Goods Act 1979.

Checkpoint 1

Use cases to explain why the contract is void in instances of *res extincta*.

Res sua (the thing is his own) is an extension of the principle of *res extincta*. It will rarely arise, but in the case of *Cooper v Phibbs* (1867) a lease was drawn up to transfer a fishery, and unknown to both parties at the time, the buyer was already the owner.

Mistake over the quality of subject matter

If a contract turns out to be a bad bargain for one party, the contract will generally not be void, although there has been disagreement over this amongst judges – see *Associated Japanese Bank v Credit du Nord* (1988) and *William Sindall v Cambridgeshire County Council* (1994). Also remember that the law only requires sufficiency of consideration, not the market value. See *Bell v Lever Bros* (1932) – the defendants were mistaken over the cost of ending an employment contract.

Leaf v International Galleries (1950) – a painting thought by both parties to be valuable was later found to be a copy. This is reasonable if we think what would happen if the situation were reversed. If a painting was bought at a jumble sale, and some years later turned out to be a valuable one, the buyer would not wish to avoid the contract!

"A mistake . . . as to the existence of some quality which makes the thing without the quality essentially different from the thing as it was believed to be."

Lord Atkin

Checkpoint 2

Can you explain the difference between mistake over existence of subject matter and mistake over quality of subject matter?

Common mistake in equity

Sometimes a decision that the contract is either valid as agreed or void does not really provide a fair solution, so the court provides an equitable solution. In *Cooper v Phibbs* (1867) an order was made to repay in time the amount that the 'seller' had spent on maintenance.

Mutual mistake ●●●

This is sometimes known as shared mistake, where the parties are at cross purposes and not really in agreement. If there is total ambiguity the contract is held void, as seen by the following cases:

→ *Raffles v Wichelhaus* (1864) A cargo of corn, to be found on a ship named *Peerless* in Bombay, was sold. There were two ships of the same name loaded with corn in Bombay, and the court held the agreement too ambiguous to enforce.
→ *Wood v Scarth* (1858) A buyer of a pub believed the only payment to be the rental of £63. The seller had also intended a premium of £500 to be paid. The contract was upheld, because of the 'extra' evidence of statements of the seller's clerk that misled the buyer.

Unilateral mistake ●●●

Here one party knows of the false assumption of the other, in some cases having encouraged it. A bad bargain alone is not fundamental enough to avoid the contract, *Smith v Hughes* (1871). However some mistakes are fundamental and one party will be taken to have known about the mistake of the other, *Hartog v Colin and Shields* (1939).

Mistaken identity

This often arises when one person poses as someone else in order to persuade a seller to part with goods on credit. The cases include:

→ *Inter absentes* – where the parties are not in each other's presence, or are dealing 'at arm's length', *Cundy v Lindsay* (1878).
→ *Inter praesentes* – where the parties are in each other's presence, or face to face, *Phillips v Brooks* (1919), *Ingram v Little* (1961), *Lewis v Avery* (1971). Generally the parties are held to deal with the person seen before them, but see *Shogun Finance v Hudson* (2001).

Mistakes over documents ●●●

→ Rectification, an equitable remedy, may be allowed to amend a written agreement, so that it reflects more accurately what the parties previously agreed in an oral contract, *Joscelyne v Nissen* (1970), *Saunders v Anglia Building Society* (1971).
→ The plea of *non est factum* may be available, although it is used very rarely now. It literally means 'not my deed'; *Foster v Mackinnon* (1869) concerned an elderly man with poor eyesight.

Checkpoint 3

Can you explain the different decisions made in the two cases mentioned under mutual mistake?

The jargon

Inter absentes means not in each other's presence (often contracting by post).
Inter praesentes means face to face, or in each other's presence.

Checkpoint 4

List similarities between these three cases of *inter praesentes* mistaken identity.

Exam questions   answers: page 120

1   Consider the circumstances which will decide whether a common mistake will make a contract void. (45 min)

2   Discuss the factors that will affect the validity of a contract formed on the basis of a unilateral mistake. (45 min)

Examiner's secrets

Use plenty of cases to illustrate your answer.

Duress and undue influence

> *"No true consent..."*
>
> Lord Wilberforce

It has long been recognized at common law that a party might have been coerced, or pressed, into a contract. The resulting contract cannot be regarded as a true agreement between the parties.

Duress

Duress was originally a narrowly defined common law doctrine: a contract formed under threat of violence to the person or unlawful constraint (holding someone against their will).

It also extended to threats to those close to the person: *Cumming v Ince* (1847), an old lady's 'agreement' was held void as it was formed under the threat of confinement to a mental hospital. At common law, threats to property were not within the definition of duress, *Skeate v Beale* (1840). However, more recently the approach to this has changed somewhat, and in *The Siboen and the Sibotre* (1976) it was suggested that some very serious threats, such as the threat to burn down a house or slash a valuable painting, may amount to duress.

Economic duress

Threats to property have led to the extension of the doctrine to cover a threat to a party's financial situation. In many circumstances in business life, commercial pressure to contract is great, but legitimate, as there is still a choice over forming the contract. This should not be regarded as duress. It is therefore difficult to draw the line at the boundaries of economic duress, but some principles emerge through case law.

→ *North Ocean Shipping v Hyundai Construction* (1979) – also known as *The Atlantic Baron*   The court recognized the possibility of economic duress, based on unreasonable commercial pressure, in a valuable shipping contract.

→ *Pao On v Lau Yiu Long* (1980)   The threat of a breach of contract alone was seen as a normal problem of commerce.

→ *Universe Tankships of Monravia v ITWF* (1982) – also known as *The Universe Sentinel*   A union's threat to 'black' a ship unless certain conditions were met was held to be economic duress.

→ *Atlas Express v Kafco* (1989)   A threat to a small firm to breach a contract to transport goods was held to be economic duress.

→ *Williams v Roffey* (1991)   Economic duress was considered but not found, as the builders made a reasonable commercial choice.

→ *CTN Cash and Carry v Gallaher* (1994)   Again, no economic duress given the commercial circumstances.

The effect of duress

Duress at common law made the contract void. However, as the courts are using their discretionary, or equitable, powers when dealing with economic duress, this makes contracts formed under economic duress voidable, and therefore subject to other principles, such as lapse of time and third party rights.

Checkpoint 1

Define common law duress in your own words.

Checkpoint 2

Explain the position on duress regarding threats to property.

> *"No practical choice..."*
>
> Lord Scarman

Test yourself

Try to remember these economic duress cases. Write down their names and a brief summary of the facts.

Checkpoint 3

Write down the facts of *Williams v Roffey* from your revision of consideration. If you can't remember these turn to that section and read it again (see pages 93 and 116–17).

The jargon

A *void* contract is invalid and ceases to exist.
   Voidable means that the contract *may* be brought to an end, if other more important factors do not override that action.

Undue influence

Because the common law doctrine of duress was so narrow, the courts developed, through equity, the doctrine of undue influence for any unfair pressure on a party to enter into a contract which does not amount to duress. The cases on undue influence can be divided into two groups:

→ no special relationship between the parties exists – here the burden is on the party claiming undue influence to prove it
→ there is a **fiduciary relationship**, either (a) generally (parent/child, solicitor/client), or (b) on this particular occasion – here undue influence is presumed, *Allcard v Skinner* (1887).

The presumption is rebuttable if evidence exists that the weaker party was free to exercise independent will in entering the contract, *Re Brocklehurst* (1978). Four ways are suggested: full disclosure of all material facts (a full explanation), independent advice, adequate consideration, and spontaneity of a gift.

The effect of undue influence

As undue influence is an equitable doctrine it makes the contract voidable. Equitable principles will therefore apply, as well as the bars to rescission, and in *Allcard v Skinner* (above) the nun was unsuccessful because of a long time delay.

The 'banking' cases

A series of cases, mainly concerning loans from banks, have arisen. The following principles emerge:

→ the relationship between a banker and client may be fiduciary if the bank is given particular trust, *Lloyds Bank v Bundy* (1975)
→ the husband and wife relationship is not generally a fiduciary one, *Midland Bank v Shepherd* (1988), but see *BCCI v Aboody* (1989)
→ there may be a requirement of disadvantage to the weaker party – *National Westminster v Morgan* (1985)
→ *Barclays Bank v O'Brien* (1993) raised important issues concerning a spouse or cohabitee and the *doctrine of notice*
→ to help define the limits of the doctrine, see the recent cases of: *TSB v Camfield* (1994); *Cheese v Thomas* (1993); *Banco Exterior v Mann* (1994); *Midland Bank v Serter* (1994); *Dunbar Bank v Nadeem* (1998)
→ for a summary of banking principles see *Royal Bank of Scotland v Etridge* (2001)

Exam questions
answers: page 120

1 'The doctrine of economic duress suffers from a lack of definition.' Discuss the development of this doctrine. (45 min)

2 Examine the doctrine of undue influence in the light of the recent line of banking cases. (45 min)

"Unfair pressure on a weaker party . . ."

Checkpoint 4

Explain why the doctrine of undue influence was developed.

The jargon

A *fiduciary relationship* is one where one party places particular trust in the other.
To *rebut a presumption* means to show that something assumed is not true on this occasion.

Checkpoint 5

The presumption of undue influence is important – where does it arise?

Checkpoint 6

What effect does undue influence have on the contract?

"The Law must . . . reduce the risk of error, misunderstanding or mishap."

Lord Bingham

The jargon

Here the *doctrine of notice* means that the bank should be aware of the rights of a weaker party (e.g. Mrs O'Brien).

Action point

It is really important to make brief notes on the facts and decisions of the cases on these two pages.

Examiner's secrets

In question 2 be very clear about the presumption of undue influence in *fiduciary relationships,* and how it can be *rebutted.*

Restraint of trade

The new specification for Contract 2 (OCR) includes restraint of trade. This is an aspect of illegality – another vitiating factor which declares that if the nature of a contract is either illegal or against public policy it will not be upheld by the courts.

Illegality

A contract may be illegal in its very nature, such as a contract to steal information for reward. Equally a contract can become illegal in the way in which it is carried out, such as a contract to deliver goods by road, where the lorry owner drives without insurance.

Checkpoint 1

Explain the meaning of a term which is 'in restraint of trade'.

Restraint of trade

A contract can also be declared void if it is not generally in the public interest, and an agreement which prevents a person trading or earning their living comes within this category. This kind of restraint often arises in an employment contract, where an employee is restricted from working for a competitor. It also arises when a seller of a business is prevented from opening a competing business nearby.

If a term in a contract restricts a party's freedom to trade it is *prima facie* void, unless it can be justified in some way. The person wishing to rely on the term must show that it is reasonable between the parties and in the public interest. The term may

Checkpoint 2

What must a party show in order to justify a restraint?

→ protect a trade secret, *Forster v Suggett* (1918)
→ protect a range of clientele, *Fitch v Dewes* (1921), *White v Francis* (1972), *Lansing Linde v Kerr* (1991)
→ create an exclusive dealing arrangement, *Schroeder Music v Macaulay* (1974), *Esso v Harper's Garage* (1968)

The restraint often takes the form of a time limit or geographical limit – not allowing a party to work in a locality for a certain time. This must be reasonable in the eyes of the court – trying to enforce too great a restraint will result in it being void, *Mason v Provident Clothing* (1913).

The courts are clearly willing to consider difficulties in modern contracts, e.g. how much knowledge an employee has, *Faccenda Chicken v Fowler (1987)* and data held electronically has complicated the issue further, *McKenna Breen v James* (2002). Sometimes the employment issues are quite complex, e.g. the employment bureau in *Office Angels v Rainer-Thomas* (1991).

Test yourself

Write down a list of the reasons why a clause in restraint of trade may be seen as reasonable.

Inducement to accept a restraint

Sometimes a clause is upheld because it is freely negotiated, or because payment is made in exchange for an acceptance of the restriction, *Allied Dunbar v Weisinger* (1988).

Businesses and the needs of society ●●●

In order to allow businesses to serve the needs of society, the court
may allow a restriction that would otherwise be void. This may be
considered according to the state and breadth of the market.

In *Nordenfelt v Maxim Nordenfelt* (1894) a world-wide restraint for
25 years was upheld, given the nature of the business of manufacturing
guns and ammunitions, and the limited number of clients.

The House of Lords set the following guidelines:

- As a starting point a restraint of trade clause is void, the burden
  being on to the party seeking to enforce it to show that it should
  be valid.
- There must be evidence that the restraint is reasonable both
  (a) between the parties and (b) regarding the public interest
  (the general good of the public).
- The courts will uphold a restraint if it protects a legitimate interest.

The effect of a clause in restraint of trade ●●●

If a restraint of trade is found to be unreasonable, then it will be void as
far as it is against public policy. So this does not necessarily mean that
the whole contract is void. Severance may be possible, if the offending
clause can be removed without altering the essential meaning of the
contract. The court traditionally will not rewrite the contract, but may
be willing to strike out offending words, retaining the general nature
of the contract. However, there is an apparent slight relaxation of this
strict approach, by interpretation of the offending clause in a way
which makes it reasonable – *Littlewoods v Harris* (1978).

Note that under European law there is a move to uphold the free
movement of workers and any practices which adversely affect
competition within the European Union will be void.

Checkpoint 3

Compare the two restrictions in the case
of *Esso Petroleum v Harper's Garage*
(1967). Why was only one upheld?

Examiner's secrets

Compare the restrictions in the cases:
How many years was the restriction
for? How wide was it geographically?
Was the restriction upheld?

Exam questions   answers: pages 120–21

1   Consider the circumstances in which a clause in a contract which is in
    restraint of trade will be upheld. (45 min)

2   Alex is a manager in a large catering business, Bakeright, and is one of
    the employees who has knowledge of the secret recipes used to produce
    the puddings for which Bakeright is famous. He decides to leave his
    employment as he has been offered employment with one of Bakeright's
    competitors at a higher salary. Bakeright point out that there is a clause
    in Alex's contract with them preventing him from taking up any similar
    employment in England within three years of leaving his work with
    Bakeright.

    Advise Alex as to whether this clause is likely to be upheld by the court.
    (45 min)

Discharge of a contract

"Bringing a contract to an end . . ."

Discharging a contract means bringing it to an end in some way. The way this is done is often important because of the burden of any loss that may fall on the parties.

Performance ●●●

A contract is discharged when both parties have totally performed their obligations.

Checkpoint 1

Use these cases to explain what is meant by 'exact' and 'complete'.

→ Performance must match *exactly* and *completely* what the parties agreed, *Re Moore Co. and Landauer Co.* (1921), where the correct goods were delivered in wrong sized cases; *Cutter v Powell* (1795), where a seaman died so performance was not complete.
→ Severable contracts are those where duties are divisible, *Vlierboom v Chapman* (1884); *Ritchie v Atkinson* (1808).
→ Substantial performance is where a party has largely performed the duties of the contract and can enforce appropriate payment, *Boone v Eyre* (1779); *Hoenig v Isaacs* (1952).
→ Acceptance of partial performance may arise where the parties agree not to continue further, *Christy v Row* (1808); *Sumpter v Hedges* (1898). Payment is made on a *quantum meruit* basis.
→ Tender of performance is a proposal to perform, and may be the equivalent of performance, *Startup v Macdonald* (1843).
→ Prevention of performance by one party may make it impossible for the other to complete performance, *Planche v Colburn* (1831).
→ Time of performance may be 'of the essence' – if not, performance must be within a reasonable time (see the Sale of Goods Act 1979).
→ Vicarious performance is where a party arranges for someone else to carry out duties on their behalf, *Edwards v Newland* (1950).

The jargon

Payment on a *quantum meruit* basis is payment in proportion to work done so far.
Time is 'of the essence' if performance within a certain time is vital to one party and made known, or is obvious, to the other.

Agreement ●●●

A contract is formed by agreement and can be discharged by agreement. To vary or end the contract, both parties must provide consideration, *Berry v Berry* (1929), where a deed of separation was modified by a new contract.

Breach ●●●

Checkpoint 2

When does breach of contract arise?

Checkpoint 3

What are the different types of terms within a contract, and the effect when they are breached? (If you can't remember, refer back to the section on the terms of a contract, page 99.)

Breach of contract arises when there is non-performance, defective performance, or an untrue statement within a contract, and may be implied from actions or statements, *Frost v Knight* (1870). Breach can be in two forms: **actual**, where one party has not performed, or **anticipatory**, where one party indicates, before the date on which performance is due, that performance will not take place. The other party can then sue immediately, *Hochster v de la Tour* (1853).

The consequences will depend on the type of term breached. A **repudiatory** breach is where a condition is breached and the innocent party may repudiate or claim damages. A **non-repudiatory** breach is where a warranty is breached and the innocent party may only claim damages.

Frustration

●●●

The doctrine of frustration provides a remedy where, during the life of the contract, and without the fault of either party, some event occurs that makes further performance impossible, illegal or radically different.

Impossibility

A contract may become impossible to carry out in three ways:

→ the subject matter is destroyed, *Taylor v Caldwell* (1863)
→ the subject matter is unavailable, *Morgan v Manser* (1948)
→ a party dies

Illegality

Frustration will discharge a contract if, during its lifetime, the law is changed in such a way that the basis of the contract becomes illegal, *Metropolitan Water Board v Dick Kerr* (1916).

Radical change in circumstances

Many cases arose out of the postponement of a coronation, where some contracts had become completely pointless. Compare *Krell v Henry* (1903) with *Herne Bay Steam Boat Co. v Hutton* (1903).

Limits to frustration

Certain limits, or restraints, are imposed by the courts.

→ If a contract becomes more onerous it will not be frustrated, *Tsakiroglou v Noblee Thorl* (1962).
→ If a party induces the frustrating event, the contract will be breached, *Maritime National Fish v Ocean Trawlers* (1935).
→ If an event is expressly provided for in the contract, frustration does not apply, *Metropolitan Water Board v Dick Kerr and Co.* (1918).
→ Where an event is foreseen, or should have been foreseen because a party has special knowledge, frustration may not apply, *Walton Harvey v Walker and Homfrays* (1931).

The legal effect of frustration

The Law Reform (Frustrated Contracts) Act 1943 provides that:

→ money paid before the frustrating event is returned
→ money payable before the frustrating event is no longer owed
→ where expenses have been incurred, payment may be ordered
→ payment may be required for any valuable benefit obtained

Exam questions

answers: page 121

1 Evaluate the circumstances in which a party may wish to claim that a contract is frustrated rather than breached. (45 min)

2 Critically assess the ways in which a contract may be brought to an end. (45 min)

"A way to share losses fairly where nobody is to blame..."

Checkpoint 4

How may a contract be frustrated through impossibility?

Checkpoint 5

Why was the contract held frustrated in *Krell v Henry* but not in *Herne Bay v Hutton*?

Test yourself

Try to list the limits to frustration and illustrate each with a case.

Checkpoint 6

Can you explain the main provisions of the Law Reform (Frustrated Contracts) Act 1943?

Examiner's secrets

In question 1 the examiner will be impressed if you show a good understanding of the provisions of the Law Reform (Frustrated Contracts) Act 1943.

Remedies

The most usual remedy for an innocent party to seek as a result of a breach of contract is damages, and this may be claimed as a right at common law. However, this may not provide a reasonable solution, so repudiation (ending the contract) is allowed in some circumstances, and alternative remedies are available, many based in equity, to suit the needs of the situations which arise.

Damages ●●●

→ *Liquidated damages* where the amount awarded has already been decided by the parties as a genuine pre-estimate. Distinguish from penalty clauses, which are not allowed, *Dunlop v New Garage* (1915).
→ *Unliquidated damages* where no fixed amount has been decided. These can be further divided into: substantial damages (a normal claim reflecting the amount lost); nominal damages (a minimum amount, acknowledging that a party has won, but not ordering a large payment); and exemplary damages (an unusually large amount, representing more than the actual loss, awarded to show the court's disapproval – not used very often).

Checkpoint 1

Explain the difference between liquidated and unliquidated damages, and outline the three types of unliquidated damages that are awarded.

Basis of assessment

→ The normal basis for awarding damages in contract is for loss of bargain. The aim is *restitutio in integrum*, where the court aims to put the claimant into the position that would have been achieved if the contract had been performed correctly, *Robinson v Harman* (1848). This supports the view that the idea behind the law of contract is to uphold contracts where possible.
→ In some circumstances damages are awarded on a reliance basis. This is the basis used normally in tort, restoring the injured party to the position which would have existed if the contract had not been formed – see misrepresentation, both fraudulent and under the Misrepresentation Act 1967, *Royscott v Rogerson* (1991).
→ The 'market rule' is that for non-delivery a person can claim the difference between what would have been paid and what the item would now cost to buy on the open market.

The jargon

Restitutio in integrum means to return to the original position.

Checkpoint 2

(a) Explain the loss of bargain basis of assessment and the reliance basis of assessment.
(b) What is meant by the market rule?

Contributory negligence

While it is established that in tort damages can be apportioned by the court on the ground of contributory negligence under the Law Reform (Contributory Negligence) Act 1945, this does not extend to breach of contract, *Basildon D. C. v J. E. Lesser (Properties) Ltd* (1985). However the Law Commission has reported that this could be a useful measure for the future. Note also that sometimes apportionment can be achieved via a different route, e.g. in capacity and frustration, by giving the courts discretion in awarding damages under a statute.

Take note

It is a good idea to make a summary of the main points concerning damages, including examples from cases.

Mental distress

The situation has traditionally been that damages could not be recovered in contract for mental distress – something tangible had to be shown, such as pain and suffering from personal injury, or physical inconvenience. However, where the very nature of the contract indicates that the benefit is not of a tangible nature, and the loss ensuing will be *non-pecuniary*, such as enjoyment of a holiday, damages can be recovered for disappointment, vexation and mental distress. See *Jackson v Horizon Holidays* (1975) and *Jarvis v Swann Tours* (1973), both concerning compensation for holidays. However, regarding contracts of employment, damages will not be awarded for injury to feelings for wrongful dismissal, *Addis v Gramophone Co. Ltd* (1909). After some uncertainty this was confirmed by the Court of Appeal in *Bliss v S. E. Thames Regional Health Authority* (1985).

Remoteness of damage

The court has to decide whether the expenses for which compensation is claimed are a direct result of a breach of contract. The principle is generally that losses are recoverable if they are reasonably within the contemplation of the parties as a probable result of the breach, *Hadley v Baxendale* (1854). However, particular unforeseen losses will not be recoverable, *Victoria Laundry v Newman* (1949).

Mitigation

There is a duty on the party claiming damages to mitigate loss where reasonable – but not an obligation to take extreme steps or to mitigate before the date of performance, *White and Carter v McGregor* (1962).

Other remedies ●●●

Other remedies are available where common law remedies do not provide a just outcome.

→ Rescission is a remedy for misrepresentation.
→ Specific performance may be ordered if the court believes that it is appropriate to enforce an obligation under a contract. The sanction for not complying is a fine or imprisonment for contempt of court.
→ An injunction may be ordered to stop a person from acting in breach of contract. This may be temporary (an interlocutory injunction) until a case goes to trial.
→ A Stop Now order, available since 2001, can be used by the Office of Fair Trading to prevent unfair business practice.

The jargon

Non-pecuniary loss is loss that is not measured directly in terms of money.

Checkpoint 3

Use cases to explain the position regarding damages for mental distress.

The jargon

Mitigation means to reduce the amount of harm caused by something.

Checkpoint 4

Can you explain how the concepts of remoteness and mitigation limit the award of damages?

Links

Rescission is discussed in full on page 105.

Test yourself

Explain when these equitable remedies may be awarded.

Exam questions   answers: page 121

1   Briefly compare the award of damages with other remedies available. (15 min)

2   Critically evaluate the principles of awarding damages for breach of contract. (45 min)

Answers
The law of contract

Offer and acceptance

Checkpoints

1 An expression of willingness to contract on certain terms, made with the intention that it will become binding on acceptance.
2 General offer (*Carlill*); a bus journey (*Wilkie*); promotional campaigns (*Esso*); dealing with a machine (*Thornton*).
3 Agreement to all the terms of the offer.
4 Does the communication arrive more or less immediately? Is the communication entrusted to a third party for delivery? Is there acknowledgement of receipt?
5 In *Clarke* the reward had been forgotten, they wanted to avoid accusation, and a reward was not paid (an Australian case). In *Williams v Carwardine* information was given with mixed motives and a reward was paid.

Exam questions

1 An offer is capable of acceptance, whereas an invitation to treat is usually a negotiating point, not as clear or definite. Some decisions are based on freedom to contract or to avoid the problem of exhausted stock. Cases include:
   - shop window, *Fisher v Bell*
   - supermarket display, *Boots*
   - auctions, *Payne v Cave*
   - tenders, *Spencer v Harding*
   - general offer, *Carlill*
   - promotional campaign, *Esso*
2 First explain the situations which amount to termination: termination by refusal; acceptance (postal rule, modern communications, acceptance over a period of time – *Errington v Errington*); counter offer (*Hyde v Wrench*); death; lapse of time (*Ramsgate v Montefiore*); revocation (*Byrne v van Tienhoven, Butler v Excello, Dickinson v Dodds, Shuey v US*); and failure of a precondition.
   It is important not just to state the law, but to think about any problems, and whether the law is fair or practical. Think about the reasoning behind the cases, and make an attempt to explain them.
3 Define acceptance, as a working beginning. Then discuss the different means of communication.
   Principles of acceptance (*Yates v Pulleyn, Entores v Miles Far East Corp.* – the offeror should not be at a disadvantage).
   Postal rule (*Adam v Lindsell, Re London v Northern Bank*) and reasonable occasions to use the post (*Henthorn v Fraser, Hollwell v Hughes*).
   Telegrams (*Cowan v O'Connor*).
   Telexes (*Entores v Miles Far East Corp.*).
   Time of 'arrival' of message (*The Brimnes*).
   Think about what may be taken into account when comparing other methods. See Checkpoint 4. Consider how fax, email, courier services and answering machines fit in with the current law. Most cases are quite old – the law on new situations therefore only exists by precedent and analogy.

4 This is based on the knowledge required in question 1, but turned into a full essay – so be analytical, and compare and contrast cases to explain the points you make.

Consideration

Checkpoints

1 Base your answer on *Dunlop v Selfridge* (1915). 'An act of forbearance of one party, or the promise thereof, is the price for which the promise of the other is bought.'
2 Although the consideration in *Re Casey's Patents* looked like past consideration, it was understood all along that if Casey did some work he would be paid. The promise of a share in the patents was given instead of this money.
3 • Existing duty under the law of the land: *Collins v Godefroy, Glasbrook v Glamorgan, Ward v Byham*.
   • Existing duty under a contract: *Stylk v Myrick, Hartley v Ponsonby, Scotson v Pegg, Williams v Roffey*.
4 A firm of builders agreed to renovate some flats, a financial penalty being due if they were late completing.
   The builders subcontracted work to carpenters who were unable to finish on time unless more money was paid than that originally agreed. The builders agreed to the extra payment for completion on time, but later refused to pay.
   It was held that they were obliged to pay, as even though the carpenters were only completing their original existing duty, the builders were (a) obtaining the benefit of not having to find new carpenters, and (b) avoiding a financial penalty.

Exam questions

1 Explain the need for consideration – to provide evidence of the bargaining side of a contract (something exchanged on both sides). Consideration:
   - must be sufficient, although it need not be adequate
   - must not be past – unless done at the request of the other party
   - must not be illegal
   - must not be vague
   - must not be an existing duty – unless something 'extra' is done, or some benefit can be seen to the other party
   All of these should be illustrated with cases.
   Decide if the rules are sensible, and if there are any which conflict, e.g. *Ward v Byham* and *White v Bluett*.

Examiner's secrets

In essays, do not simply 'drop' case names on a page. Explain the facts briefly, and think about why the decision was made.

2 Start by explaining why an existing duty is not generally good consideration, but that something added to the existing duty *may* be. This 'extra' can be viewed either as new consideration for a new promise, or consideration to vary the agreement. It is what will amount to 'extra' that is at the heart of this essay.

Examine a duty owed under the law of the land, followed by a contractual duty, then a duty owed to a third party, and lastly the important case of *Williams v Roffey* (see Checkpoint 4).

In *Ward v Byham* very little was held to be 'extra'. Apply this to *Williams v Roffey*. Draw your points together in a conclusion.

Legal intent

Checkpoints

1 The presumption in social and domestic arrangements is that the parties do not intend their contracts to be legally binding. This is rebuttable by clear evidence.

2 It is presumed that in commercial agreements the parties intend their contracts to be legally binding. This is again rebuttable, but in a commercial context very strong and clear evidence is needed, particularly if it affects a consumer.

3 An honourable pledge clause is an example of rebutting the presumption in a commercial context. It is often used in football coupons.

4 It could be unfair on a consumer if they had paid in expectation of an agreement being honoured. They would not be aware of the legal significance of the clause.

5 To facilitate negotiations between trade union representatives, employers and employees.

Exam questions

1 To ensure that (a) a trivial or purely domestic matter does not unintentionally turn into a contract and (b) contracts made in a commercial context are enforceable.

2 By applying the presumption of no legal intent, and comparing the facts with existing cases to see if there is evidence of rebuttal (see Checkpoints above).

3 By applying the presumption of legal intent, and comparing the facts with existing cases to see if there is evidence of rebuttal (see Checkpoints above).

4 Briefly explain the need for legal intent – to protect commercial agreements and to prevent domestic arrangements becoming contracts without that intention.

Explain the presumption in social and domestic arrangements and its rebuttal.

Explain the presumption in commercial arrangements. Here it is *not* necessary to prove legal intent, it is *presumed*. Reasoning – to hold those in commerce to

agreements, and ensure consumers are protected. Explain rebutting the presumption.

Discuss honourable pledge clauses. Is it right that these are allowed?

Conclude – draw together both areas. It is not always necessary to prove legal intent, as it is presumed to exist in commercial contracts. However, it does need to be proved in agreements made in social and domestic circumstances.

Capacity

Checkpoints

1 Corporations (organizations, such as universities and companies); diplomats and sovereigns; those who are drunk or of unsound mind; minors.

2 He was a student at Cambridge at the turn of the century, and he was the son of a wealthy architect, so the waistcoats were 'suited to his condition in life'.

3 In *Doyle v White City Stadium* (1935) a clause in a boxer's training contract prevented him from keeping the prize money in competitions, but the contract was on the whole for his benefit, and therefore binding.

In *de Francesco v Barnum* (1889) a contract to train a young dancer was held to be oppressive because of the unreasonable restrictions in it, e.g. she was not allowed to perform outside the school, travel, or marry. The contract was therefore unenforceable.

4 Restitution is not possible if the money representing the goods has been spent, or the subject matter has been consumed, e.g. food eaten, or a taxi ride taken.

Exam questions

1 Members of society who may be vulnerable, e.g. minors, those who are drunk or of unsound mind.

2 It is binding if it is on the whole beneficial to the minor. See Checkpoint 3.

3 Contracts of a continuing nature, e.g. payment for mobile telephone service provision on a monthly basis. These may be repudiated by a minor before or on reaching 18.

4 The Minors' Contracts Act 1987 made the remedy of restitution available (see notes) and made guarantees of loans to minors enforceable against an adult guarantor.

5 Define minors and examine the various forms of necessaries for which the minor may be liable:
- goods and services
- contracts of employment, training and education, if beneficial to the minor
- contracts of continuing obligation and the general common law position on loans

Explain the provisions of the Minors' Contracts Act 1987:
- for non-necessaries the court now has the power, at its discretion, to order restitution of the goods or any property representing them
- guarantees by an adult are now enforceable

Compare the previous common law position with the present position and show that the common law continues to protect an adult who supplies necessaries to a minor, statute adding fairness and flexibility.

6 Use the points in the above answer, briefly, then apply the law to Nadine and Olivia.
- Nadine's contract with the stage school is a contract of education so it may be binding (examine the terms).
- Olivia's loan may not be enforceable if it is not guaranteed.
- Trade contracts with a minor are not enforceable.
- Olivia's mobile phone could come into the category of 'luxurious items of utility'.
- Her dance lessons may be regarded as training.

Draw together these points in a conclusion for both Nadine and Olivia.

The terms of a contract

Checkpoints

1 How soon before the contract was the statement made? Does the representor have special knowledge? Is special importance placed on an issue? How persuasive is the statement?

2 By custom, by statute or by the courts.

3 (a) For a breach of warranty the innocent party can claim damages.
(b) For a breach of condition the innocent party can choose whether to affirm the contract and claim damages, or to repudiate.

4 In *Poussard v Spiers and Pond* (1876) a singer was ill and missed both rehearsals and opening performance, so this was held to be a breach of condition, whereas in *Bettini v Gye* (1876) a singer only missed rehearsals, so this was held to be a breach of warranty.

5 The Sale of Goods Act 1979, amended by Sale and Supply of Goods Act 1994, in sections 12–15 implies conditions that the seller has a right to sell the goods, goods will be as described, goods will be of satisfactory quality, goods will be fit for a purpose made known to the seller, and the sample will correspond with the whole of the goods in quality.

Exam questions

1 The court will consider whether statements should be terms rather than representations, taking into account the following points:
- how soon before the contract the statement was made
- whether the representor has special knowledge
- whether special importance was placed on an issue
- how persuasive the statement is

They will then consider:
- the degree of notice (how effectively was the term brought to the other party's attention?)
- whether there was a 'course of dealings'; if so, the party suing may be deemed to have had the chance to read the notice
- the time at which notice was given – the terms must be seen or mentioned at or before the point of contract, not after the acceptance is made

2 Terms are of different types according to how important or fundamental they are to the contract. Explain the difference between conditions and warranties, and the effect of breaching each type (Checkpoint 3).

Illustrate your answer with cases (Checkpoint 4).

Now explain the innominate term, and the approach used in *Hong Kong Fir* and the cases following it (see your notes on this, made after reading the section on types of terms).

3 If conditions and warranties were the only types of terms, uncertainty would be minimal. The use of innominate terms means that it is difficult to predict the status given to a term when a breach arises.
- Sometimes types of terms are determined by statute, and here the process is straightforward.
- Terms may be labelled by the parties – but labelling is not necessarily conclusive.
- Some terms are not easily classified as they could be breached in a variety of ways. See *Hong Kong Fir*. The court looks at the seriousness of the breach, and then treats the breach as a breach of condition or warranty.

Sometimes parties do need to know where they stand *if* a breach should occur, especially when in the same line of business and on equal terms (*The Chikuma, Bunge v Tradax* (1981)). Otherwise the use of the innominate term helps to bring about justice, but introduces some uncertainty.

Exemption clauses

Checkpoints

1 Because the clause may have been imposed on a party without free negotiation, e.g. in a consumer contract.

2 The term must not be too late (*Olley v Marlborough Court*); it must be brought to the notice of the other party (*Thornton v Shoe Lane Parking*); and there may be a 'course of dealing' (*Hollier v Rambler Motors*).

3 In *Glynn v Margetson*, if the clause had been valid, allowing the ship to call at any port *en route*, the contract to carry oranges in good condition would have defeated the main purpose of the contract (the main purpose rule).

In *Houghton v Trafalgar* the word 'load' was interpreted strictly, against the insurance company, so as not to include an excess of passengers (the *contra proferentem* rule).

4 The legislation on exemption clauses generally protects the consumer and anyone who has been a victim of a standard term contract (where terms have been inserted without free negotiation).

5 The bargaining power of the parties, and available supplies, any inducement to agree to the term, e.g. a favourable price, trade custom and previous dealings, and the difficulty of the task.

Exam questions

1 • Incorporation – see Checkpoint 2.
  • Construction – see Checkpoint 3.
  • Legislation – write about the main provisions in Unfair Contract Terms Act 1977 and in the Unfair Terms in Consumer Contract Regulations 1994.
  • Reasonableness – see Checkpoint 5.
2 Use the material in question 1 as the factual basis of your essay.
  Explain how the need arose to protect the consumer – Checkpoint 1 – and how legislation has now added to the role of the courts.
  There are still some occasions when exemption clauses are reasonable and therefore valid, not 'outlawed' – see 'Is the exemption clause valid?' in the main text and Checkpoint 5.
3 Explain incorporation briefly, and the main provisions of the legislation, and then apply this to Anneliese.
  At first sight the exemption clause regarding late delivery could be reasonable because Anneliese chose this option. However, if the goods become so late that, knowing the circumstances, the contract becomes pointless, it may be defeated by the main purpose rule and unreasonable under Unfair Contract Terms Act 1977 section 2(2).
  The clause excluding liability for injury would probably not be incorporated following *Thornton v Shoe Lane*, but in any case would now not be valid under section 2(1) of Unfair Contract Terms Act 1977.

Privity of contract

Checkpoints

1 Dunlop would have been able to sue the wholesaler to whom he sold tyres, since there was a contract between them. Dunlop could not however sue the wholesaler's customers, and Selfridge was one of these. Only a party to a contract can normally sue.
2 The contract for the holiday had been made by Mr Jackson for the benefit of the family. At that point only Mr Jackson could sue, although the Court of Appeal allowed damages for the family. Now the Contracts (Rights of Third Parties) Act 1999 would allow the family to recover damages.
3 It was argued that if rights could be 'attached' to land, they could be 'attached' to other forms of property.
  It was argued that the rights under a contract could be held on trust, and enforceable by the law of trusts rather than by contract law.
  It was claimed that a term of the Law of Property Act 1925 would allow rights in any kind of property, not just land-related matters, to be passed to a third party.
4 A person who is not a party to a contract may enforce a term of the contract in his own right if the contract expressly provides that he may, or if it purports to confer a benefit on him.

Exam questions

1 The doctrine of privity: only a person who is party to a contract may sue on it.
  Exceptions: statute; agency; collateral contracts; contracts which run with the land; price restrictions (use cases to illustrate these); and the right of a third party to enforce a right expressly intended for that person – Contracts (Rights of Third Parties) Act 1999.
2 Explain the doctrine of privity – see Checkpoint 1. Briefly explain the established exceptions – see Question 1.
  Discuss the problems created by the doctrine – see Checkpoint 2.
  Consider briefly the ways in which attempts had been made to avoid the doctrine – see Checkpoint 3. Explain the provisions of the Contracts (Rights of Third Parties) Act 1999.
  Discuss the situations in which the new statute will alleviate the problems caused by the rule of privity.

Misrepresentation

Checkpoints

1 To provide a remedy for a person who has suffered as a result of untrue statements made before a contract is formed.
2 An untrue statement of fact, made by one party to a contract to another, which, while not forming a term of a contract, has an inducing effect on it.
3 Misleading conduct; concealing a defect; half-true statements; changed circumstances; fiduciary relationship; contracts *uberrimae fidei*.
4 • Affirmation (*Long v Lloyd*).
  • Lapse of time (*Leaf v International Galleries*).
  • Restitution impossible (*Vigers v Pike*).
  • Supervening third party rights (*White v Garden*).
  • Statutory unfairness (Misrepresentation Act 1967).
5 (a) Section 2(1) gives a remedy of damages where a misrepresentation has occurred, without the need to prove fraud.
  (b) Damages are assessed on a tort (reliance) basis. Section 2(2) gives the court discretion to award damages in lieu of rescission.

Exam questions

1 Define misrepresentation, and consider why a doctrine is needed – see Checkpoints 1 and 2.
  Explain the statements for which a person will not be liable (opinion, etc.).
  Explain that silence is normally not misrepresentation. Discuss the circumstances when it may be – Checkpoint 4.
  Consider the extra duty imposed in a fiduciary relationship or one of *uberimma fides*.
  Explain that the statement must have induced the other party.

2 Explain why a remedy is needed, see Checkpoint 1.
   Explain rescission and the bars, see Checkpoint 4, and consider whether they are reasonable.
   Explain how damages are available for fraudulent misrepresentation, but that it is difficult to prove.
   Explain how damages are available under the Misrepresentation Act 1967, see Checkpoint 5.
   Consider the basis of assessment, and the position in which this will now leave the innocent party.
3 Introduce misrepresentation, define it, and say generally why Tom may be able to sue.
   Consider each of the three statements:
   • 'superb condition' – opinion?
   • 'serviced regularly' – half true?
   • 'four new tyres' – untrue.
   There may be a misrepresentation over the first two, but definitely over the third. Apply the remedies, concentrating on the right to rescind and damages under the Misrepresentation Act 1967.

Mistake

Checkpoints

1 The subject of the contract no longer exists, e.g. the corn could no longer be sold (*Couturier v Hastie*).
2 See Checkpoint 1. If the subject matter can be exchanged, but is merely a bad bargain (of lesser quality), then the contract can be upheld.
3 In *Wood v Scarth* there was extra evidence, so that the contract was not as ambiguous as in *Raffles v Wichelhaus*.
4 All three involved an imposter; some check of his identity; payment by cheque; disappearance of buyer; and attempts to recover goods from a third party.

Exam questions

1 Explain false assumption in forming the contract.
   The mistake must be fundamental – use Lord Atkin's statement.
   Explain *res extincta* cases where the contract will be void, e.g. *Couturier v Hastie*.
   Examine *res sua* where the court is likely to use an equitable remedy, *Cooper v Phibbs*.
   Discuss the effect of a mistake over quality of subject matter – you can be discursive here – see main text.
   Form a conclusion on whether there are circumstances when the doctrine is useful.
2 Explain mistake generally, and define unilateral mistake.
   Stress the importance of one party knowing of the fundamental mistake of the other.
   Discuss the effect of mistake over quality of subject matter.

Duress and undue influence

Checkpoints

1 Persuasion to enter a contract under the threat of violence to the person or unlawful constraint, or to someone close.
2 At common law – not duress.
   Suggestions in *The Siboen and the Sibotre* that some very serious threats, such as the threat to burn down a house or slash a valuable painting, may amount to duress.
3 See Checkpoint 4 in Consideration (pages 93 and 116–17).
4 To deal with situations which were obviously unfair but which did not fall within the strict definition of duress.
5 When there is a fiduciary relationship (in banking cases, when a customer has 'crossed the line into an area of confidentiality').
6 It makes it voidable (can be ended if none of the bars to rescission applies).

Exam questions

1 Define duress – see Checkpoint 1.
   What about property? See Checkpoint 2.
   Using cases, explain how this extended to finance, earning a living and threats to breach a contract.
   Examine the effect of economic duress, and the uncertainty as to when it will be found to exist.
2 Explain the need for the doctrine – see Checkpoint 4.
   State the presumption clearly – see Checkpoint 5.
   Explain the effect of the doctrine – see Checkpoint 6.
   Following *Lloyds v Bundy*, examine the cases, especially *Barclays v O'Brien*. Show how the most recent cases help to define the responsibility of the bank.

Restraint of trade

Checkpoints

1 A term within a contract that has the effect of preventing a person trading or earning their living.
2 Show that the restraint is reasonable both between the parties and in the interest of the public.
3 One was much shorter than the other.

Exam questions

1 • Explain the idea of a term that restrains a person from trading.
   • Explain that these are *prima facie* void as against public policy.
   • Consider how a party might show that the term is reasonable (parties' interest, public interest).
   • Look at the practicalities – protection of a trade secret, range of clientele, allowing a business to operate, reasons for exclusive dealings.

- Consider the way in which this may work – geographical limits, time limits, etc.
2 • Use all of the material in question 1 (but be quite brief as you also need to apply it).
  • Apply each point to Alex and Bakeright.

Discharge of a contract

Checkpoints

1 In *Cutter v Powell* the sailor had not reached his destination so his obligations were incomplete.
  In *Re Moore and Landauer* the delivery was complete but not exact as it was in the wrong size cases.
2 When there is non-performance, defective performance or untrue statements within a contract.
3 See Checkpoint 3 and question 2 in The terms of a contract (pages 99 and 118).
4 The subject matter may be destroyed or unavailable, or a party may have died.
5 In *Krell v Henry* there was now no point at all to the contract, but in *Herne Bay v Hutton* some benefit could still be enjoyed.
6 Money paid is returned; money owing is no longer owed; payment may be ordered for expenses; payment may be required for valuable benefits.

Exam questions

1 Explain that the benefit of claiming frustration rather than breach is to share loss. The alternative of breach imposes liability on one party. Frustration is therefore a defence to a claim of breach.
  Examine in turn:
  • impossibility – see Checkpoint 4
  • illegality – e.g. when war is declared
  • radical difference – see the coronation cases
  Consider the limits to frustration, i.e. more onerous duties, event foreseen, provided for or induced.
  Discuss the effect of frustration – Checkpoint 6.
2 Examine each method of discharge:
  • performance – Checkpoint 1 and main text
  • agreement – both parties provide consideration

- breach – Checkpoints 2 and 3
- frustration – Checkpoints 4, 5 and 6
Assess when these circumstances may arise.

Remedies

Checkpoints

1 • Liquidated: an amount has been decided in advance by the parties.
  • Unliquidated: an amount is decided by the court, and may be substantial, nominal or exemplary.
2 (a) Putting the injured party in the position which they would have been in if the contract had been performed, as opposed to putting them in the position which they would have been in if the wrong had not occurred.
  (b) The market rule is that damages may be claimed which represent the difference between what would have been paid and what the item would now cost on the open market.
3 Damages were given for disappointment, vexation and mental distress in both *Jackson* and *Jarvis*.
4 • Losses are recoverable which were within the reasonable contemplation of the parties (i.e. not too remote).
  • A duty exists to act reasonably to keep the loss to a minimum.

Exam questions

1 Damages is money for the wrong which has occurred, while other remedies may prevent any further wrong, e.g. injunction, repudiation, specific performance.
2 Explain and evaluate the following issues:
  • substantial or other damages – Checkpoint 1
  • basis of assessment – Checkpoint 2
  • mental distress – Checkpoint 3
  • remoteness – Checkpoint 4
  • mitigation – Checkpoint 4

Consumer protection refers to areas of the law which protect consumers from abuse of power by big businesses. The main Acts of Parliament you must know are the Sale of Goods Act 1979, the Supply of Goods and Services Act 1982, the Consumer Protection Act 1987 and the Trade Descriptions Act 1968. However, there are other areas of the law which give rights to consumers. The most important is the tort of negligence and, in addition, you should be aware of contract law on exclusion clauses.

Consumer protection

Exam themes

→ Terms implied into contracts for the sale of goods

→ Terms implied into contracts for the supply of goods and services

→ Protection of consumers through the control of terms of a contract

→ Protection from dangerous goods

→ Protection against misleading information

Topic checklist

	AQA	OCR	WJEC
○ AS ● A2			
Sale of goods	●	●	●
Supply of goods and services	●		●
Consumer protection	●		●

Sale of goods

Many sale of goods contracts are made by consumers. Items bought in a shop or through a catalogue or via the internet will come under this heading. The normal rules on formation of a contract apply (offer and acceptance, consideration, intention and capacity). But, in addition, the law gives consumers extra protection.

Sale of Goods Act 1979 ●●●

The first Act regulating the law on sale of goods contracts was passed in 1893. In the over 100 years since then it has been realized that consumers need more protection and the law is now contained in the 1979 Act as amended by the Sale and Supply of Goods Act 1994.

Implied terms ●●●

Sections 12 to 15 of the 1979 Act imply five key terms in contracts for the sale of goods. These cover title, description, satisfactory quality, fitness for a particular purpose and sale by sample.

Title
Section 12 implies a condition that the seller has a right to sell the goods. In *Rowland v Divall* (1923) this was breached when a stolen car was sold. Section 12 also implies a warranty that there is no charge on the goods.

Description
Section 13 implies a condition that the goods will match their description. The section also states that a sale can be a sale by description even though the buyer selected the items, e.g. from a supermarket shelf.

Satisfactory quality
Section 14(2) implies a condition that goods will be of satisfactory quality. This condition applies only where goods are sold in the course of a business. In *Stevenson v Rogers* (1999) where a fisherman whose normal business was selling fish sold his boat it was held that, even though the sale was a 'one-off' of its particular type, it was a sale in the course of business. Satisfactory condition takes into account any description of the goods, fitness for normal purposes (*Priest v Last* (1903), a hot water bottle which burst), appearance and finish, freedom from minor defects, safety and durability.

Fitness for a particular purpose
Under section 14(3), where goods are sold in the course of business, if a buyer expressly or by implication makes known a particular purpose, then there is an implied condition that the goods will be fit for that purpose. However, this section does not apply where it can be shown either that the buyer did not rely on the seller's skill or judgement or that it was unreasonable for him to do so.

Checkpoint 1

Can you explain what is meant by 'invitation to treat' and when it might occur in a consumer situation?

Checkpoint 2

Can you give the definition in section 2 of the Sale of Goods Act 1979 of a contract of sale of goods?

Action point

Make a spider diagram showing the implied terms in sections 12 to 15.

Checkpoint 3

Can you give two other cases that show a breach of the implied terms in sections 13 or 14?

Check the net

Look at the Sale and Supply of Goods to Consumers Regulations 2002 at www.legislation.hmso.gov.uk. These add extra conditions to section 14 that the goods must conform to advertising claims.

Sale by sample

Section 15 implies conditions that the bulk of the goods will correspond with the sample, that the buyer will have a reasonable opportunity to compare the bulk with the sample and that the goods will be free from any defect, making their quality unsatisfactory, which would not be apparent on reasonable examination of the sample.

Excluding implied terms ●●●

Section 12 cannot be excluded from any contract for the sale of goods. Sections 13 to 15 cannot be excluded from a consumer contract and can be excluded from other contracts only if it is reasonable.

Acceptance of goods ●●●

Under section 35 of the Sale of Goods Act 1979 a buyer is assumed to have accepted the goods when he intimates to the seller that he has done so; or he does any act which is inconsistent with the ownership of the seller; or retains the goods after the lapse of a reasonable time without intimating rejection to the seller. In *Clegg v Anderson* (t/a *Nordic Marine* (2003)) it was held that a three-week delay in rejecting a yacht was reasonable. The buyer is not deemed to have accepted the goods unless he has a reasonable chance of examining them. If there are faults with the goods and the buyer asks for or agrees to them being repaired, the buyer is not assumed to have accepted them.

Passing of property ●●●

If the goods have not been ascertained or are not yet in existence, then the property cannot pass. For specific goods the parties can agree when the property passes, or else section 18 of the Sale of Goods Act 1979 applies. The main rules are:

→ goods in a deliverable state – property passes on contract
→ not in a deliverable state – property passes when they are ready and the seller tells the buyer of this
→ goods on approval – property passes on acceptance by buyer or after lapse of a reasonable time

Passing of risk

The risk involved with damage to, or loss of, goods may be specifically agreed by the parties, but otherwise the risk passes when the property in the goods passes.

Exam questions answers: page 130

1 Explain the importance of the terms implied by the Sale of Goods Act 1979. (40 min)

2 Zara has a day out shopping. She buys an umbrella, but the first time she uses it she finds it will not stay open. She also buys material to make a soft toy for her baby son. When she makes the toy she finds that the material tears easily and is not suitable for a child's toy. Advise Zara. (30 min)

Checkpoint 4

Can you explain the difference between a warranty and a condition?

Checkpoint 5

Can you give the legal definition of consumer in a consumer contract?

Checkpoint 6

Can you name and explain a case about acceptance of a new car?

The jargon

Passing of property means the ownership of the goods is transferred from the seller to the buyer.

Examiner's secrets

If the examiner uses the word 'buys' in a scenario question then you should consider the Sale of Goods Act.

Supply of goods and services

Supply of goods covers situations which are not sales or hire-purchase such as an exchange of goods or a collateral contract. It is also important to protect consumers where there is a supply of services and there are implied terms for this type of contract. Finally there are also regulations which cover specific situations such as package holidays.

Supply of goods ○○○

Terms are implied in these contracts by the Supply of Goods and Services Act 1982. The same type of conditions are implied as for sale of goods. These are:

→ right to transfer title in the goods (section 2)
→ that the goods match any description (section 3)
→ that the goods are of satisfactory quality and fit for any particular purpose (section 4)
→ that the goods match any sample (section 5)

Sections 4 and 5 apply only where the supplier is acting in the course of a business.

Hire of goods ○○○

The Supply of Goods and Services Act 1982 also implies terms in contracts for the hire of goods, e.g. the hire of a car or the hire of a television. Sections 7 to 10 imply the same conditions of a right to transfer the goods, that the goods will match their description, that they will be of satisfactory quality and fit for any particular purpose.

Supply of services ○○○

Sections 13 to 15 imply terms in contracts for services. Services includes a wide variety of things such as electrical rewiring, fitting new windows, dry-cleaning clothes, processing photos, hairdressing, hotel accommodation and professional services such as doing accounts or providing legal services. The implied terms are:

→ that the supplier will carry out the service with reasonable care and skill (section 13) (*Lawson v Supasink* (1984) poor fitting of a kitchen)
→ that (if no time has been agreed) the supplier will carry out the service in a reasonable time (*Charnock v Liverpool Corporation* (1968) eight weeks to repair car)
→ that (if no charge has been agreed) the supplier will charge a reasonable amount (this is a question of fact)

Sections 13 and 14 apply only where the supplier is acting in the course of a business. They are innominate terms.

Negligence

As well as the implied term that the services will be carried out with reasonable care and skill, the tort of negligence also applies. This is important where someone other than the person making the contract with the supplier is injured through lack of care.

Checkpoint 1

Do you know which Acts imply terms into contracts for the sale of goods and contracts of hire-purchase?

Checkpoint 2

Can you list the type of matters that are considered when deciding whether the quality is satisfactory?

Test yourself

Write out from memory the terms implied into a contract for services.

Checkpoint 3

Using cases, can you explain what is meant by 'acting in the course of business'?

Checkpoint 4

Can you explain the phrase an innominate term?

Goods supplied with services

In some contracts for supply of services, goods will also be supplied. If these are part of the service, e.g. a small amount of wire used in an electrical repair, then terms are implied by sections 2 to 5 of the Supply of Goods and Services Act 1982. Where the goods are a separate item and clearly charged as such to the consumer, e.g. a new oven in a contract to fit a new kitchen, then this is a sale of the oven and, while terms are implied in the fitting by the Supply of Goods and Services Act 1982, the oven is covered by the Sale of Goods Act 1979.

Excluding terms ●●●

The Unfair Contract Terms Act 1977 prevents the implied terms for the supply of goods being excluded from any consumer contract. For supply of services the implied terms can be excluded only if this is reasonable.

Standard terms contracts

Unfair Terms in Contracts Regulations 1999 apply to standard terms in consumer contracts and state that any unfair term is not binding on the consumer. The regulations do not apply to negotiated terms.

Package Holiday Regulations ●●●

Contracts for package holidays are covered by the Package Holiday Regulations. Normal contract rules and the Supply of Goods and Services Act 1982 also apply. A key point in the regulations is that package organizers or retailers must not supply any misleading descriptive material. They are liable even though they are not the actual suppliers of the services (e.g. the hotel abroad is actually supplying the services). The Regulations also create criminal liability.

Contracts for unsolicited goods or services ●●●

Sometimes goods are sent to people without their having asked for them as a method of trying to force people to buy the goods. This problem has been dealt with by the Unsolicited Goods and Services Act 1971. This states that if the person receiving the goods sends a written notice to the sender that the goods were not requested, then if the sender does not reclaim them after 30 days, the recipient can claim them as a free gift. Where no written notice is sent then the recipient has to wait six months before they can claim the goods.

Checkpoint 5

Can you state which sections of the Sale of Goods Act 1979 imply terms in the sale of goods?

The jargon

The *Unfair Contract Terms Act 1977* is often referred to as *UCTA*.

Checkpoint 6

Which European Union directive led to the Unfair Terms in Contracts Regulations 1999?

Action point

Make a list of the different areas of law that could be involved in a contract for a package holiday.

Exam questions answers: page 131

1 To what extent does the law give adequate protection to consumers of services? (30 min)

2 Krazy Kits Ltd are fitting a new kitchen for Yolande at an agreed cost of £6 500. One of the cupboards is fitted so badly that it falls off the wall. The new freezer does not work. When the bill arrives, the full cost charged is £7 000. Advise Yolande. (30 min)

Examiner's secrets

Don't forget that questions on this topic can include general contract rules and other areas such as sale of goods.

Consumer protection

Consumers can sue under the tort of negligence, but this depends on the proof of fault. The Consumer Protection Act 1987 has given additional protection for consumers by widening the category of people who are liable and imposing strict liability on them. Criminal law also plays a part in consumer law by making traders liable for false descriptions of goods or services and for misleading prices.

Consumer Protection Act 1987 ●●●

This Act was passed as a direct result of the European Product Liability Directive and section 1 provides that the Act should be interpreted in accordance with the directive. The Act gives the buyer or anyone else who has suffered loss or damage through a defective product the right to claim from the producer.

The producer
The Act defines producer as including:

→ manufacturers
→ first importers into the European Union
→ own-branders who hold themselves out as producers
→ suppliers who do not on request identify the producer

The product
All manufactured products are included but the definition is much wider than this as it includes anything that has been processed in any way. It does not cover unprocessed agricultural products. So an orange is not covered but orange juice is because this has been processed.

The defect
This can be a fault in manufacturing, design or instructions. A product is defective when 'the safety of the product is not such as persons generally are entitled to expect'. The test is objective considering:

→ the manner in which the product is marketed
→ any instructions or warnings given with it
→ what might reasonably be expected to be done with it

In *A and others v National Blood Authority* (2001) blood was held to be defective because the defendants knew that some of it might be contaminated with Hepatitis C and failed to inform the public that this could be the case.

Damage covered
The Act covers liability for death, personal injury and damage to property (over £275). The property must be of a type ordinarily intended for private use and actually intended for this by the person suffering the damage. Damage to the product itself is not covered.

Checkpoint 1

What three basic points must be proved to establish a case in negligence?

Test yourself

Write out the different meanings of 'producer' from memory.

Action point

Make your own notes on the key points that have to be proved under the Consumer Protection Act 1987.

Checkpoint 2

Can you give examples of property that is normally intended for private use?

Defences

Liability can be avoided if it can be shown that:

→ the producer is not in business (e.g. sale of home-made products for charity)
→ the defect did not exist at the time of manufacture
→ the defect was caused by complying with the law
→ scientific and technical knowledge at the relevant time was not such that the defect might be expected to have been discovered

Misleading prices

Part III of the Consumer Protection Act 1987 makes it a criminal offence to give consumers a misleading price indication about goods, services or accommodation.

Trade Descriptions Act 1968

This makes it a criminal offence for any person in the course of trade or business to apply a false trade description to any goods or to supply or offer to supply any goods to which a false trade description is applied. False means to a material degree and includes misleading descriptions.

Trade description

This covers such matters as quantity, size (e.g. of shirts/shoes), composition (e.g. 65% polyester/35% cotton), method of manufacture, fitness for purpose (e.g. waterproof), strength, performance, testing or approval and other history.

Description of services

It is a criminal offence for any person to make a statement which he knows to be false, or recklessly make a false statement, as to the nature or provision or location of any services, accommodation or facilities.

Defences

It is a defence if it was due to a mistake, or reliance on information supplied, or the default of another or some cause beyond the person's control *and* he took all reasonable precautions and due diligence to avoid the commission of the offence.

Director-General of Fair Trading

The Director-General's role is to supervise trading practices and take action against traders who are persistently unfair to the consumer. He also recommends new legislation to improve consumer protection.

Exam questions   answers: pages 131–2

1 Explain and comment on the improvements to consumer protection brought about by the Consumer Protection Act 1987. (40 min)

2 Dodgy Garages sold a car to Sam. The car was described as 'in immaculate condition' and showed 24 000 miles on the clock. In fact the car had done 84 000 miles and there were several faults so that Sam had to spend £800 to make it roadworthy. Advise Dodgy Garages as to their civil and criminal liability. (40 min)

The jargon

The last defence in this list is known as the *state of the art* defence.

Checkpoint 3

Who enforces the provisions of Part III of the Consumer Protection Act 1987 and the Trade Descriptions Act 1968?

Checkpoint 4

Can you give other examples that come within the meaning of trade description?

Checkpoint 5

Which Act gives the Director-General of Fair Trading his powers?

Examiner's secrets

If the examiner asks for civil and criminal liability make sure you cover both.

129

Answers
Consumer protection

Sale of goods

Checkpoints

1 An invitation to treat is an invitation to the other person to make an offer. It is not an offer in contract law. One example in a consumer situation is goods in a shop window. These are an invitation to the shopper to make an offer to buy (*Fisher v Bell* (1961)). Another example is the display of items on the shelves of a supermarket. This is an invitation to treat and the consumer makes the offer at the checkout (*Pharmaceutical Society of Great Britain v Boots Chemists* (1953)).

2 Section 2 of the Sale of Goods Act 1979 states that a contract of sale of goods is:

'a contract by which the seller transfers or agrees to transfer the property in goods to the buyer for a money consideration called the price.'

3 Cases include:
- *Beale v Taylor* (1967) where a car was described as a 'Herald, convertible white 1961'. It was in fact the back half of a 1961 car welded to the front of an older car. This was a breach of section 13.
- *Godley v Perry* (1960) in which a small boy was injured when he used a catapult he had bought. It was held that this was a breach of section 14 as the catapult was not fit for its ordinary use.
- *Griffiths v Peter Conway Ltd* (1939) in which a woman with an exceptionally sensitive skin suffered skin problems through wearing a fur coat she had bought. This was not a breach of section 14 as she had not made known to the seller that she had an abnormally sensitive skin and the coat was fit for normal people to wear.

4 A *condition* is a fundamental term of the contract. It is such an important term that, if it is broken, the buyer can choose whether to repudiate (cancel) the contract or continue with it and claim damages.

A *warranty* is a less important term. Breach of a warranty only allows the buyer to claim damages.

5 A person is defined as dealing as a consumer by the Unfair Contract Terms Act 1977 where:
- he neither makes the contract in the course of business nor holds himself out as doing so, and
- the other party does make the contract in the course of business, and
- the contract involves the supply of goods which are of a type ordinarily supplied for private use or consumption

6 *Bernstein v Pampson Motors* (1987)

Mr Bernstein bought a new Nissan car. After three weeks and some 140 miles, the engine of the car 'seized up' because of some sealant which had got into the lubrication system when the car was being assembled. This was a breach of section 14 but because he had used the car for three weeks he had accepted the car. It was held that he could not repudiate the contract and was only entitled to damages. The law on acceptance was amended in 1995 and it is uncertain whether Mr Bernstein would now have been held to have accepted the goods. The present law states that the buyer is not deemed to have accepted the goods unless he has a reasonable opportunity of examining them.

Exam questions

1 Start by briefly setting out the terms implied by the Sale of Goods Act in sections 12 to 15.

Then look at why such terms are needed with points such as:
- the lack of balance between the parties in consumer contracts
- the fact that individual consumers have virtually no 'bargaining power'
- businesses could choose to avoid liability for defects by using exclusion clauses
- the fact that most of the terms are conditions allows the consumer to repudiate the contract

Use some specific examples of situations where protection by the law of the consumer is needed. You could use your knowledge of cases in doing this.

2 For both these items you need to ascertain whether there has been a breach of section 14 of the Sale of Goods Act 1979. However, they involve different parts of that section so deal with them separately.

First the umbrella – this is a breach of section 14(2) as the purpose of an umbrella is to keep the rain off. If it will not stay open then it is not fit for this purpose.

Second the material – here the question does not tell you whether the material is fit for normal purposes, nor are you told whether Zara explained what she wanted the material for to the seller. So you need to deal with all possibilities.

As the material 'tears easily' it may be that it is not fit for normal purposes and there is a breach of section 14(2). If it is fit for ordinary use, then is there a breach of section 14(3)? – only if Zara explained this purpose to the seller and relied on his skill and judgement.

Explain it is important for Zara to establish that there is a breach of a condition as this allows her to repudiate the contract and/or claim damages.

> **Examiner's secrets**
>
> With the Sale of Goods Act 1979 the important point is to make sure you identify which section(s) are involved in the question.

Supply of goods and services

Checkpoints

1 Sale of Goods Act 1979, sections 12 to 15. Supply of Goods (Implied Terms) Act 1973, sections 8 to 11.

2 Satisfactory quality includes considering:
- any description of the goods
- the price, if relevant
- fitness for all the purposes for which goods of the kind are commonly supplied
- appearance and finish

- freedom from minor defects
- safety
- durability

3 Acting in the course of business is a phrase used in many Acts of Parliament in regard to consumer protection. However, it is not clearly defined and the case law has been contradictory, e.g.:
   - *R & B Customs Brokers v United Dominions Trust* (1988) it was held that a company which bought a second-hand Shogun vehicle for one of its directors was not acting in the course of business under the definition in the Unfair Contract Terms Act 1977. The evidence in the case was that this was only the second or third car that had been bought.
   - *Stevenson v Rogers* (1999) the defendant was a fisherman whose normal business was to sell fish. He sold his fishing boat to replace it with another. As in *R & B Customs Brokers* this was a rare occurrence. However, it was held that he was acting in the course of business. The Court of Appeal distinguished the case from *R & B Customs Brokers* as the case was about section 14 of the Sale of Goods Act 1979 and not UCTA.

4 An innominate term is one which may be either a condition or a warranty depending on how serious the breach is. It is not possible to say which it is until it has been broken (see also The jargon, page 99).

5 - section 12 seller has right to pass title
   - section 13 goods must match description
   - section 14 goods must be of satisfactory quality and fit for purpose
   - section 15 goods must match sample

6 Directive 93/13 on Unfair Terms in Consumer Contracts. This directive was aimed at protecting consumers of goods and services from abuse of power by the seller or supplier and from 'one-sided' contracts.

Exam questions

1 The question is only about 'services', so the focus is on the law in the Supply of Goods and Services Act 1982, though there are also other areas you can include such as the Package Holiday Regulations, the Unfair Terms in Contracts Regulations 1999 and criminal liability of traders under the Trade Descriptions Act 1968.

   Start by explaining the protection given to consumers by the implied terms in sections 13, 14 and 15 of the 1982 Act.

   Then discuss difficulties/omissions in that Act such as the use of the word 'reasonable' and the difficulty of defining this. Point out that the terms can be excluded but only if this is reasonable under UCTA. Use cases to illustrate your answer.

2 Deal with each point separately.
   - First the poor fitting of the cupboard. In fitting the cupboard the company is providing a service, so this is covered by the Supply of Goods and Services Act 1982. Under section 13 there is an implied term that the work will be carried out with due care and skill. There is

clearly a breach of this implied term so Yolande could claim the cost of putting the matter right.
   - Second the freezer which does not work. This is covered by the Sale of Goods Act 1979 as Yolande is clearly purchasing the freezer as part of the contract. As it does not work, it is not of satisfactory quality and there is a breach of section 14(2). Yolande can repudiate the contract and claim damages.
   - Finally the extra cost. The question states that the agreed cost was £6 500, so any attempt to charge more is not in accordance with the terms of the contract. This comes under basic contract law rules. Yolande would not have to pay the extra.

Examiner's secrets

In broad discussion questions the examiner likes you to look at the wider picture and include different areas of law which give protection to the consumer.

Consumer protection

Checkpoints

1 For negligence the three key points which must be proved are that:
   - the defendant owes the claimant a duty of care
   - the defendant has broken that duty of care
   - the claimant has suffered damage as a result of the breach

2 Many items can be for private use or for use in the course of business. It is usually a question of fact as to which it is, e.g. a car bought for yourself is for private use, but if the car is bought as one of a fleet for a car hire firm then it is obviously not private use.

3 Local Trading Standards Officers have powers to check for breaches of these Acts and also to take criminal proceedings against traders.

4 There are many examples such as 'one lady owner' as part of the history of a second-hand car.
   Some cases include:
   - *Yugotours Ltd v Wadsley* (1988) where the fact that a photograph of a three-masted schooner was used in a holiday brochure together with the words 'the excitement of being under full sail on board this majestic schooner' was a false statement under the Trade Descriptions Act 1968.
   - *Dixon Ltd v Barnett* (1989) where a telescope was described as capable of up to '455 x magnification', but the useful magnification was only 120 times. This was therefore a false trade description even though scientifically the telescope could achieve 455 times magnification.

5 The Fair Trading Act 1973

Exam questions

1 As this question asks you to explain *and* comment, don't forget to do both! Start with explaining the key points in the Consumer Protection Act. These are:

- that it makes a 'producer' liable to a consumer for defective products
- that is also imposes criminal liability in respect of defective goods

Point out the improvements:

- the consumer has a wider range of people to claim against; this is important where the manufacturer is abroad and there is no possibility of making a claim against them
- there is no need to prove fault; the Act tries to impose strict liability so that it is easier to establish a claim than under negligence
- that the range of claimants is wider that under the Sale of Goods Act as it includes any injured by the defective product even though they were not the purchaser

Now comment on the problems that remain:

- the state of the art defence which could mean that cases such as the Thalidomide drug claims may not be covered
- the fact that the product itself is not covered, so the Sale of Goods Act must be used for this

2 Don't forget to cover both civil and criminal liability. First look at civil liability.

Sam has the possibility of making a claim under:

- the Sale of Goods Act 1979 as the car does not match its description (section 13)
- contract law, if the phrase 'immaculate condition' was used prior to the sale, then it may be a misrepresentation

Now consider the criminal law. Dodgy Garages are probably liable under the Trade Description Act 1968 (section 1). This is shown by *Kensington and Chelsea Borough Council v Riley* (1973) where a trader was convicted of an offence where the description 'in immaculate condition' was used, yet the car needed £250 spent on it to make it roadworthy. They are also liable for the false mileage unless they can show that they relied on information given to them by the previous owner and had used all due diligence. Alternatively they may have put a disclaimer notice stating that they did not guarantee the accuracy of the recorded mileage. This would prevent liability unless it was shown that they themselves had turned back the clock.

Examiner's secrets

The examiner does not expect you to know all the cases on trade descriptions. What is wanted is clear knowledge of the provisions of the Act and sensible application to the facts.

Tort includes a number of different types of civil liability and there are numerous individual torts. There are some common features. Many torts will be about unlawful interference while many others will be about a breach of a duty created by law. It is arguable whether liability in tort is always the best way of helping the victims of 'wrongdoing'. The common remedy in tort is damages but there are other remedies available that relate more closely to the harm suffered.

Exam themes

→ Fault liability and no-fault schemes

→ Remoteness and standard of care

→ Primary victims and secondary victims in nervous shock cases

→ The circumstances in which there can be liability for a negligent misstatement

→ Problems on children, independent contractors, and trespassers in occupiers' liability

→ Pollution and *Rylands v Fletcher* and/or nuisance

→ Problems on employment status and acts in the course of employment

→ Justifications for making an employer liable for the torts of an employee

Topic checklist

O AS ● A2	AQA	OCR	WJEC
General principles in tort	●	●	
Negligence – general	●	●	
Negligence – nervous shock, etc.	●	●	
Occupiers' liability	●	●	
Vicarious liability	●	●	
Strict liability	●	●	
Nuisance	●	●	
Trespass to the person		●	
Trespass to goods and land		●	
General defences and remedies	●	●	

General principles in tort

Tort is an area of civil law. It concerns the wrongs committed by individuals and is about compensating the victims of those wrongs for the loss or damage they have suffered. It would be more accurate to talk of a 'law of torts' since there are many individual torts, all having different requirements or ingredients. Some torts are very old and are based on interference or 'trespass'; some are more recent and are based on the breach of a legal duty.

The general character and aims of tort

Tort has two principal objectives:

→ deterrence – to reduce the amount of damage caused by wrongdoings by making the wrongdoer responsible for the remedy
→ compensation – one of the main remedies in tort is damages, the purpose of which is, as far as money can, to put the victim in the position he would have been in if the tort had not happened

Tort has been given a number of definitions. The standard modern ingredients of a tort are when the defendant's wrongful act or omission causes loss, damage or injury to the claimant through the fault of the defendant, and the damage is of a type that attracts liability in law.

Comparisons with other areas of law

The general aims of tort and other areas of law such as contract and crime are quite different so it is useful to understand how tort compares.

Comparison with criminal law

There is a lot of overlap between tort and crime and there can also be liability in both, e.g. a defendant can be liable to compensate for assault and battery in tort and be punished for an assault offence in crime. Differences include:

→ the parties – the state brings the action in crime whereas an individual brings the action in tort
→ the outcomes – a criminal action may result in a conviction and punishment while an action in tort may result in liability on the part of the defendant and a remedy awarded to the claimant
→ terminology and procedure
→ the standard of proof – which is higher in crime.

Comparison with contract law

Tort and contract law are also often closely linked but there are differences which include:

→ contract law enforces contracts and provides remedies if contracts are broken whereas tort tries to prevent wrongs from happening and compensates the victims of wrongdoing

---

The jargon

Tort is a French word that simply means 'wrong' – so a tort is a wrong for which there is a legal remedy.

"Tortious liability arises from the breach of a duty primarily fixed by law; such duty is to persons generally and its breach is redressable by an action for unliquidated damages."

Winfield

Action point

Make a list of ways in which tort can act as a deterrent.

Checkpoint 1

Name some torts that are also crimes.

Checkpoint 2

Who are the different parties in a tort action and a criminal action and what are the different standards of proof?

→ in contract the rights and duties are those agreed upon by the parties when the contract is made whereas in tort the rights and duties are set by law

→ damages in contract are to put the victim of the breach in the position he would have been in if the contract had been properly performed whereas tort damages are to put the victim of the tort in the position he would have been in had the wrong not happened

The interests that tort can protect ●●●

Torts can be grouped by the type of interest they protect.

1 *Personal security*, e.g. trespass to the person, medical negligence, and liability for nervous shock, and some employers' liability and statutory duties in health and safety, and occupiers' liability; and defamation which protects a person's reputation.
2 *Property*, e.g. land rights are protected by trespass to land, nuisance, and *Rylands v Fletcher*; personal property by trespass to goods.
3 *Economic loss* – this is more controversial and problematic but damages can be recovered for this under the rules in *Hedley Byrne v Heller & Partners* (1964) for negligent misstatement causing a financial loss.

NB Following the Human Rights Act 1988 tort law may also be important in human rights, e.g. *Marcic v Thames Water plc* (2002) and Article 8 the right to respect for private and family life.

Fault liability ●●●

Proving fault on the part of the defendant is an essential aspect of many torts including negligence. In these torts, if the claimant cannot prove fault on the part of the defendant then there is no claim and no compensation for the loss or injury suffered.

Defects with the tort system ●●●

There are a number of problems with the system of liability in tort:

→ it does not compensate the victims of all wrongs, but generally only those who can show fault
→ it is an expensive system to operate, e.g. costs equal 85% of damages
→ it is subject to many delays and people are put off claiming or eventually drop their claims
→ there is no point suing 'a man of straw' so the financial means of the defendant can determine whether a claimant has a remedy
→ claimants may be forced into accepting much lower settlements than the loss they have suffered

Exam questions
answers: page 154

1 Consider the main arguments for and against establishing a 'no-fault' system of compensation for personal injury. (45 min)

2 In what ways is tort different to other areas of law such as crime and contract? (20 min)

Test yourself

Try to remember the different reasons for awarding damages in tort and in contract.

The jargon

'*Pure economic loss*' is a loss which is only financial rather than involving physical damage or personal injury.

Checkpoint 3

Do you know the facts of the *Hedley Byrne* case?

Action point

Identify how the Woolf reforms might help to reduce the costs of the tort system.

Checkpoint 4

What is a 'man of straw'?

Examiner's secrets

Try to use cases to illustrate some of the problems caused by the fault principle.

Negligence – general

Negligence is a very modern tort and a very important one. It can cover a variety of situations from car crashes to badly manufactured products and from carelessly performed operations to carelessly prepared accounts. Lord Atkin identified the ingredients of negligence in the case of *Donoghue v Stevenson* (1932).

A successful negligence claim depends on three things:

→ a *duty of care* owed by the defendant to the claimant
→ *breach* of that duty by the defendant
→ *damage* suffered by the claimant and *caused* by the defendant's breach that is a *foreseeable* consequence of the breach

The duty of care ●●●

Lord Atkin originally determined how a duty of care could be identified in his '*neighbour principle*'.

The modern test is now the three-part test from *Caparo v Dickman* (1990):

→ *foresight* – there is no duty unless it is reasonably foreseeable that the defendant's act or omission will cause damage to the claimant
→ *proximity* – the parties must be sufficiently closely connected for the duty to exist
→ *fair and reasonable* – it must be just to impose the duty

Public policy has also been important in determining whether or not judges will say that a duty of care exists, e.g. in *Rondel v Worsley* (1969) the court was not prepared to make a barrister liable for his conduct of a case in court; in *Hill v Chief Constable of West Yorkshire* (1988) the court would not accept that the police could be liable to the victims of crime for failing to catch the criminal.

Breach of the duty of care ●●●

Once a claimant has proved the duty of care is owed he must then show that the defendant breached that duty. This is merely when the defendant falls below the standard of care appropriate to the duty. Breach of duty is measured objectively by the 'reasonable man test'. There are, however, many factors that can be taken into account:

→ the magnitude of the risk – degree of care expected depends on the likelihood of the risk; compare *Bolton v Stone* (1951) and *Haley v London Electricity Board* (1965)
→ the practicability of precautions – the reasonable man has to do only what is reasonable to avoid harm, *Latimer v AEC* (1953)
→ social utility of the activity – if the defendant's act is to avoid greater harm then there is no liability, *Watt v Herts CC* (1954)
→ inexperience – the same standard of care regardless of the experience of the defendant, *Nettleship v Weston*

Where professionals are concerned the standard expected is that of the reasonable competent professional, *Bolam v Friern Hospital MC* (1957).

Checkpoint 1

Can you remember the actual duty owed in this important case?

"You must take reasonable care to avoid acts or omissions which you can reasonably foresee would be likely to injure your neighbour."

Lord Atkin in *Donoghue v Stevenson*

Test yourself

Try to remember the cases that illustrate the three-part test.

". . . the omission to do something which a reasonable man would do or doing something which a prudent and reasonable man would not do . . ."

B. Alderson in *Blyth v Birmingham Waterworks*

Checkpoint 2

Compare the usual standard of care and that owed by professionals.

Damage caused by the defendant ●●●

The defendant must have caused the damage suffered by the claimant or he is not liable. *Causation* is measured by the *'but for test'*. So if but for the defendant's negligent act or omission the claimant would not have suffered loss or damage then the defendant is liable as in *Barnett v Chelsea & Kensington Hospital Management Committee* (1969).

Where there is more than one possible cause then the court may feel unable to impose liability on the defendant, *Wilsher v Essex AHA* (1988). However, where there is more than one cause of the damage a defendant may still be liable for 'materially increasing the risk of the damage', *Fairchild v Glenhaven Funeral Services & Others* (2001).

Sometimes an intervening act can break the *chain of causation* between the defendant's negligent act and the damage suffered by the claimant so that the defendant is not liable. This can be:

→ an intervening act by claimant, *Wieland v Cyril Lord Carpets* (1969)
→ an intervening act of nature, *Carslogie Steamship Co. v Royal Norwegian Government* (1952)
→ an intervening act by a third party, *Knightly v Johns* (1982)

Remoteness of damage ●●●

The courts have always been careful to avoid compensating a claimant for damage that is too far removed from the defendant's negligent act or omission. Since *The Wagon Mound* (1961) the test is whether or not the damage was *'reasonably foreseeable'* by the defendant.

The precise extent of damage need not be foreseen as long as the defendant could have foreseen damage of the general type suffered by the claimant, *Bradford v Robinson Rentals* (1967).

Proof of negligence and *res ipsa loquitur* ●●●

The burden of proof is always on the claimant. Sometimes it is very difficult for a claimant to prove the exact details of negligence because there is insufficient information available. However, where it seems obvious that there must have been negligence, the defendant must show why he is not negligent and therefore liable. There are three key elements to the plea:

→ the thing causing the damage was under the defendant's control at all material times, *Gee v Metropolitan Railway Co.* (1873)
→ no other explanation, *Barkway v South Wales Transport* (1950)
→ the damage could apparently only have been caused by negligence *Scott v London & St Katherine Docks* (1865)

Exam questions   answers: pages 154–5

1   Discuss with reference to decided cases how the courts determine that there has been a breach of the duty of care in negligence cases. (45 min)

2   Evaluate the part played by 'public policy' considerations in the law of negligence. (45 min)

Checkpoint 3

Explain why the defendant was not liable in this case.

The jargon

Novus actus interveniens – simply means a new act intervenes.

Checkpoint 4

Explain the connection between causation in fact (the but for test) and causation in law (remoteness of damage).

The jargon

Res ipsa loquitur simply means 'the thing speaks for itself'.

Action point

Try to work out why *res ipsa loquitur* is so important in medical negligence cases.

Examiner's secrets

The examiners like to see a balanced argument in essay questions with points for both sides of the argument.

Examiner's secrets

An examiner will be impressed if you can comment on the similarity or difference between 'public policy' and 'fair and reasonable'.

Negligence – nervous shock, etc.

Most duty of care situations are based on fairly straight-forward relationships as between, e.g. doctor and patient, employer and employee, fellow motorists, manufacturers and consumers (the original duty owed in *Donoghue v Stevenson*). On occasions, however, the judges have been prepared to accept that there can be a duty of care in some fairly novel situations.

Nervous shock ●●●

This is a difficult area of negligence which was originally rejected in the 19th century and which developed in fits and starts in the 20th century so that it is an uncertain area of law.

The three main issues you need to consider are:

→ what type of harm amounts to nervous shock
→ who is entitled to recover damages for nervous shock
→ and in what circumstances

Definition of nervous shock

For a person to recover damages for nervous shock he must have suffered a *recognized psychiatric disorder* such as *post-traumatic stress disorder* or *acute anxiety syndrome*. Ordinary human emotions and conditions such as grief or insomnia are insufficient to create liability, *Reilly v Merseyside Regional Health Authority* (1994).

Primary victims and secondary victims

It has been possible for **primary victims** to succeed in claims for a long time. These are people who are involved in the accident caused by the defendant's negligence who either suffer some other personal injury as well or who are at risk of injury, *Dulieu v White* (1901).

Liability to **secondary victims** has been more problematic. The rules are now contained in *Alcock v Chief Constable of South Yorkshire* (1991) from the Hillsborough disaster and there are three key questions to ask:

→ was there a close tie of love and affection between the claimant and the victim of the defendant's negligence?
→ was the claimant sufficiently close in time and space to the event?
→ did the claimant witness the incident or its immediate aftermath?

The most generous example to a claimant was that in *McLoughlin v O'Brien* (1981) where witnessing the aftermath two hours after the event counted.

Traditionally *rescuers* have been able to claim successfully, e.g. *Chadwick v B R Board* (1993) – but not mere bystanders, e.g. *McFarlane v E E Caledonia* (1994). Now *White v Chief Constable of South Yorkshire* (1999) imposes stricter conditions on professional rescuers because of the unfair comparison with relatives in *Alcock*. Now a rescuer must be either a genuine primary victim or, according to *Greatorex v Greatorex* (2000), can be a genuine secondary victim.

Checkpoint 1

Say why nervous shock claims were originally not accepted and try to give an early case example.

Test yourself

Make a list from memory of those sorts of conditions that will count as nervous shock and those that will not.

The jargon

A *secondary* victim is one who is not injured or at risk as a result of the defendant's negligence.

Test yourself

See if you can make a list of cases illustrating what is meant by the 'immediate aftermath'.

Action point

Make brief notes on all of these nervous shock cases so that you will remember them.

Test yourself

Make sure you have a good understanding of the differences between primary victims and secondary victims for the exam.

Pure economic loss ●●●

Generally a claimant will not be able to recover damages for a *pure economic loss*. This is because this type of loss is more appropriate to contract rather than tort claims. So in *Spartan Steels v Martin & Co.* (1973) a claim for loss of profit arising from a negligently caused power cut failed. The two-part test from *Anns v Merton LBC* (1978) briefly confused this point, most notably in *Junior Books v Veitchi* (1983). But *Murphy v Brentwood DC* (1990) overruled the *Anns* case.

Economic loss caused by negligent misstatements ●●●

The House of Lords accepted this type of duty in *Hedley Byrne v Heller & Partners* (1964). A claim is possible only if certain criteria apply:

→ a *special relationship* exists between the parties, *Mutual Life & Citizens Assurance Co. v Evatt* (1971)
→ the maker of the misstatement possesses the type of knowledge needed by the claimant, *Harris v Wyre Forest DC* (1988)
→ the defendant is aware that the claimant will rely on the statement and the claimant does so, *Chaudhry v Prabhakar* (1988)

Liability under this principle is common with surveyors, *Smith v Eric S Bush* (1989), and also accountants, *Caparo v Dickman* (1989). In the last case Lord Oliver identified the facts that might be considered in establishing liability:

→ the purpose for which the statement was made and communicated
→ the relationships between advisor, advisee and any third party
→ the size of the class of people to which the advisee belongs
→ the state of knowledge of the advisor
→ reliance by the advisee

Loss caused by omissions ●●●

Usually there is liability only for **misfeasance** and not for **non-feasance**. Sometimes though when a defendant has a duty to act he can be liable for a failure to act or omission:

→ if the defendant has a contractual duty, *Stansbie v Troman* (1948)
→ or owes a special duty to or has a special relationship with the claimant, *Home Office v Dorset Yacht Co.* (1976)
→ or fails to control third parties that he is in some way responsible for, *Haynes v Harwood* (1935)
→ or fails to control dangers that he is responsible for, *Goldman v Hargrave* (1967)

Exam questions   answers: page 155

1 Critically discuss the different ways in which the law on nervous shock deals with primary and secondary victims of a defendant's negligent act or omission. (45 min)

2 When will a person be liable for failing to act? (20 min)

Action point

See if you can remember what the 'two-part test' from *Anns* was and say why it was overruled in *Murphy*.

Checkpoint 2

Explain why the principle in *Junior Books v Veitchi* can still apply.

Checkpoint 3

Why does *Chaudhry v Prabhakar* seem a harsh result?

Test yourself

Try to make a list of the extra points added in *Henderson v Merrett Syndicates* (1994).

The jargon

'*Misfeasance*' is a wrongful act, '*non-feasance*' is a wrongful omission.

Checkpoint 4

Explain why there was liability in each of these four cases.

Examiner's secrets

Be sure to add comment as well as detail if you are asked to critically discuss.

Occupiers' liability

"... the 1957 Act has always been regarded as particularly well drafted because it is one of the few statutes to give illustrations..."

Vivienne Harpwood

Occupiers' liability is a straightforward area developing from and similar to negligence. It is based on two Acts: the Occupiers' Liability Act 1957 in respect of lawful visitors, and the Occupiers' Liability Act 1984 in respect of trespassers. Key issues include:

→ what counts as premises
→ who can be a defendant (i.e. who is an 'occupier') or a claimant
→ the nature of the duty owed
→ the position of children
→ the position of professionals coming on to the premises
→ liability for the work of independent contractors
→ the defences available

Premises, defendants and claimants

Premises are not defined in either Act so the common law applies and the cases have included things such as ships, aircraft, and vehicles, and even a ladder leaning against a wall in *Wheeler v Copas* (1981). Potential defendants are **occupiers** of premises. This is a broad term and includes anyone who is in control of premises, *Wheat Lacon* (1966). The 1957 Act simplified the existing law and distinguished between two classes of visitor to premises:

→ lawful **visitors** – who are protected by the 1957 Act
→ persons who are not lawful visitors – the most common category here being **trespassers** who have no protection under the 1957 Act but have limited protection in the 1984 Act

The 1957 Act and the common duty of care

By section 2(1) an occupier of premises owes the same duty, the common duty of care to all his visitors except insofar as he is free to and does extend, restrict, modify or exclude his duty to any visitors by agreement or otherwise.

The nature of the duty is identified in section 2(2) and is to take such care as in all the circumstances is reasonable to see that the visitor will be reasonably safe for the purpose for which he is invited to be there. The appropriate standard of care is the same as for negligence cases generally, so there is no need to guard against unforeseeable risks.

Occupiers' liability towards children

The 1957 Act recognizes that children are less careful than adults and section 2(3) states that premises must be reasonably safe for a child of that age. So an occupier must take greater care of children:

→ and must be aware that unthreatening objects to adults may be dangerous to a child, *Moloney v Lambeth LBC* (1966)
→ and must avoid **allurements**, *Glasgow Corporation v Taylor* (1922)
→ but can expect parents to be responsible for younger children, *Phipps v Rochester Corporation* (1955)

Don't forget

Occupiers' liability is very similar to negligence, but if you mistake a problem question on OLA for negligence there are only limited marks available to you.

Checkpoint 1

Make a list of those people who are lawful visitors covered by the 1957 Act.

The jargon

A *'common duty'* is owed to all lawful visitors. Before the Act there were different duties.

Action point

Try to think why the Act makes it the visitor rather than the premises themselves that must be kept safe.

Checkpoint 2

Why does the law treat children differently?

The jargon

An *allurement* is something that attracts. The Act recognizes that children may be drawn towards dangers.

Provided some damage to the child is foreseeable then the occupier is liable, *Jolley v London Borough of Sutton* (2000).

Liability to people carrying out a trade ●●●

Section 2(3)(b) says such people 'will appreciate and guard against any risks'. So tradespeople are expected to avoid any of the risks associated with their trade, *Roles v Nathan* (1963).

Liability for the torts of independent contractors ●●●

Generally, under section 2(4), the occupier has no liability for 'the faulty execution of any work or construction, maintenance or repair by an independent contractor'. The occupier is able to avoid liability if:

→ it was reasonable to hire a contractor, *Haseldine v Daw* (1941)
→ the contractor was competent, *Ferguson v Welsh* (1987)
→ where it is possible the occupier has checked to see that the work was carried out properly, *Woodward v Mayor of Hastings* (1945)

Checkpoint 3

Briefly state some reasons why occupiers are not usually liable for the torts of independent contractors.

Avoiding liability ●●●

There are three possibilities:

→ warnings – if sufficient to safeguard the visitor, so sometimes a barrier may be needed instead, *Rae v Mars* (1990)
→ exclusion clauses – but good notification of these must be given and the Unfair Contract Terms Act 1977 may restrict their use
→ common law defences of contributory negligence, *Sayers v Harlow UDC* (1958), and consent *Simms v Leigh RFC* (1960)

Action point

Write down some warnings that would be sufficient and some that would not, or when a barrier would be necessary.

Trespassers and the 1984 Act ●●●

Because of the danger associated with some premises in modern times the common law developed **the common duty of humanity** in *B R Board v Herrington* (1972) where the trespassers were young children. The 1984 Act protects any trespasser against personal injury providing the occupier is aware of the danger and of the likelihood of trespassers and appreciates that the risk is one requiring protection for the trespasser.

Checkpoint 4

Why is this case important?

Exam questions   answers: pages 155–6

1   Danger World, a pleasure theme park, has a sign at the entrance:
    'All rides are dangerous and people enter the park at their own risk.'
    Advise Danger World of their liability if:
    a) Sarah, aged 11, catches her heel in a hole in the floor of a ride while alighting and is injured
    b) Graham, an electrician repairing one of the rides, is electrocuted when Daisy who controls the ride carelessly plugs it in
    c) Tim, aged 8, sneaks through a hole in the perimeter fence and cuts himself and rips his trousers on broken glass (45 min)

2   Discuss the ways in which an occupier can avoid liability under the Occupiers' Liability Act 1957. (20 min)

Examiner's secrets

Remember that problem questions on occupiers' liability are quite easy to spot because they will usually involve some injury to a child or some negligence by a contractor who has worked on the premises. Remember also that questions might involve both lawful visitors and trespassers.

Examiner's secrets

Remember to explain the nature and scope of the duty in section 2(1) and section 2(2) of the 1957 Act. Doing so will gain marks.

Vicarious liability

Liability in tort can arise not just for a person's own actions or omissions but sometimes for the torts of another. This is *vicarious liability* which is most common where an employer is held liable for the torts of his employee. This was originally said to happen because the 'master' had control over the 'servant' and took the benefit of the work.

The essential ingredients of vicarious liability

There are three key questions in determining liability:

→ was the thing complained of a tort? – there is rarely vicarious liability for a crime or a fraud
→ was the **tortfeasor** in the employment of the defendant? – there is usually no liability for the torts of an independent contractor who is responsible for his own tortious acts and omissions
→ did the tortfeasor carry out the tort *in the course of employment*?

Tests of employment status

An employee must be distinguished from an independent contractor who is self-employed. Often whether or not a person is an employee is obvious but sometimes it is not so clear and judges over the years have devised tests for determining the issue.

1 *The control test* – originated from the master/servant relationship, this test is based on whether the employer has control of the way in which the employee carries out the work – this is not a good test when the work is sophisticated, e.g. surgeons, but it can be useful in determining who is responsible for a worker who is hired out, *Mersey Docks & Harbour Board v Coggins and Griffiths* (1947).
2 *The integration test* – this determines that a worker is an employee if his work is an integral part of the business, whereas if the work is only ancillary to the business the person is self-employed, *Whittaker v Minister of Pensions* (1967).
3 *The economic reality or multiple test* – under this test from *Ready Mixed Concrete v Minister of Pensions* (1968), the court looks at each factor pointing to employment or self-employment and weighs up which is the more likely, including: ownership of tools; tax and national insurance; method of payment; self-description; and who benefits financially if the work is carried out efficiently

Even so some workers defy easy description:

→ casual workers, *O'Kelly v Trust House Forte* (1983)
→ outworkers, *Nethermere (St Neots) v Taverna* (1984)

In the course of employment

An employer may be liable in any of the following situations:

→ where the employee's act is authorized, *Poland v Parr* (1927)
→ where the employee is carrying out an authorized act in an unauthorized way, *Limpus v London General Omnibus Co.* (1862)

The jargon
Master and *servant* are old-fashioned words to describe employer and employee.

The jargon
A *tortfeaser* is the person who actually carries out the act or omission.

Checkpoint 1
Can you think of any other reason why we may need to distinguish an employee from a self-employed person?

Action point
Make brief notes on why the tests before the economic reality test are inadequate to cover all situations.

Checkpoint 2
Say how each of these features points toward employment or self-employment.

The jargon
An *outworker* is one who works at home rather than at the employer's place of business.

→ or even where the act has been prohibited but the employer will benefit from the act, *Rose v Plenty* (1976)
→ where the employee does an authorized act in a careless manner, *Century Insurance v Northern Ireland Transport Board* (1942)
→ now, following *Lister v Hesley Hall* (2001), an employer can be liable to compensate for criminal acts of employees who have sufficient connection with the employment

Not in the course of employment ●●●

An employer will not be liable where the employee's tortious act falls outside of the scope of employment as when:

→ the employee is merely travelling to or from work, unless the journey forms part of the employment, *Smith v Stages* (1989)
→ the employee does something which is not his job, *Beard v London General Omnibus Co.* (1900)
→ the employee is on 'a **frolic** of his own', as in taking an unauthorized break, *Hilton v Thomas Burton* (1961)

Justification for imposing liability on an employer ●●●

Vicarious liability is often called 'rough justice' because the employer is liable for something that he did not do, and because it contradicts the general fault principle in tort. But there are many justifications:

→ traditionally an employer did have 'control' over the worker
→ the employer is more capable of bearing the loss
→ the employer can and must insure against such events
→ it allows a claimant a reasonable prospect of compensation
→ the employer is responsible for choosing the workforce and should select competent people
→ the employer is likely to ensure higher standards of behaviour within the organization if liable for employees' actions

Checkpoint 3

Why were *Limpus* and *Beard* decided differently?

The jargon

A *frolic* is something that the employer will not be liable for as it relates only to the employee and the employer takes no benefit at all from it.

Test yourself

Identify why vicarious liability 'contradicts the general fault principle in tort'.

Checkpoint 4

How can an employer achieve this last point?

Exam questions   answers: pages 156–7

1   Tom is a delivery driver for Pegasus Delivery. Under his contract Tom must work such hours as instructed and can accept work from nobody else. He must wear a uniform and pays his own tax. The company deducts National Insurance and also money from Tom's wages so that he can buy the van from them. After delivering a parcel to a customer of Pegasus, Nigel, Tom is asked by Nigel to deliver a parcel to another company urgently for them. He cannot contact Pegasus so takes the parcel anyway. On the way he injures a pedestrian, Roger, through his negligent driving.
    Advise Roger of any claim against Pegasus Delivery. (45 min)

2   Critically discuss the circumstances in which an employer will be liable for the torts of his employee. (45 min)

Examiner's secrets

Usually in questions on vicarious liability you will need to consider the employment tests as well as whether the tort was in the course of employment.

Strict liability

Strict liability exists in torts when the claimant does not have to prove fault. This means that the defendant can be liable even without any bad intention merely because he owns a particular thing or is responsible for a particular thing. So it is something like strict liability in crime. There are two areas of particular interest at A-level. These are the tort of *Rylands v Fletcher*, which came from the case of the same name, and liability for animals.

Strict liability and *Rylands v Fletcher* ●●●

The tort of *Rylands v Fletcher* (1868) is all to do with the *escape* of *dangerous things* out of the defendant's control that then harm the claimant. The escape in the case that the tort comes from was of water from a reservoir that flooded a neighbouring mine because the contractors building the reservoir had not blocked off existing shafts. In the House of Lords, Lord Cairns also added that the thing brought on to the land must involve a **non-natural** use of the land. So the tort could have been particularly appropriate in controlling the dangers brought about by industrialization and ought to be a means of controlling pollution.

The essential ingredients of the tort of Rylands v Fletcher

There are four:

→ a bringing on to the defendant's land
→ of a thing likely to be dangerous if it escapes
→ which amounts to a non-natural use of the land
→ and the thing does escape and causes damage

After *Cambridge Water Co v Eastern Counties plc* (1994) there is now a fifth, that the damage is foreseeable.

Bringing on to the land

There is usually no liability for things that are naturally there, so there may be no liability for the spread of weeds, *Giles v Walker* (1890). Nor is there usually liability for things that naturally accumulate on the land such as rainwater, *Ellison v Ministry of Defence* (1997). Also the thing must be brought on to the land for the defendant's benefit or purpose, *Dunne v North Western Gas Board* (1964).

A thing likely to do mischief if it escapes

The thing in question must be a source of foreseeable harm as with the fairground ride in *Hale v Jennings* (1938).

Non-natural use of land

This is a difficult area because of the way society, and particularly technology, changes and develops. There are though some clear points:

→ domestic uses are natural even if dangerous, e.g. fire, *Sokachi v Sas* (1947); electricity, *Collingwood v Home & Colonial Stores* (1967)

→ the way in which something is stored may make it a non-natural use of land, *Mason v Levy Autoparts* (1967)

→ but some things are always classed as non-natural use, *Cambridge Water Co. v Eastern Counties Leather plc* (1994)

The escape

There is dispute whether the escape should be from a place which the defendant occupies to one he does not, *Read v Lyons* (1947); or from circumstances within the defendant's control to those not within his control, *British Celanese v A. H. Hunt* (1969).

Defences

There are available defences that include act of God, act of a stranger, consent, common benefit and statutory authority.

Strict liability and animals ●●●

This was originally a common law area but is now mostly contained in the Animals Act 1971. Liability under the Act is strict. The Act draws a distinction between **dangerous species** and **non-dangerous species** and the appropriate duty is different for each.

Dangerous species

These are defined in section 6(2) of the Act as any species 'not commonly domesticated in the UK' and with 'such characteristics that they are likely, unless restricted, to cause severe damage'. So it could include animals that are actually tame or domesticated in their natural country, e.g. a camel, *Tutin v Chipperfield Promotions* (1980). By section 2(1) a **keeper** of such an animal is always liable for damage caused by it.

Non-dangerous species

The rules here are much more complex. By section 2(2) a keeper is liable if:

→ the damage is of a kind that the animal is likely to cause if unrestrained or is likely to be severe if caused by that animal and

→ likelihood of severe damage is due to characteristics peculiar to that animal or common in the type of animal at certain times and

→ those characteristics were known to the keeper

Defences

These include consent under section 5(2), *Dhesi v Chief Constable of the West Midlands* (2000), contributory negligence under section 10 and under section 5(1) there is no liability to a person who is wholly responsible for his own injury.

Exam questions
answers: page 157

1. To what extent can *Rylands v Fletcher* still be said to be a tort of strict liability? (45 min)

2. Explain the difference between 'dangerous' and 'non-dangerous' species of animals. (20 min)

Checkpoint 2

State the brief facts and points of this important case.

Checkpoint 3

Try to identify how each of these defences could apply.

The jargon

Non-dangerous species are ones that are domesticated or native to the UK.

The jargon

A *keeper* is the owner of the animal or the head of a household where a person under the age of sixteen owns the animal.

Checkpoint 4

Can you think of a certain time when an animal might be dangerous?

Examiner's secrets

Before answering question 1 remind yourself what strict liability means and then list all of those factors that seem to contradict the idea of strict liability in the tort.

Examiner's secrets

Always try to give the examiner a full and proper definition of the tort as well as your argument on the question.

Nuisance

A nuisance may be of two types: private nuisance, involving neighbours, and public nuisance, involving the community in general, and usually to do with the highway. The two are quite different and the area is also complicated still further in modern times because there are a number of statutory nuisances controlling things like noise and pollution. Nuisance involves indirect interference.

Private nuisance

Private nuisance is an action between neighbours and involves one neighbour unreasonably interfering with the other neighbour's use or enjoyment of their land. So it is sometimes called the 'law of give and take' because the judges will try to strike a sensible and fair balance between competing interests. The test is always: does the conduct justify legal intervention? The tort is really more about prevention than compensation so injunctions can be an appropriate remedy as well as damages if damage has been caused. The major requirements of the tort include the following.

An unreasonable use of land
It is usually referred to as an 'unlawful' use of land, but this actually means *unreasonable*. A number of factors need consideration:

→ The nature of the *locality* – a nuisance is more likely to be found in a residential area than in one that is built-up or industrialized, *Laws v Florinplace* (1981) – where the locality has mixed uses, the court may try to reach a compromise between the parties, *Dunton v Dover DC* (1977).
→ The seriousness of the interference – where the nuisance causes damage other factors such as locality need not be taken into account, *St Helens Smelting Co. v Tipping* (1865).
→ The duration of the nuisance – an actionable nuisance needs to arise from a *continuous* state of affairs rather than an isolated event unless there is physical injury, *Bolton v Stone* (1950).
→ The sensitivity of the claimant – if the claimant's interests are abnormal then it would be unfair to prevent the other party from carrying out their lawful business, *Robinson v Kilvert* (1889).
→ Acts of **malice** can also be a consideration – whether by the claimant, *Christie v Davey* (1893), or the defendant, *Hollywood Silver Fox Farm v Emmett* (1936).

Nuisance is one way of protecting privacy but since the Human Rights Act 1988 an action is also now possible under Article 8, *Marcic v Thames Water plc* (2002).

Indirect interference
Nuisance involves *indirect* interference whereas trespass involves *direct* interference. Many things count as indirect interference including:

Example

Statutory nuisances are found in the Environmental Protection Act 1990 and the Environment Act 1995.

". . . a continuous, unlawful and indirect interference with a person's enjoyment of land or some right over it."

Winfield

". . . what would be a nuisance in Belgrave Square would not necessarily be so in Bermondsey."

L. J. Thesiger *Sturges v Bridgman*

Checkpoint 1

Explain why there was no nuisance in *Bolton v Stone*.

The jargon

Malice in this sense does mean acting spitefully or unreasonably.

Links

See pages 150–1.

→ smells and fumes drifting over the land, *Bliss v Hall* (1838)
→ vibrations from machinery, *Sturges v Bridgman* (1879)
→ smuts and smoke, *Halsey v Esso Petroleum* (1961)

The use or enjoyment of land

There is no nuisance where the interference is merely with a recreational use of land such as watching television, *Hunter v Canary Wharf Ltd* (1997). Though there may be for interference with an ancillary function, *Crown River Cruises Ltd v Kimbolton Fireworks Ltd* (1996).

Who can sue and who can be sued

Nuisance is actionable only by people with an interest in land, so a landowner can sue, but his family cannot and nor can a lodger, *Malone v Laskey* (1907) and *Hunter v Canary Wharf* (1997).

A number of people besides the occupier or owner can be sued:

→ the creator of the nuisance if different, *Esso Petroleum v Southport Corporation* (1953)
→ a person who adopts a nuisance, *Tetley v Chitty* (1986)
→ a landowner who fails to deal with an act of a stranger or a natural event he is aware of, *Sedleigh Denfield v O'Callaghan* (1940)

Defences

The most common defence is statutory authority as many activities are now licensed by Parliament, but there is also:

→ act of a stranger, *Sedleigh Denfield v O'Callaghan* (1940)
→ 20 years' prescription or long use, *Sturges v Bridgman* (1879)
→ public policy, *Miller v Jackson* (1977)
→ consent

Public nuisance ●●●

This is quite different to private nuisance since liability extends beyond immediate neighbours, and also because it can be a crime as well as a tort which would be prosecuted by the Attorney-General. There must be a substantial class of people affected before action is brought and the claimant must suffer *special damage* above that suffered by other citizens, e.g. personal injury, *Castle v St Augustine Links* (1922).

The tort usually involves the highway either by:

→ obstructions to the highway as by rowdy pickets
→ the poor state of the highway
→ projections which fall on to the highway such as overhanging trees

Checkpoint 2

Try to explain the difference between these two cases.

Action point

See if you can identify why this principle operates unfairly in the *Hunter* case.

Checkpoint 3

How does a person 'adopt' a nuisance?

Action point

Think of some modern activities that might be a nuisance but would be protected by statute.

Checkpoint 4

Explain the term 'public policy' and how it applied in *Miller v Jackson*.

". . . something which affects a reasonable class of Her Majesty's citizens materially or in the comfort and convenience of life . . ."

Winfield

Examiner's secrets

If you are asked to compare elements of different torts be careful that you answer on both.

Exam questions   answers: pages 157–8

1   Using cases critically, discuss what is meant by the terms 'unlawful use of land' in private nuisance and 'non-natural use of land' in the tort of *Rylands v Fletcher*. (45 min)

2   Discuss the effect of malice in a nuisance action. (20 min)

Trespass to the person

Trespass to the person is one of the oldest torts. As with all forms of trespass it involves an interference with a person's rights. In this case the interference is with the person's personal security. All trespasses are actionable *per se* and so there is no need to prove that damage has occurred. The tort can be committed in one of three ways:

→ assault
→ battery
→ false imprisonment

Assault and battery

These are separate torts but very often go together, the assault coming before the battery. But the individual definitions need to be considered.

Assault

Assault occurs where a person apprehends an immediate battery or other unwanted physical force. It is a completely free-standing tort so that it does not matter that the defendant does not go on to commit a battery. It is the effect it has on the claimant that is important.

→ If the claimant apprehends a battery then there is an assault, *Smith v Superintendent of Woking* (1983).
→ If the defendant attempts to carry out a battery but is restrained from doing so it is still an assault, *Stephens v Myers* (1830).
→ But a mere passive state is usually not an assault, as where a police officer merely blocked a doorway, *Innes v Wylie* (1844). Some threatening behaviour is needed, *Read v Coker* (1853).
→ It has always been said that words on their own cannot be an assault. However, it is possible that the words used can show that there is no assault, *Tuberville v Savage* (1669). In recent criminal cases silent telephone calls have been classed as assault, *R v Ireland*, *R v Burstow* (1996).

Battery

If assault is the fear of some force or violence then battery is the actual application of the force. Force is seen as any physical contact so that it can include areas such as intrusive medical treatment without consent which do not require any form of hostile touching, *Re F* (1990). Professor Winfield has said that technically all of the normal day-to-day brushes of life are batteries. It is unlikely, however, that we could sue every time somebody bumped into us in the street. Indeed 'schoolboy horseplay', even though it caused severe injury, has been held not to amount to a battery in *Wilson v Pringle* (1987). Lord Goff, in *Collins v Wilcock* (1984), felt the right test was 'whether the contact was acceptable in the ordinary contact of daily life'.

The jargon

Per se simply means 'in itself'.

The jargon

The false here simply means without lawful authority.

"A person commits assault where he intentionally and directly causes the claimant to apprehend that he is to be the victim of a battery."

Baker

Checkpoint 1

Why could a passive state not amount to an assault?

Checkpoint 2

Say why there was no assault in *Tuberville v Savage*.

Action point

Make brief notes on the ways in which these criminal appeals have affected the way that assault is defined in tort.

". . . the least touching of another in anger is battery."

C. J. Holt in *Cole v Turner* (1704)

Battery generally involves the *direct* and *intentional* application of force. Though in the past fireworks thrown into a crowd and then re-thrown amounted to a battery, *Scott v Shepherd* (1773), now an indirect cause of harm is probably negligence rather than battery, *Letang v Cooper* (1965). Intention is a fairly recent requirement, *Fowler v Lanning* (1959).

Defences to assault and battery

→ *volenti non fit injuria* (consent) – particularly appropriate in contact sports, *Simms v Leigh RFC* (1969) and *Condon v Basi* (1985), and also in medical treatment since patients with full capacity can refuse treatment, *Re T* (1992)
→ necessity – i.e. to prevent a greater harm, *Leigh v Gladstone* (1909)
→ self defence – if reasonable force is used, *Lane v Holloway* (1968)
→ inevitable accident – if beyond the defendant's control, *Stanley v Powell* (1891)
→ lawful arrest, see *PACEA* 1984

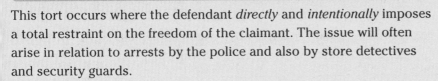

False imprisonment

This tort occurs where the defendant *directly* and *intentionally* imposes a total restraint on the freedom of the claimant. The issue will often arise in relation to arrests by the police and also by store detectives and security guards.

→ the restraint must be total, *Bird v Jones* (1845)
→ and no means of escape must be possible, *Wright v Wilson* (1699)
→ indirect restraint may be negligence, *Sayers v Harlow UDC* (1958)
→ a claim is possible even where the claimant was unaware of the restraint at the time, *Meering v Graham White Aviation* (1919)
→ and there is no action merely because the claimant has to pay to leave, *Robinson v Balmain New Ferry Co.* (1910)
→ or where an employer can reasonably expect an employee to remain at work, *Herd v Weardale Steel, Coal and Coke Co.* (1915)

Defences include consent, and lawful arrest (remember that the police and private citizens have different powers of arrest).

Exam questions
answers: page 158

1 In a football match, Littlebridge's centre forward, Mark Alan, is frequently fouled by Mudchester's Danny Blagham. Just on half time, Mark prevents Danny from scoring with a well-timed tackle. Going into the tunnel Danny then hits Mark from behind, knocking him out. A first aider, Cecil, rushes to help Mark but Danny shakes his fist at Cecil and threatens to hurt him. Stan, a steward, then seizes Danny and locks him up till after the game. Discuss the liability of all the parties. (45 min)

2 To what extent is 'hostility' a requirement of battery? (20 min)

Checkpoint 3

Say how assault or battery could be carried out without the other.

The jargon

Volenti means a legal claim cannot be made where the claimant willingly took the risk of injury.

Test yourself

Try to memorize a list of factors that would turn an arrest into a battery.

Checkpoint 4

What is the difference between *Bird v Jones* and *Wright v Wilson*?

Action point

The police can arrest on suspicion that an offence has been or may be committed but a private citizen cannot. Write down the other requirements of lawful arrest.

Don't forget

Problem questions on trespass to the person usually involve at least two if not all three ways of committing the tort.

Examiner's secrets

In your answers always give full definitions of the torts to get best marks.

Trespass to goods and land

Trespass to goods and trespass to land are two of the oldest torts and perhaps have less relevance today because there are statutory remedies available. They are both torts based on an unlawful interference with a person's rights as with trespass to the person. Because of their character, remedies other than damages may be appropriate.

Trespass to goods ●●●

There were originally two torts that covered interferences with goods: trespass to goods and conversion.

Trespass to goods is very similar to trespass to land, it can be defined as 'the unlawful, direct and immediate interference with goods in the possession of another'.

→ The interference must be direct such as scratching a panel on a coach in *Fouldes v Willoughby* (1841).
→ There is no need to show that the goods have been damaged or taken, just moving them is sufficient.
→ It must be intentional as when the defendant shot a dog thinking it was a wolf in *Ranson v Kitner* (1888).
→ It is only necessary to show possession, not ownership, as with the bracelet in *Parker v British Airways Board* (1982).

The Torts (Interference with Goods) Act 1977 removed many anomalies and overlaps in the common law and also contributory negligence as a defence. It introduced a general concept of liability for interference. Under the Act it is possible to dispose of goods which are not claimed for, and people who have improved the goods can claim for this also. Remedies include damage for any loss or damage to the goods and possibly recovery of the goods.

Trespass to land ●●●

Again this is one of the oldest torts. It can be defined as the unlawful and direct interference with the rights of an owner of land or a person in possession of it. So it can involve entering the land without permission or staying on the land after permission has been withdrawn. There are a number of other important points to note:

→ trespass is actionable *per se* so there is no need to prove damage and the purpose of the action may merely be to end the trespass
→ a person may become a trespasser even after entering lawfully by acting in an unauthorized way or by entering prohibited parts
→ while people in possession of the land can bring an action they may be unable to bring an action against a superior owner as with the forcible re-entry after a lease ended in *White v Bayley* (1861)

The other things that require explanation include:

→ what amounts to a trespass
→ what counts as land for the purposes of trespass
→ what are the available defences

Test yourself

Why do you think remedies other than damages may be appropriate?

Checkpoint 1

Distinguish between ownership and possession and say why the claimant won in *Parker v British Airways Board*.

Checkpoint 2

Can you remember a case where a person became a trespasser after entering lawfully?

Test yourself

Try to give a definition of land before going on to the next page.

What amounts to a trespass to land?

Trespass is entering the land without permission or staying after permission is withdrawn. It clearly includes straightforward acts such as walking or driving over it and standing on it, but it can include some less obvious things such as:

→ being carried on to the land against your will as in *Smith v Stone* (1647) although this case was successfully defended
→ leaning on a wall as in *Gregory v Piper* (1829)
→ an advertising hoarding overhanging neighbouring land as in *Kelsen v Imperial Tobacco Co. Ltd* (1956)
→ and the least contact may be enough as with the ladder leaning against the wall in *Westripp v Baldock* (1938)

But the interference must be direct or nuisance might be the better tort as in *Lemon v Webb* (1894) where the interference was from tree roots.

What counts as land in trespass?

The traditional Latin maxim was *cuius est solum ejus est usque ad coleum et ad inferos*. Clearly the surface of the land itself presents no problem and we have seen that this may include its boundaries. The subsoil beneath it and the air space above it may be more problematic but there are cases that consider these.

Rights over the subsoil would probably now be limited by the rights to excavate given to bodies such as British Coal, but there may be rights as in *Hickman v Maisey* (1900), where spying on training horses from the road was trespass as the road ran over the claimant's land. A similar point applied in *Harrison v Duke of Rutland* (1893) in relation to protesters trying to disrupt a grouse shoot.

Rights over air space are similarly restricted in modern times, particularly now that air travel is common and the Civil Aviation Act 1982 might apply. There are some rights in the air space though. In *Woolerton & Wilson v Richard Costain* (1970) there was a trespass when a crane swung out over the claimant's land; however, in *Lord Bernstein of Leigh v Skyways* (1977), an action against a firm of aerial photographers failed.

Defences

These might include entering with a legal right, e.g. a meter reader; licences, e.g. when you invite your friends; and even necessity if the defendant enters to prevent some catastrophe.

Checkpoint 3

Why do you think that the defendant won in *Smith v Stone* (1647)?

Test yourself

What other tort might be appropriate if trespass does not apply?

The jargon

This Latin maxim means that the rights in the land extend to the air space above the surface and the subsoil below.

Checkpoint 4

Can you remember what Lord Bernstein was complaining about?

Exam questions   answers: pages 158–9

1 To what extent does the law on trespass to land protect a person's privacy? (45 min)

2 Explain and illustrate how a lawful visitor may become a trespasser. (20 min)

Examiner's secrets

A discussion on privacy might also include when the paparazzi camp out to photograph the rich and famous.

General defences and remedies

Some defences are only available to specific torts such as abatement of a nuisance. However, there are a number of defences that can be raised in more than one tort and these are known as 'general defences'. Damages is a common remedy in tort but there are other remedies that are more appropriate in some circumstances.

General defences

The defences obviously act as a lawful excuse for what otherwise might amount to tortious behaviour. They are quite varied. Some act as a total defence but others are only partial.

Consent (*volenti non fit injuria*)

The rule is basically that no claim can be made by one who consents to the risk of harm. This means that a person will not have consented who is given no understanding of the risk or who is forced into taking it as in *Smith v Baker* (1891) where injury was unavoidable in the employment.

Consent is particularly appropriate to sporting contests where the competitors accept the normal risks of the sport, *Simms v Leigh RFC* (1969), and in medical treatment, though the patient need not be given all of the facts, *Sidaway v Governors of Bethlem Royal Hospital* (1985).

Inevitable accident

A defendant will not be liable for an event totally beyond his control as with the injury to the grouse beater in *Stanley v Powell* (1891).

Act of God

This defence really refers to extreme weather conditions and the defendant is not liable because it is out of his control as with the violent storm bursting the banks of the pool in *Nicholls v Marsland* (1876).

Statutory authority

This may be very appropriate in nuisance with many industrial processes being under licence and therefore lawful as with the smells and noise from the oil refinery in *Allen v Gulf Oil* (1981). But it can apply also to negligence and other torts. While not as straightforward as statutory authority, local authority planning permission is another possible defence, *Gillingham Borough Council v Medway (Chatham) Dock Ltd* (1993).

Illegality (*ex turpi causa non oritur actio*)

A defendant may not be liable when the claimant has suffered harm while engaged in an illegal activity, *Ashton v Turner* (1981). Although this did not stop the trespasser from receiving damages when he was shot by the defendant in *Revill v Newbury* (1996).

The jargon

Abatement simply means that the claimant is entitled to act to stop the nuisance himself.

Checkpoint 1

What is the effect of a 'partial' defence?

Watch out!

Consent is not available for sporting injuries falling outside the rules of the game as with the foul tackle in *Condon v Basi* (1985).

Checkpoint 2

Discuss whether severe storms could result in a successful defence of an act of God in England.

Links

See pages 146–7.

Test yourself

Try to write down from memory all the defences on this page and brief facts from all the cases.

Necessity

This defence succeeds because the defendant commits the tort to avoid a worse harm occurring as in the injury to the fireman in *Watt v Herts CC* (1954) and justifying force-feeding in *Leigh v Gladstone* (1909).

Self-defence

A person is entitled to defend himself, his family and property but only by using reasonable force so the defence failed in the vicious attack by the husband of the 'monkey-faced tart' in *Lane v Holloway* (1968).

Novus actus interveniens (a new act intervenes)

Particularly appropriate to negligence, the defence succeeds because it breaks the chain of causation. The intervening act can be by the claimant, an act of nature and a third party as we have already seen in cases such as *Knightley v Johns* (1982) in negligence.

Test yourself

Try to write down from memory the other cases on *novus actus interveniens* from negligence.

Contributory negligence

Now by the Law Reform (Contributory Negligence) Act 1945, a claimant's damages can be reduced if he was partly responsible for the harm suffered. Damages were reduced by 25% for climbing on the toilet roll holder in *Sayers v Harlow UDC* (1958), and passengers failing to wear seat belts in cars, *Froom v Butcher* (1975), or crash helmets while on motorbikes have had their damages reduced.

Checkpoint 3

Say whether it is possible to have 100% contributory negligence.

Remedies

There are two main remedies available in tort: damages and injunctions, although there are other remedies such as abatement of a nuisance, and distress damage feasant in trespass, etc.

Test yourself

Say which of damages or injunctions is more likely to act as a deterrent and which acts as compensation.

Damages

The purpose of tort damages is to put the claimant, as far as money can do so, in the position he would have been in if the tort had not occurred. So the remedy is artificial and also speculative in that future losses may have to be calculated such as loss of earnings in the case of personal injury. This is done using *multiplicands* and *multipliers*. Damages may also have to be calculated after death and the deceased can claim through his personal representatives under the Law Reform (Miscellaneous Provisions) Act 1934 and dependants can claim, including a sum for bereavement, under the Fatal Accidents Act 1976.

The jargon

The '*multiplicand*' is what the court reckons is the claimant's annual net loss and the '*multiplier*' is the number of years they will multiply it by.

Injunctions

This is a discretionary remedy. Injunctions are usually **prohibitory**. They may be **interim** or **perpetual** but their purpose is to stop the tort from reoccurring.

Checkpoint 4

What are 'interim' injunctions and what are 'perpetual' injunctions?

Exam questions   answers: page 159

1   To what extent do the general defences represent a proper apportionment of blame? (45 min)

2   Examine the effects of death on a claim in tort. (20 min)

Examiner's secrets

Questions purely on defences are rare but it is useful to know the defences well for the other questions.

Answers
Tort

Checkpoints

1 Libel, public nuisance, trespass.
2 *Tort*: Claimant sues defendant; standard of proof is on a balance of probabilities. *Crime*: The Crown prosecutes the defendant; standard of proof is beyond a reasonable doubt.
3 A small company, Easipower, approached Hedley Byrne who, before they would contract, asked for a credit reference from Easipower's bankers, Heller. Heller carelessly gave a good reference even though Easipower were in difficulties and Hedley Byrne lost money as a result.
4 A person of no financial means.

Exam questions

1 A tough question and one requiring some thought, as it is in any case quite a controversial subject.

The first thing to do is to show what fault liability is by explaining the principle of negligence: existence of a duty of care, breach of the duty, and foreseeable damage caused by the defendant, *Donoghue v Stevenson*.

Next the concept of no-fault schemes can be explained: proof of injury, but no requirement to prove fault. Schemes such as the New Zealand system (making claims through the Accident Compensation Commission – with 80% of pre-accident earnings possible) or that suggested by the Pearson Commission 1978 here.

The advantages of the scheme should be discussed: victim does not have to prove fault, only the accident and injury, so covers a wider range of accidents; costs less to administer than the tort system; no lump sum payment means account can be taken of worsening medical conditions more easily; simpler and not subject to as many delays as the tort system.

And the disadvantages: an unfair distinction is made between accidents and diseases; involves spending public money as in a benefit system; compensation for pain, suffering and loss of amenities would be lower than in a fault system; there is no deterrence to the person causing accidents and no apportionment of blame; the Pearson recommendations were fairly limited; the New Zealand system has been modified.

Comment also on other strict liability torts.

> **Don't forget**
>
> It may sound obvious but don't go straight into a discussion on no-fault schemes without first defining what fault means in tort.

2 This is a straightforward short question requiring only a simple comparison with other areas of law.

Tort could be defined as an area of civil liability involving classified 'wrongs'.

There can be overlaps between both tort and crime, and tort and contract, and examples given, e.g. assaults, negligent misstatement, etc.

The main differences with crime involve a difference in process and terminology, the parties to the action, i.e. the state is involved in criminal actions, the outcomes of the action, i.e. remedies as opposed to punishment, and the standard of proof, i.e. beyond reasonable doubt, as opposed to on balance of probabilities.

The main differences with contract law are who sets the duty (the parties or the law), the way in which damages are used if awarded, and tort has more of a deterrent purpose while contract is more about regulating arrangements.

The possibility of dual liability could be raised.

Checkpoints

1 A manufacturer owes a duty not to harm users or consumers of his products.
2 The usual standard is objectively measured according to the standards of the 'reasonable man'. Professionals are measured against the standard of other professionals in the same field, so they effectively judge their own standard.
3 Because even though the doctor failed to examine the patient he could not have prevented his death.
4 The defendant must have actually 'caused' the damage (this is causation in fact), and the damage must be 'reasonably foreseeable' (this is causation in law – referred to as remoteness of damage).

Exam questions

1 This is a fairly straightforward question on the standard of care in negligence. Two points are clearly important, it asks for a discussion and for cases by way of illustration.

Breach of duty is falling below the standard of care appropriate to the particular duty owed. The standard is usually set against the standards of the 'reasonable man', an objective standard, *Blyth v Birmingham Waterworks*.

A range of factors affecting the duty can be explained and illustrated: depends on magnitude of risk, *Bolton v Stone*; practicability of precautions, *Latimer v AEC*; social utility of the act or omission, *Watt v Herts CC*; inexperience does not reduce the standard, *Nettleship v Weston*; same standard is expected of trainees as of experienced people, *Wilsher v Essex AHA*; children may be expected to maintain the same standard, *Morales v Ecclestone*; common practice may not be an excuse, *Brown v Rolls-Royce*; a defendant need only have guarded against the foreseeable, *Roe v Minister of Health*.

A different standard of care is applied to professionals, the standard appropriate to a competent professional, *Bolam v Friern Hospital Management Committee*.

There should be some discussion of these points.

2 This again is quite a controversial area so there is potential for a lot of discussion.

Policy decisions should be defined as those the judges suggest they make in the public interest, e.g. protecting the cricket club in *Miller v Jackson*.

It can also be noted that policy considerations can apply to all aspects of negligence: duty, breach, and remoteness.

It is also worth noting that Lord Wilberforce's two-part test from *Anns* was overruled because policy was said to play too much of a part in it giving too much discretion to judges. But it can be shown that a number of factors influence judges to make policy decisions, e.g. loss allocation and the presence of insurance, *Nettleship v Weston*; moral considerations, protection of professionals, *Bolam*; and the fear of 'opening the floodgates' is the most common of all, *Alcock v Chief Constable of South Yorkshire*.

In any case judges have always been prepared to use policy as a reason for not imposing a duty of care on a defendant, e.g. limiting the liability of lawyers, *Rondel v Worsley*, and of judges, *Sirros v Moore*, and of the police, *Hill v Chief Constable of West Yorkshire*, and in respect of the unborn, *McKay v Essex Area Health Authority*.

Negligence – nervous shock, etc.

Checkpoints

1 Because there was little knowledge of psychiatry at the time, *Victoria Railway Commissioners v Coultas*.
2 Because the relationship between the parties was 'almost contractual' so could be relied on.
3 Because the defendant was only a friend of the family, not a person giving professional advice.
4 Because the defendant owed a duty to the claimant in each case and failed to do what the duty required.

Exam questions

1 This question has two parts: identifying what primary and secondary victims are, and comparing how well or how badly they are treated.

First it is important to state that nervous shock is a duty of care situation in negligence so the principles of negligence still apply: existence of the duty, breach, and foreseeable damage caused by the defendant.

Next nervous shock should be defined as a recognized psychiatric disorder such as post-traumatic stress disorder, but not including mere grief or other common emotions, *Reilly v Merseyside RHA*. The test for who can and cannot claim is now contained in the Hillsborough litigation, *Alcock v Chief Constable of South Yorkshire*.

A primary victim should be defined as one present at the scene and suffering injury, *Page v Smith*, or at risk, *Dulieu v White*, and rescuers should now come under this category, *White v Chief Constable of South Yorkshire*.

A secondary victim should be defined as one who satisfies three criteria: a close tie of love and affection to the victim, *Hambrook v Stokes*, close proximity in time and space to the incident or 'immediate aftermath',

McLoughlin v O'Brien, and witnessed (heard or saw) the event or immediate aftermath, *Hale v London Underground*.

Discussion can include whether it is unfair to exclude people who have suffered on these grounds and whether the floodgates argument is appropriate here.

2 This is a straightforward short question.

Omission should be defined as a wrongful failure to act (non-feasance) rather than a wrongful act (misfeasance).

It should be explained that liability is imposed only because there is a duty to act and the breach of the duty is the failure to act, and that imposing such liability will be rare.

The general classes of actionable omissions are now contained in Lord Goff's judgment in *Smith v Littlewoods Organization Ltd*. They include: a breach of a contractual duty, *Stansbie v Troman*, or a legal duty, *Barnett v Chelsea & Kensington Hospital*; or breach of a duty arising out of a special relationship, *Dorset Yacht Co. v Home Office*; or breach of an ethical and legal duty, *Bland v Airedale NHS Trust*; a failure to control a third party for whom the defendant is responsible, *Haynes v Harwood*; or over land or dangerous things within the defendant's control, *Goldman v Hargrave*.

Occupiers' liability

Checkpoints

1 People invited to enter, people entering under a contract, people with a legal right to enter, e.g. meter readers, people exercising a private right of way.
2 Because they have not yet developed a full awareness and they are more vulnerable.
3 Because they did not carry out the work, and would have little control over them. Also the independent contractors should carry their own public liability insurance.
4 Because it accepted the fact that more may be required to prevent injury to child trespassers where the occupier realized the likelihood of the trespass and the danger that existed.

Exam questions

1 This is a problem question and the guidance in 'Answering problem questions' in the resources section should be followed.

The area should be identified as Occupier's Liability and definitions offered, i.e. a statutory area of negligence, with the same principles on standard of care applying.

Occupier should be defined as one in control of premises, *Wheat v Lacon*; premises, using the common law, is broadly defined and may include a ladder, *Wheeler* v *Copas*; potential claimants are lawful visitors under the 1957 Act and trespassers under the 1984 Act. The definitions of occupier and premises are satisfied here.

Section 2(1) 1957 Act states that a common duty of care is owed to all visitors and the scope of the duty is defined in section 2(2) as keeping the visitor safe for the legitimate purposes of the visit.

Sarah is a lawful visitor and a child so by section 2(3) greater care must be taken for her safety, *Moloney v Lambeth LBC*. There is an obvious danger and Danger World are probably liable.

Graham is exercising a trade and under section 2(3)(b) must guard against the risks associated with his trade, *Roles v Nathan*. But here the injury is beyond his control and Danger World are liable.

Tim is a trespasser and is not therefore a visitor under the 1957 Act. He can claim under the 1984 Act if Danger World would have been aware of the danger and the likelihood of trespassers, *B R Board v Herrington*. The Act applies to injury only so there will be no claim for the trousers.

2 This is a straightforward descriptive short question.

Section 2(1) says that an occupier can 'extend, restrict, modify or exclude' his liability.

There are three ways liability can be avoided.

- *Warnings*: though these must be sufficient to keep the visitor safe, so may be inadequate for children and sometimes barriers are more appropriate, *Rae v Mars*.
- Exclusions of liability are possible but they must conform with the Unfair Contract Terms Act 1977.
- Two common law defences are appropriate: *volenti* (consent) – but the visitor must have agreed to the actual risk, *Simms v Leigh RFC*; contributory negligence, where damages may be reduced by the extent to which the visitor helped to cause the injury, *Sayers v Harlow UDC*.

It is also worth noting that it is possible, e.g. in contractual terms, to offer a higher standard.

Vicarious liability

Checkpoints

1 In employment law most employment protection rights do not apply to the self-employed.

2 You are more likely to buy your own tools if self-employed. Self-employed pay schedule D tax annually and pay their own Class 2 stamp. Employed people have tax and NI deducted by the employer. Employees usually receive wages, self-employed a price for the job. People usually describe themselves accurately.

3 Because the one involved the employee doing his own job in an unauthorized fashion but the other involved the employee doing something that was not part of his job.

4 By giving proper instructions and by using disciplinary proceedings.

Exam questions

1 This is a common type of vicarious liability problem requiring consideration both of Tom's employment status and whether his act was in the course of employment.

Vicarious liability should be identified as the area and defined as fixing an employer with liability for the torts of his employee committed in the course of employment.

The appropriate tests for employment should be introduced and applied to Tom. The control test and integration test may be mentioned but here the economic reality test seems the most appropriate. Working hours as instructed, being unable to work for someone else, and wearing a uniform all limit Tom's independence, and Pegasus paying his NI points to employment. On the other hand he pays his own tax and is buying his own van. On balance though he is probably an employee.

Tom is delivering, which is his work, so he may be acting in the course of his employment. He is certainly doing an unauthorized act, *Limpus v London General Omnibus Co.*, and a prohibited act also, *Rose v Plenty*, since he is not to work for anyone else. The question is whether he is doing something totally outside of his employment, *Beard v London General Omnibus Co*, or indeed whether he is on a frolic on his own, *Hilton v Thomas Burton*. He is likely not to be in the course of employment when delivering for Nigel.

2 This is an essay question asking for discussion so it requires more than explaining the two requirements of being an employee and the tort occurring in the course of the employment. It requires also some evaluative comment on the justifications for vicarious liability or arguments against it.

Again vicarious liability should be defined as an employer being liable for the employee's torts. The tests of employment status including control test, integration test, and economic reality test should also be outlined. Difficult categories of worker could also be considered such as casual workers, *O'Kelly v Trust House Forte*, and outworkers, *Nethermere (St Neots) v Taverna*.

What amounts to in the course of employment should also be considered. Authorized acts, *Poland v Parr*, and acts done in an unauthorized manner or prohibited acts where the employer takes a benefit should be explained and compared with a frolic. Comparisons can be made between *Limpus*, *Beard*, *Century Insurance*, *Hilton v Thomas Burton*, *Twine v Beans Express*, *Rose v Plenty*, etc.

Discussion should focus on the justifications for imposing liability on the employer: better able to stand the cost; ensures claimant has someone solvent to sue; employer can improve standards to avoid torts, etc. The disadvantages can also be considered: contrary to fault principle; unfair to impose liability on someone other than the tortfeasor. These can be applied to the cases.

Don't forget

In questions that call for a discussion the best answers are balanced. Giving an account of one side only loses you some of the available marks.

Strict liability

Checkpoints

1 *Giles v Walker*; *Hale v Jennings*; *Cambridge Water v Eastern Counties Leather*; *Read v Lyons*.
2 Chemicals from a tanning process seeped through the floor into the ground and over many years contaminated a 'bore hole'.
3 Extreme weather causes a landslide, *Nicholls v Marsland*; a trespasser blocks up a sink, *Peters v Prince of Wales Theatre*; gas was brought on to land for the benefit of the claimant's use, *Dunne v North Western Gas Board*; burst water main was seen as an inevitable consequence of supplying water so no liability, *Green v Chelsea Waterworks*.
4 An obvious example is when a female animal has recently given birth to young and is keen to protect them.

Exam questions

1 This question requires a discussion of the various elements of the tort and some discussion of the ways in which these erode the original principle of strict liability.

    Rylands v Fletcher can be defined in Blackburn's words where 'a person brings on to land and keeps there anything likely to do mischief if it escapes is answerable for all the damage which is a natural consequence of its escape'.

    Lord Cairns in HL added 'non-natural use' of land.

    The ingredients can be discussed and illustrated: bringing on to land, *Giles v Walker*; likely to do mischief if it escapes, *Musgrove v Pandelis*; the escape and the damage, *Read v Lyons*; non-natural use of land, *Cambridge Water v Eastern Counties Leather*.

    There are many factors making it less than full strict liability: if *Read v Lyons* is correct then the escape must be from land controlled by the defendant to that not controlled by him, though *British Celanese v Hunt* should be mentioned; it is often seen as an extension of nuisance so there is no general strict liability for dangerous things; the requirement of 'non-natural use of land' is a major limitation; the requirement of foreseeability in *Cambridge Water*; the number of defences – consent, *Peters v Prince of Wales Theatre*; common benefit, *Dunne v North West Gas Board*; act of a stranger, *Perry v Kendricks Transport*; act of God, *Nicholls v Marsland*; statutory authority, *Green v Chelsea Waterworks*.

2 This is a short question requiring a simple explanation of the definitions of dangerous and non-dangerous species under the Animals Act 1971.

- Dangerous species are identified in section 6(2)(a) and (b) – one not commonly domesticated in Britain; and, whose fully grown animals are likely to cause damage unless restrained or any damage caused is likely to be severe, *Behrens v Bertram Mills Circus*. This includes any 'foreign' animal even if normally tame, *Tutin v Chipperfield Promotions*, and a keeper is always liable.
- Non-dangerous are native domesticated animals. Liability under section 2(2) is possible if damage is of a kind that the animal unless restrained was likely to cause or was likely to be severe; likelihood of damage was due to an abnormal characteristic known to the keeper. A good example is the guard dog in *Cummings v Grainger*.

Examiner's secrets

Cases are a very useful illustration here.

Nuisance

Checkpoints

1 Because it was shown that balls had only come out of the ground on six occasions in 30 years so any nuisance was occasional rather than continuous.
2 In *Hunter*, claimants failed when a large building interfered with TV reception because it was only a recreational use of land and many claimants had no proprietary interest so could not sue. In *Kimbolton* the claimants succeeded because the barge that was set on fire by fireworks had a functional use although attached to other recreational purposes.
3 Failing to do something about a nuisance you are aware of and being responsible for a nuisance someone else has created. Here it was allowing go-kart racing.
4 Public policy means that judges feel it would be against the public interest. Here Miller asked for an injunction, but because granting it would lead to the Cricket Club being closed it was felt not to be in the public interest.

Exam questions

1 This is an essay question asking for a comparison of elements of two torts, but also calls for discussion.

    Unlawful use in nuisance should be identified as meaning unreasonable and that the courts are trying to balance the competing interests of neighbouring landowners.

    A number of factors have an effect: locality, e.g. Thesiger in *Sturges v Bridgman* – compare *Laws v Florinplace* and *St Helens Smelting v Tipping*; presence of damage, *Halsey v Esso Petroleum*; continuous nuisance, *Bolton v Stone*; malice by one party, *Christie v Davey* and *Hollywood Silver Fox Farm v Emmett*; oversensitivity of the claimant, *Robinson v Kilvert*.

    Non-natural use in *Rylands v Fletcher* is inevitably a fluid concept and changes over time. It will not include normal domestic uses, *Rickards v Lothian*; and it is the nature of the use that makes it non-natural, *The Charing Cross* case; and sometimes the context in which the thing is accumulated, *Mason v Levy Autoparts*; but some things are always a non-natural use of land, *Cambridge Water v Eastern Counties Leather*.

Some discussion should also be made on the fairness of the definitions, e.g. policy may leave a person without any remedy in nuisance, *Miller v Jackson*, and technical development makes many dangerous things natural, *Musgrove v Pandelis*.

2 A simple short question or part of a larger question. It only requires simple explanations of nuisance, unreasonable use of land, and cases in illustration.
- Nuisance is defined as an indirect and unlawful interference with another person's enjoyment or use of their land.
- Unlawful merely means unreasonable.
- Motive normally plays no part in liability in tort, *Mayor of Bradford v Pickles*.
- But malice can be relevant in nuisance, as it may turn what might be a reasonable use of land into unreasonable use. Malice can be by the person creating the nuisance, *Hollywood Silver Fox Farm v Emmett*, or by a person responding to a nuisance, *Christie v Davey*, which may then defeat his own complaint.

Trespass to the person

Checkpoints

1 Because it is unlikely that doing nothing at all could put a person in fear of a battery taking place.
2 Because the defendant actually indicated that there would be no battery by his words, 'If it were not assize time I would take such language from you'. Because it was assize time therefore he intended to do nothing.
3 Threatening somebody but not actually touching him – assault. Hitting him from behind – battery.
4 In *Bird* the claimant was prevented from crossing a bridge one side but could leave on the other. In *Wright* the claimant was locked up but could escape through a low window.

Exam questions

1 This is a typical trespass to the person problem involving all three aspects of the tort: assault, battery and false imprisonment.

Trespass can be identified as actionable *per se*.

The definitions and requirements of each tort can also be identified. Assault – intentionally putting someone in fear of immediate battery by threatening behaviour, *Read v Coker*, and whether or not the attack will be carried out is irrelevant, *Stephens v Myers*; words alone were not originally an assault, *Tuberville v Savage*, but criminal cases may have altered this. Battery – directly and intentionally applying unlawful force to a person, *Cole v Turner*; it is arguable whether hostility is needed – compare, *Wilson v Pringle* and *Collins v Wilcock*.

Defences include self-defence if reasonable force is used, and consent if the actual risk is known. False imprisonment must be a total restraint with no chance of escape, *Bird v Jones*, and any arrest must conform to the rules.

In the problem, Mark's tackle is within the rules so there is no battery. Danny hitting Mark is a battery without any assault. Danny physically as well as verbally threatens and thus assaults Cecil. Stan has no legal right to lock Danny up and this is false imprisonment. If he was making a citizen's arrest he should have called the police immediately.

2 This is another short essay which merely asks for a discussion of one controversial aspect of the law on battery.

Battery should be defined as an area of trespass to the person. It is an unlawful, direct and intentional physical interference with a person's personal security by some form of unwanted touching. It has been said that 'the merest touching of another in anger is battery', *Cole v Turner*, but it is unlikely to include 'everyday collisions'.

Whether or not battery requires an element of hostility for liability is open to some debate. In *Wilson v Pringle* it was said that mere horseplay was not battery because there was no hostility. However, in *Collins v Wilcock* Lord Goff preferred the test of 'whether the contact was acceptable in the ordinary contact of daily life'. A requirement of hostility in any case would prevent intrusive medical treatment in the absence of consent from being battery.

> **Don't forget**
>
> In trespass to the person, problems on sport or on medical treatment consent are usually an issue but some candidates forget to discuss consent in relation to sporting injuries and what establishing it entails.

Trespass to goods and land

Checkpoints

1 Ownership involves legal title, possession does not. Parker won because he had the rights of a finder in possession which were superior to any claim by the company as occupiers.
2 *Chic Fashions v Jones*.
3 Because he had no control over being on the land.
4 The company took aerial photographs of his estate and then tried to sell them to him.

Exam questions

1 This is a discussion of the relevance of the law of trespass to a very real modern concern.

The tort should be defined as an unlawful and direct interference with the rights or interests of an owner or occupier of land without permission. Trespass is actionable *per se* so there is no need to show any damage.

What amounts to land for the purposes of trespass should also be considered. It obviously includes the surface and anything on the surface, *Hickman v Maisey* and *Harrison v The Duke of Rutland*, but it can also, within certain limits, include the subsoil below, and the air space above – compare *Kelsen v Imperial Tobacco* with *Lord Bernstein of Leigh v Skyways.*

Justification for entry can be a defence so should also be considered as well as the principle of trespass *ab initio* (from the start). There are limitations on the rights of a mere licensee, but some licensee rights will improve under the Human Rights Act which includes more safeguards against public authorities.

The discussion focuses on whether trespass law is useful to protect privacy. Any discussion on the limitations will be valid, e.g. some comment on Lord Bernstein's complaint. Some protection of airspace is obviously available but not sufficient to prevent photographs being taken from aircraft. Discussion of the way public figures are hounded by the press and stalkers is also useful and whether the remedies available are effective enough. Other statutory procedures may be more useful. In any case, remedies are not instantaneous and do not immediately resolve the difficulty.

2 This is a very straightforward short question merely asking for some discussion of the ways in which a lawful visit can become a trespass. The principle of trespass *ab initio* should also be considered.

Trespass should again be defined as an unlawful and direct interference with the rights of an owner or person in possession of land.

Again it should be identified as being actionable *per se* so that when the lawful purposes of a visit are exceeded a remedy can be sought even if there is no damage although there usually will be.

A lawful visitor can become a trespasser by staying on the land after the time for the legitimate visit has ceased, *Hey v Moorhouse*. A person might also cease to be a lawful visitor by going beyond the legitimate purposes of the visit as when an invited friend sneaks into your bedroom and goes through your things.

The principle of *ab initio*, or from the start, should also be explained. This originally applied where the entry was by authority of law but was then abused, *The Six Carpenters Case,* though this principle will not now mean that everything done becomes or is unlawful, *Chic Fashions v Jones.*

General defences and remedies

Checkpoints

1 It does not relieve the defendant of liability but it may reduce damages.

2 It is unlikely these days. Since the 1980s we have had some very severe storm weather and so it is not really extreme and unforeseeable weather any longer. To be successful would probably require something like a hurricane.

3 Yes it is possible. The defendant can still be liable because of a breach of a strict liability duty but the claimant is entirely responsible for his own damage. As in *Jayes v IMI (Kynoch)* where the company was in breach of their obligation to ensure that machinery was fenced but the claimant took the fence off and put his hand in to clear it.

4 Interim injunctions are used to prevent something from happening before the main issue is tried; with perpetual injunctions all of the relief is gained by the injunction.

Exam questions

1 This question requires an explanation of each of the general defences and some discussion of how fair their application is in given situations.

Each of the main general defences can be considered, defined and illustrated, and some comment made on how fairly they operate.

- *Volenti non fit injuria* (consent) can be explained as when the claimant has actually agreed to and accepted the risk of harm. The claimant must have understood and accepted the actual risk, *Smith v Baker*. There are many possible weaknesses – the possibility of coercion in relation to risk in employment; what falls within legitimate sporting injuries, *Simms v Leigh RFC*; should a patient undergoing treatment be given all information necessary for an informed consent, *Sidaway v Governors of Bethlem Royal and Maudsley Hospitals?*
- Inevitable accident – must be beyond the defendant's control, but was that the reality in *Stanley v Powell*?
- Necessity, *Watt v Herts CC*, and Act of God, *Nicholls v Marsland* – does this mean a person can have no remedy at all even though suffering the injury or loss?
- Contributory negligence. This is now under the Law Reform (Contributory Negligence) Act 1945 and damages are reduced by the amount the claimant is at fault for his own harm, *Sayers v Harlow UDC*, but again this could be abused.
- Illegality. The claimant loses his rights because of being involved in the illegal act, *Ashton v Turner,* but again is this allowing a tortfeasor to avoid liability unfairly? Here it allowed the insurer to avoid making payment.

2 This is a straightforward short question or part question.
It should be stated that it is only fair that a person's claim in tort survives his death but that such actions were not always possible.

The two possible actions that are now available should be described as follows:

- An action on behalf of the estate of the deceased under the Law Reform (Miscellaneous Provisions) Act 1934 can be brought by the personal representatives and is similar to a personal injury claim.
- An action can be brought by certain dependants who are also relatives under the Fatal Accidents Act 1976 which includes a sum for bereavement.

> **Don't forget**
>
> Sometimes you are asked a question on both *volenti* and contributory negligence together. Remember that this will usually involve contrasting their application.

Two of the exam boards have units on Human Rights. This has become a much more important area of law since the passing of the Human Rights Act 1998. It is also an area of law which is developing as new cases test the extent of the rights given by the Human Rights Act. Showing knowledge of the latest cases will impress the examiners.

Rights and freedoms

Exam themes

→ The protection of freedoms nationally and internationally

→ Restrictions on the right to exercise freedoms

→ The Human Rights Act 1998

→ The concept of civil liberty

→ Sacrificing individual rights to the common good

Topic checklist

○ AS ● A2	AQA	OCR	WJEC
The European Convention	●		●
The Human Rights Act 1998	●		●
Restrictions on freedoms	●		●
Protection of rights and enforcement of rights	●		●

The European Convention

Until fairly recently a citizen of the UK was protected in the case of human rights mainly by the European Convention on Human Rights. To use the Convention was a very long-winded process and meant exhausting all possible national channels first. For a long time civil libertarians called for the introduction of a Bill of Rights to incorporate the Convention into English law. The Government has now done so by passing the Human Rights Act 1998.

The background to the Convention

The European Convention on Human Rights was drawn up after World War Two with a view to preventing events such as the holocaust from happening again. It was drawn up and is overseen by the Council of Europe. It has twenty-five members, including the members of the European Union, although the two bodies are entirely separate. Each member has signed the Convention and later *ratified* it, although this does not mean that the Convention is incorporated into the national law of the countries that have signed it. The Convention has its own court in Strasbourg, the European Court of Human Rights, where actions for breaches of human rights can be brought. This court has nothing to do with the European Court of Justice, the court of the European Union.

Human rights under the Convention

The original agreement is divided into a number of Articles, each of which represents an individual human right. These include:

→ Article 2 – the right to life
→ Article 3 – freedom from torture or inhuman or degrading treatment
→ Article 4 – freedom from slavery
→ Article 5 – the right to liberty apart from lawful arrest
→ Article 6 – the right to a fair trial
→ Article 7 – freedom from any retroactive penal laws
→ Article 8 – the right to respect for private and family life, home and correspondence
→ Article 9 – freedom of thought, conscience and religion
→ Article 10 – freedom of expression
→ Article 11 – freedom of peaceful assembly and association
→ Article 12 – the right to freely marry
→ Article 13 – the right to an effective remedy in a national court
→ Article 14 – freedom from discrimination

A number of other rights were added by protocol, including the right to peaceful enjoyment of possessions; the right to an education; the right to free elections; and the right to free movement within a state. However, the UK has not ratified these protocols. Many of the rights also allow for states to impose restrictions such as protecting national security.

Watch out!

The European Convention is not part of the European Union.

Checkpoint 1

What is a 'civil libertarian'?

The jargon

Ratified simply means confirming the agreement.

Test yourself

See if you can write down the rights from memory, particularly Articles 3, 6, 8, and 10, which are ones the UK is often accused of breaching.

Checkpoint 2

What legitimate restrictions do you think can be imposed on Article 11?

Bringing a claim for breach of a human right

A citizen of a state covered by the Convention can eventually complain to the European Court of Human Rights (ECHR). Petitions are made initially to the European Commission of Human Rights. It determines whether the petition can be heard, which depends on all possible national remedies having been exhausted. The petition must also be lodged within six months of the petitioner being turned down for the final time in his own country. The Commission also rejects petitions that contain no real case. Admissibility does not mean that the case goes straight to the court because the Commission first tries to reach a 'friendly' settlement with the state in question. If the country then refuses to comply the complaint can go to the ECHR. The process can take a very long time. One petitioner was executed while admissibility was being decided.

The European Court of Human Rights

The court sits in Strasbourg and is comprised of judges representing the different member states. They should act independently rather than representing the interests of their own countries. There are twenty-one judges in all, and a panel of seven usually hears a case. They can declare that a state has breached the Convention and can also award compensation. However, they tend to rely on the co-operation of the state in question as there are no real means of enforcing their rulings.

Breaches of the Convention by the UK

The UK has a worse record of complaints against it than most other states, although this may merely reflect greater access. However, it has also lost more cases than it has won. The cases involve many Articles:

→ in *Golder v UK* (1975) there was a breach of Article 6, the right to a fair hearing, when a prisoner was denied access to a solicitor
→ in *Republic of Ireland v UK* (1978) the method of interrogating IRA suspects during internment breached Article 3 and was degrading treatment though it was not torture
→ in *Sunday Times v UK* (1979) preventing publication of details of the thalidomide scandal by using contempt law breached Article 10
→ more recently in *Thompson & Venables v UK* (1999) the child killers of Jamie Bulger had their right to a fair trial under Article 6 breached
→ in *Cossey v UK* however, a transsexual failed in her attempt to prove that preventing her from marrying breached Article 12

Exam questions   answers: page 170

1 What obstacles stand in the way of proving a breach of human rights under the European Convention? (20 min)

2 'The UK has one of the worst records of breaching the Convention.' Discuss. (45 min)

Checkpoint 3

What is the other important body that helps to administer the Convention besides the Commission and the Court of Human Rights?

Watch out!

The only ultimate sanction that can be taken against a state in breach of the Convention is expulsion and this would do nothing for the human rights of its citizens.

Checkpoint 4

In what way was this trial a breach of Article 6?

Examiner's secrets

Question 1 focuses particularly on procedure, so there is no need for you to give masses of detail on the Articles themselves. Use cases in Question 2.

163

The Human Rights Act 1998

The Human Rights Act was passed in 1998. This is the first specific Act on rights that the United Kingdom has had. The Act incorporates most of the Articles of the European Convention on Human Rights into the law of the United Kingdom. However, there are criticisms as there are some omissions and it is also possible for Parliament to legislate in a way that is inconsistent with the Convention.

Purpose of the Act ●●●

This is stated in the Act as being 'to give further effect to the rights and freedoms guaranteed under the European Convention on Human Rights'. Schedule 1 of the Act specifically includes Articles 2 to 12 and Articles 14 and 16 of the Convention within the definition of Convention rights. The Act came into effect in October 2000.

Limitations

Although most Articles are included, Parliament has chosen to derogate from Article 5(3) (which entitles a person who has been detained to be brought promptly before a court). The reason for this is to allow the longer detention of suspected terrorists under the Prevention of Terrorism Act 1989.

Also Article 13 (the right to an effective remedy) is omitted from the Schedule, though it may be argued that the provisions of the Act itself in section 8 provide an effective remedy.

Effect of the Act on UK legislation ●●●

Section 19 states that any new Bill going through Parliament must contain a written declaration that it is compatible with the Convention or a declaration that although it may not be compatible the Government still wish to proceed with it. This second part has been criticised as it allows the Government to avoid the Convention in future.

Declarations of incompatibility by the courts

Under section 4 of the Act where a court at the level of the High Court or above decides that an existing Act of Parliament is not compatible with the Convention, that court can make a declaration of non-compatibility. This declaration draws the attention of the Government to the problem but does not affect the parties to the case. Under section 10 of the Act a statutory instrument (delegated legislation) can be used to amend the law and bring it into line with the Convention. This is meant as a fast-track way of altering the law, but the statutory instrument must be laid before Parliament for its approval.

Interpretation of UK law

Section 3 of the Human Rights Act says that, so far as possible, legislation must be interpreted in a way which is compatible with Convention rights. Even before the Act came into force the courts

164

showed their willingness to interpret legislation in this way. In *R v DPP ex parte Kebilene* (1999) the Queen's Bench Division Court ruled that sections of the Prevention of Terrorism Act 1989 which effectively reverse the normal burden of proof in criminal trials were contrary to Article 6 of the Convention.

Decisions of the European Court of Human Rights

Section 2 of the Human Rights Act requires a UK court which is making a decision which involves a Convention right to take into account the opinions and decisions of the European Court of Human Rights in previous cases.

Individual rights under the Act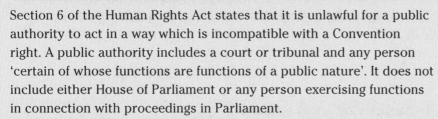

Section 6 of the Human Rights Act states that it is unlawful for a public authority to act in a way which is incompatible with a Convention right. A public authority includes a court or tribunal and any person 'certain of whose functions are functions of a public nature'. It does not include either House of Parliament or any person exercising functions in connection with proceedings in Parliament.

If a public authority is in breach of this duty, then section 7 gives a right to any individual who is the 'victim' of the unlawful act to bring proceedings against the public authority for breach of section 6.

Remedies

If a court finds that a public authority has infringed an individual's rights by acting in a way which is incompatible with the Convention, then the court can 'grant such relief or remedy, or make such order ... as it considers just and appropriate'. However, damages can only be awarded when the court is 'satisfied that the award is necessary to afford just satisfaction to the person in whose favour it is made'.

Criticisms of the Human Rights Act

The main criticisms are that:

→ Interest groups have no rights to bring an action under the Act.
→ Government ministers exercising functions connected to Parliament are not within the definition of public authority.
→ There is no mechanism for forcing action when an Act has been declared incompatible with the Convention.
→ The Act does not establish a Human Rights Commission to keep the way in which the law is working under scrutiny.

Check the net

The case of *R v DPP ex parte Kebilene* is likely to be appealed to the House of Lords. You can check the House of Lords judgments on the internet to find out when this happens.

Checkpoint 3

Can you explain why it is important that the courts consider decisions of the European Court of Human Rights?

Checkpoint 4

Can you give examples of people or organizations which would come within the definition of 'public authority'?

Examiner's secrets

As this is a new area of law the examiner will be impressed if you can use recent examples of cases.

Exam questions   answers: pages 170–1

1   Discuss the extent to which the Human Rights Act 1998 gives effect to the European Convention on Human Rights. (40 min)

2   Using examples explain what effect the Human Rights Act 1998 will have on English law. (40 min)

Restrictions on freedoms

There are many areas known as civil liberties that involve basic freedoms, for example freedom of speech. However, individual freedoms must always be balanced with the rights of other people so on occasions the law needs to limit the extent to which a particular freedom can be exercised. A simple example is where it is an abuse of freedom of speech to use it to spread false and malicious rumours about a person. So many laws place restrictions on these civil liberties, some being more justified than others.

Checkpoint 1

Can you think of two basic rights that are not generally protected? One particularly affects public figures.

Balancing rights

Not every basic right is protected. Some rights have limited protection because exercising the right may interfere with another person's freedom. A good example of a conflict between rights and freedoms is the right to life of an unborn child. This is denied in order to allow the mother the freedom to make decisions over her own body.

Freedom of expression

We are all said to have freedom of expression, and this is guaranteed by Article 10 of the European Convention on Human Rights. However, the right is subject to many restrictions:

The jargon

In the context of defamation, *publication* merely means repeating to a third party.

→ The law of defamation prevents the **publication** of false statements that may damage a person's reputation. It can also have a profound impact on freedom of speech as suggested in the 'McLibel' case.

→ Both broadcasting and the press have Standards Commissions that dictate what is acceptable. There is also a Board of Censors for films and videos, and an Obscene Publications Act. 'D' notices are also a powerful tool of government used to restrict press comment.

→ The Official Secrets Act 1911 can prevent people who have signed it from speaking out on issues that concern them as in the 'Spycatcher' case. It may also be used to prevent the public from finding out important information as in the case of Clive Ponting.

Action point

Make brief notes on how freedoms were being abused in these cases.

→ Criminal actions such as incitement can be used to prevent the spread of racial hatred as in *R v Jordan & Tindal* (1963) or to prevent an incitement to soldiers to defect as in *R v Arrowsmith* (1975), or to prevent blasphemy as in *R v Lemon* (1979).

Checkpoint 2

What apparent contradiction or unfairness in the law is seen in the law on blasphemous libel?

Freedom of movement

This is a freedom we all take for granted but it does have restrictions.

→ A person can be lawfully detained while under arrest, and while on remand, even though the person is still considered to be innocent.

→ A person can be lawfully detained against their will by an order under the Mental Health Act 1983.

→ Immigration law is used to deport people. People may be denied passports. Even Article 39 (ex Art 48) of the EC Treaty ensuring free movement enables member states to deny entry on grounds of public security, public policy or public health as in *Van Duyn v The Home Office* (1984).

→ In 1984 striking miners were prevented from travelling to picket lines elsewhere to prevent breaches of the peace.
→ People have been prevented from entering clubs if they are not public places as in *R. R. Board v Dockers Labour Club* (1972).
→ The tort of trespass may also prevent people from straying on to other people's land without permission.

Freedom of association and freedom of assembly ●●●

Both rights are protected by Article 11 of the European Convention. Freedom of association is being able to meet with like-minded people to form organizations and to pursue common goals. This means bodies such as trade unions and pressure groups. While everyone is free to join such groups, restrictions on the freedoms include:

→ workers at GCHQ were banned from being members of unions by the Government as confirmed in *CCSU v Civil Service* (1984)
→ membership of terrorist groups is prohibited by the Prevention of Terrorism Act 1989
→ membership of a paramilitary group or wearing uniforms is banned by the Public Order Act 1936 section 1 and section 2
→ the law of conspiracy

Freedom of assembly refers to the right to meet with other people to peacefully protest in meetings or marches. The freedom has limitations:

→ The most important are in the Public Order Act 1986. In the Act a 'public assembly' is defined as twenty or more people in a public place partly or wholly open to the air. Section 14 gives the police wide powers to restrain such assemblies or to move them on. Under section 12 the police can apply to stop marches or to postpone them. The Act also includes the offences of **riot** (twelve or more people who use or threaten violence); **violent disorder** (three or more people who use or threaten violence); and **affray** (using or threatening violence). These terms are open to interpretation.
→ The Criminal Justice and Public Order Act 1994 also gives the police wide powers to deal with 'criminal trespasses', a measure mainly aimed at 'new age travellers', 'raves', and 'hunt saboteurs'.

Freedom from discrimination ●●●

This freedom is limited because, although it applies to areas like race, sex and disability, it does not include areas like religion and age.

Exam questions   answers: page 171

1   What justifications are there for limiting freedom of speech in a modern society? (45 min)

2   How and why is freedom of association restricted within English law? (20 min)

Checkpoint 3

Can you remember why Miss Van Duyn was legally denied entry into the UK?

Watch out!

It is now untrue to say that trespass is an area of civil law only. See below.

Action point

Make a note that the 1936 Act was passed to prevent fascist sympathizers from marching in their uniforms. It also makes it an offence to train a body to carry out the functions of a police force or armed service.

Test yourself

See if you can write down these offences and their essential elements from memory.

Checkpoint 4

What other areas of law can be used to control assembly?

Examiner's secrets

It is important to use examples to illustrate your arguments in these questions.

Protection of rights and enforcement of rights

Many rights can be enforced through normal court proceedings. An important development for the enforcement of rights within the English Legal System has been the use of judicial review proceedings. If there is no satisfactory remedy in our home courts then cases where there is a breach of human rights can be taken to the European Court of Human Rights.

Checkpoint 1

Can you name the Acts of Parliament which give protection from discrimination?

Domestic law

Some areas of human rights are protected by a specific English law. Examples include anti-discrimination laws on the grounds of sex, race or disability and protection against harassment. Where there is a breach of the English law then the aggrieved person can take action under our domestic law in the appropriate court or tribunal. As well as being able to claim compensation there are other remedies available, such as an injunction.

Human Rights Act 1998

Under this Act individuals have the right to apply to the English courts if they are the victim of an unlawful act by a public authority. Unlawful in this context means acting in a way that is incompatible with the European Convention on Human Rights. If a court finds that there has been an infringement of a Convention right, then it can make any order it considers appropriate. The only limitation on this is that damages will be awarded only if this is necessary to 'afford just satisfaction' to the victim.

Checkpoint 2

Can you give the definition of 'public authority' in the Human Rights Act?

Judicial review

This is a review by the courts of the decision-making process of any public body or official. It can be used to challenge the decisions of a wide variety of bodies such as local authorities or one of their departments (e.g. the housing department), government departments, Inland Revenue Commissioners and even the Football League. It can also be used to challenge decisions made by the lower courts such as the Magistrates' Courts. An application for permission to take judicial review proceedings is made to a judge in the High Court.

"Judicial review . . . provides the means by which judicial control of administrative matters is exercised."

Lord Diplock

Principles of judicial review

There are three main grounds for judicial review. These were summarised in *Council of Civil Service Unions v Minister for the Civil Service (1984) (GCHQ case)* as:

→ illegality – where an error of law has been made or the act is beyond the powers of the body concerned

→ irrationality – where the decision is so unreasonable that no reasonable authority would have made the decision

→ irregularity – where the correct procedure has not been followed or the rules of natural justice have been breached

The jargon

Another phrase for 'beyond the powers' is *ultra vires*.

Wednesbury unreasonableness

A court cannot interfere with a decision just because it would have come to a different one. Even if the court thinks that the decision is wrong it still has no right to strike it out. If the decision is within the powers and the correct procedure has been followed, then the only basis for judicial review is that the decision is *Wednesbury* unreasonable. This comes from *Associated Provincial Picture Houses v Wednesbury Corporation (1948)* in which it was said that a decision would be struck out if it was so unreasonable that no reasonable public body could have reached the same decision.

Remedies

As well as the normal private law remedies available in English law, the courts have the public law remedies which they can use. These are the prerogative orders of:

→ *certiorari* – which allows the court to quash a decision
→ *mandamus* – which is an order to do something, for example, ordering a tribunal to hear a case that it has refused to deal with
→ prohibition – which is an order not to do something and is used to prevent a public body from acting unlawfully in the future

European Court of Human Rights ●●●

An individual who claims that their human rights under the European Convention on Human Rights have been infringed and that they have been unable to get satisfaction from their domestic courts may make an application to the European Court of Human Rights. One member state may also report another member state for a breach of the Convention.

Procedure

Individuals apply to the court where a committee of three judges decides whether the complaint is admissible. Only a very small number of cases are held to be admissible each year. Most fail because they have not used up all the possible appeal routes in their state. If a complaint is held to be admissible then the Government of the state concerned is asked for its comments and there may be a negotiated settlement. If not, then the case is heard in full and the court gives judgment on it.

Remedies

The court can rule that the state has breached the Convention and award compensation or other 'just satisfaction' to the complainant. Even though the court rules there has been a breach of the Convention, it cannot make the state concerned change its laws for the future and so prevent further breaches.

> *"A decision which is so outrageous in its defiance of logic or accepted moral standards that no sensible person . . . could have arrived at it."*
>
> GCHQ case (1984)

Checkpoint 3

Can you name the more common remedies available to the courts?

Test yourself

Write out these three prerogative orders from memory. Check that you have spelt them correctly.

Checkpoint 4

Do you know in which city the European Court of Human Rights sits?

Examiner's secrets

Don't forget that the Human Rights Act will make an impact on judicial review.

Exam questions answers: page 172

1 Explain why judicial review is important in English law. (40 min)

2 Discuss the role of the European Court of Human Rights. (40 min)

Answers
Rights and freedoms

The European Convention

Checkpoints

1 A person who believes that there are fundamental rights that should be guaranteed by the constitution. Usually such people are also in favour of a Bill of Rights and a written constitution.
2 Those that arise when the assembly ceases to be peaceful or has an unlawful or seditious purpose.
3 The Committee of Ministers of the Council of Europe.
4 The two boys, aged only 11 at the time of the trial, were tried in an adult court. So ECHR felt they would have been intimidated and probably would not have been able to understand the proceedings.

Exam questions

1 This is only a short question or part of a question and focuses on the procedure of petitioning.

Obviously the starting point is a brief explanation of what the Convention is and why it was created. Without too much detail or depth some rights guaranteed by the Convention can be identified.

The first obstacle is the extent to which the individual state is prepared to allow petitions. The next obstacle is the requirement that all national remedies must have been refused. This could take the petitioner a very long time during which the breach of the right may be continuing.

Once the petitioner has been allowed to go as far as petitioning, the Commission must first of all assess it for admissibility. The character of the process can be considered and also the fact that the Commission has as its first priority reaching an amicable settlement with the state. It should be mentioned that it is not unusual for a state to refuse to comply and that this is where a hearing in the court may apply. There is no guarantee that the Court will find a breach.

Finally it should be mentioned that whatever the limited sanctions available to the court, ultimately it is dependent on the co-operation of the state to achieve a remedy for the petitioner.
2 This question concerns a controversial claim about the UK and a discussion of the claim. So the cases involving the UK can be identified and also the UK position put in the context of the other members.
 • Because of the number of claims brought before the Commission the UK can inevitably be seen as having a bad record.
 • In terms of cases lost the UK has lost about three-fifths of cases brought against it and only Italy has a worse record.
 • Claims against the UK have also concerned a wide range of the individual's rights.
Any of the cases that the candidate knows can be used to illustrate the sorts of abuses of human rights that the UK has been responsible for. These could include: *Golder v UK* on Article 8 respect for family life and Article 6 the right to a fair hearing; *Ireland v UK* on Article 3 degrading treatment; *Tyrer v UK* on corporal punishment in schools and Article 3; *X v UK* on detention of mental patients and Article 5 the right to liberty; *Dudgeon v UK* on criminality of homosexual practice and Article 8 respect for private life; *Sunday Times v UK* on Article 10 freedom of expression; *Chahal v UK* on rules on deportation and Article 3; *Benham v UK* on detention for non-payment of community charge and Article 5 liberty and Article 6 right to a fair hearing; *McCann v UK* on shoot on sight of IRA members in Gibraltar and Article 2 the right to life; *Thompson & Venables v UK* on Article 6.

Finally it should be pointed out that other countries have not allowed individual petition as long as the UK, so this in part explains our record. Also the UK has now incorporated the Convention in the Human Rights Act.

The Human Rights Act 1998

Checkpoints

1 The right to a fair trial. Freedom of expression. Freedom of peaceful assembly and association.
2 Derogation means literally being able to 'take away' from legal obligations or to legally avoid them.
3 ECHR is more liberal in its interpretation of the Convention than English courts have traditionally been, e.g. *Thompson & Venables v UK* on A6; *Malone v UK* on breach of A8 by telephone tapping.
4 Local Authorities; NHS Hospital Trusts.

Exam questions

1 Start with the general picture, i.e. Human Rights Act 1998 incorporates most of the Convention into UK law. Then deal with areas where the Convention has not been given effect, e.g. non-incorporation of Article 13; derogation from Article 5(3). Then consider other gaps in the Human Rights Act such as:
 • Parliament is not included in 'public authority' so the Convention does not apply
 • it does not apply to private bodies: creating anomalies such as the Convention affecting NHS hospitals but not private hospitals
 • UK law must be interpreted to give effect where possible to the Convention but the Convention does not override our law
 • Parliament can choose to enact a law that is in breach of the Convention
Finish with a conclusion about the extent to which the Convention has been given effect.
2 The key phrase here is 'giving examples'. So you must be able to discuss specific examples. The reason the Human Rights Act has an effect on our law is because it incorporated most of the European Convention on Human Rights. Any Act of Parliament that is incompatible with the Convention is likely to be amended, especially where the courts have made a declaration of non-compatibility.

Laws that conflict with the Convention and may be affected include:

- section 10 Contempt of Court Act 1981 which according to the ruling in *Golder v UK* (1996) is incompatible with Article 10
- section 16(a) AND 16(b) of the Prevention of Terrorism Act 1989 which infringes Article 6 as shown in the decision in *Kebilene* (1999)
- Interception of Communications Act 1985 which probably conflicts with Article 8
- sections 34–7 of the Criminal Justice and Public Order Act 1994 on adverse inferences being drawn from silence probably infringes Article 8

All these laws may have to be changed due to the effects of the Human Rights Act.

Restrictions on freedoms

Checkpoints

1 Two rights with little protection are those of privacy and of freedom of information. The rich and famous rightly complain that their privacy is interfered with by the paparazzi, highlighted by the Princess of Wales' death. We have some access to certain information, but lack of a proper Freedom of Information Act means that the Government can act in relative secrecy.

2 Blasphemous libel is a crime but applies only to the Christian faith. It seems unfair in a multicultural society that Christian beliefs should be protected in this way while other religions are not. This was highlighted in the offence taken by Muslims to *The Satanic Verses*.

3 She was a 'scientologist'. The UK government felt that this was a cult and so her entry into the UK was not in the public interest and contrary to public policy.

4 There are many. The miners' strike 1984–1985 showed police have rights to take steps to prevent breaches of the peace they reasonably believe will occur. March organizers must give police advance notice. Byelaws can also apply, particularly in certain locations. Criminal law can be used for threatening behaviour, harassment, or disorderly conduct. The Police Act 1996 can also be used in relation to obstructing the police, and the Highways Act 1980 in the case of obstructions to the highway. Public nuisance is also a possibility.

Exam questions

1 This is a very wide question even though it is on a very specific freedom and full discussion is needed.

First some definition of free speech should be given, i.e. it is freedom to express views and opinions as well as artistic freedom. It also is guaranteed in Article 10 of the European Convention, although restrictions are accepted.

Defamation limits free speech and compensates a person whose reputation has been lowered by a false statement about them. It is justified since truthful statements can be legitimately made even if harmful and also it prevents 'witch hunts'.

Obscenity laws like the Obscene Publications Act 1959, Theatres Act 1968 and Protection of Children Act 1978 restrict the publishing of material likely to deprave. It is

justified because it can protect people from abuse and violence.

Restrictions on the press and broadcasters include voluntary codes of practice, licensing arrangements, and the availability of complaints procedures. These try to ensure that material is accurate and not overly offensive. Government restrictions on expression such as 'D' notices and the Official Secrets Act are supposed to prevent breaches of national security and are therefore in the interests of the public, although in some instances these are viewed as more controversial, e.g. *Ponting*, *Spycatcher*.

Copyright protects the original owner of material.

Law also prevents anything treasonous, seditious or likely to incite disaffection to preserve order.

2 This is a short question focusing on a narrow area.

Freedom of Association should be defined, i.e. the right of individuals to meet with like-minded persons to discuss or act on issues of common concern. It is a fundamental right guaranteed by Article 11 of the European Convention.

It may be worth noting that even if this right is protected restrictions may arise in other contexts, e.g. under restrictions on the right to assembly, or limitations placed on the content of literature. The obvious types of association in question are political parties, trade unions and pressure groups. The trade union movement itself had some significant limitations placed on it during the 19th century, including the Combination Acts.

Generally there is freedom of association. Restrictions are of two types: firstly associations of a particular character may be unlawful, e.g. extreme political groups intending to overthrow the state, or even criminal conspiracies; secondly while the association may be lawful what they do might become unlawful, e.g. animal rights activists may have a right to meet to air their views but not to contaminate foodstuffs or send petrol bombs to animal research laboratories.

The obvious restrictions are on specific types of organization: The Public Order Act 1936 prevents the wearing of uniforms (at the time of the Act this was fascist uniforms) and to organize as an unauthorized military group. Since then the Prevention of Terrorism (Temporary Provisions) Act 1989 has outlawed terrorist groups.

Protection of rights and enforcement of rights

Checkpoints

1 Sex Discrimination Act 1975. Race Relations Act 1976. Disability Discrimination Act 1995.

2 Public authority is defined as any court or tribunal or any person of whose functions some are of a public nature. It does not include the Houses of Parliament or any person exercising functions in connection with Parliament.

3 Damages, injunctions, declarations.

4 Strasbourg.

Exam questions

1 Start by explaining the key importance of judicial review is that it allows people to challenge decisions and the decision-making process, where no other appeals process is available. Include the point that it allows the judiciary to keep a check on the executive (you might refer to Montesquieu's theory of the separation of powers to explain the significance of this). Then use case examples to show the importance, e.g.:

- *Bromley London Borough Council v Greater London Council* (1982) where GLC was held to have gone beyond its powers in raising rates to fund a cheap fares policy
- *R v Secretary of State for Foreign Affairs, ex parte World Development Movement Ltd* (1995) where a grant of aid to Malaysia for the Pergau Dam project was held to be beyond his powers
- *R v Secretary of State, ex parte Thompson and Venables* (1997) where HL ruled that the Home Secretary should not have set a minimum period of 15 years' custody for two young offenders

2 Start with the broad idea that the role of the European Court of Human Rights is to enforce the European Convention on Human Rights. You can support this with mention of some rights given under the Convention. Then briefly explain that both individuals and other member states can refer cases to the court. To discuss role you should use cases such as:

- *Golder v UK* (1975) on breach of Article 8 by preventing a prisoner sending confidential letters to a solicitor. Comment on the fact that this case led to a change in the Prison Rules.
- *Tyrer v UK* on corporal punishment in schools and Article 3.
- *Sunday Times v UK* on Article 10 freedom of expression.
- *Benham v UK* on detention for non-payment of community charge and Article 5 liberty and Article 6 right to a fair hearing.
- *McCann v UK* on shoot on sight of IRA members in Gibraltar and Article 2 the right to life.

Examiner's secrets

Don't forget that there are overlaps between some topics. Use this to your advantage, e.g. the cases suggested in question 1 can also be used for judicial independence.

This chapter focuses on the synoptic units for AQA and OCR. The first four spreads are aimed at AQA. AQA requires you to use the law you have learnt in the earlier units to consider themes of jurisprudence. The last two spreads look at the synoptic themes for OCR. The knowledge for these is contained in earlier units and so this section links to those sections and concentrates on the types of question asked and how to approach them.

Exam themes

(AQA)

→ The purposes of law

→ The relationship between law and morality

→ The Hart/Devlin debate

→ Balancing interests

→ The concept of fault

→ The judicial role in creating law

(OCR)

→ English Legal System theme

→ A case study from your A2 option

→ Discussion of set areas of substantive law

→ Application of set areas of substantive law

Topic checklist

O AS ● A2	AQA	OCR	WJEC
Rules and morals	●		
Natural law and justice	●		
Balancing of interests and concepts of fault	●		
The OCR synoptic unit		●	

Rules and morals

Morality is generally to do with beliefs so may be affected by religion. We all have a moral code of some kind which defines what we think is and is not acceptable behaviour. Morality can differ from culture to culture and from individual to individual, although some behaviour is universally unacceptable. Inevitably morality has an impact on law, particularly the criminal law. Very often it concerns behaviour of a sexual nature and leads to controversy.

Morals

Durkheim, a French sociologist, has identified that it is impossible to find a single set of moral values that would be acceptable to all the members of a modern society. Certainly views would vary widely on issues such as *euthanasia*, pornography, use of soft drugs, *vivisection* and even things like sex before marriage and body piercing can cause controversy. There appears to be a number of core morals associated with life and death issues, but even then there is also disagreement. While most people see any form of killing as wrong, there are vastly opposing views on whether abortion is the taking of a human life or merely a woman exercising rights over her own body. Where lesser considerations such as the concept of dishonesty are concerned there are as many interpretations as there are individuals. Morals also clearly change and develop. Views on homosexuality have altered dramatically since the trial of Oscar Wilde and now the argument is more over whether or not gay couples should be able to legally parent children.

Rules

Twining and Miers defined rules as 'a general **norm** mandating or guiding conduct'. So this could include general guiding legal principles with no legal force such as rules in sport. It might also include custom or practice and involve the disapproval of the community rather than any legal sanction if such a rule is broken. Hart, however, has commented that rules should be distinguished from habit or practice. He suggests that the defining characteristic of a rule is its enforceability. Rules are generally obeyed for one of three reasons:

→ because of a sense of moral obligation
→ because the rule is reasonable and relevant
→ because a penalty may be imposed if the rule is broken

The last one explains why people obey rules that they disagree with such as when compulsory seat belt wearing was introduced.

Law and morality

Law and morality are both **normative**. In other words they both specify how people should behave. Moral viewpoints can clearly have an enormous influence on the making of laws, and some people would argue that the criminal law represents a common moral position.

Action point

Try to write down some things that you think are morally wrong but which are not legally wrong.

Checkpoint 1

Do you know what *'euthanasia'* and *'vivisection'* are?

Checkpoint 2

What types of killing are lawful under English law?

The jargon

A *'norm'* is merely a standard practice.

Action point

Try to think of a legal rule that you consider immoral, a legal rule that you consider unreasonable or irrelevant, and a law that you might be prepared to break despite the fact that it may result in a penalty.

Major moral positions are clearly represented in law, e.g. in serious crime such as murder, rape, robbery, etc. In other areas the law may appear to be based on moral positions but ones not accepted by everyone. An obvious example of this is the legalization of abortion under the Abortion Act 1967, the morality of which is contested by groups such as LIFE and the Association of Lawyers for the Defence of the Unborn. Moral contradictions can also appear in the law so that while abortion can be carried out legitimately, the courts have refused actions for '**wrongful life**' in *McKay v Essex AHA* (1982) because it is contrary to the principle of the sanctity of life. Similarly doctors have been prosecuted for openly practising euthanasia as in *R v Cox* (1992) but withdrawing feeding so that a patient in a permanent vegetative state would die was accepted in *Airedale NHS Trust v Bland* (1993).

Other contradictions involve sexual morality. The House of Lords in *R v Brown* (1993) held that a group of homosexual sadomasochists could not consent to harming each other's genitalia as it was not in the public interest to allow such behaviour. However, the Court of Appeal in *R v Wilson* (1996) held that a wife could consent to her husband branding his initials in her buttocks with a hot knife.

The difference between law and morality

Even though the law develops from a shared morality there are significant differences between the two:

→ morality develops over time while law can be introduced instantly
→ morality depends on voluntary codes of conduct whereas law is enforceable and many morals may, in any case, be difficult to enforce if not unfair, e.g. *Gillick v West Norfolk and Wisbech AHA* (1986)

The Hart/Devlin debate

Much of this debate was prompted by the Wolfenden Committee 1957 which recommended the legalization of prostitution and homosexuality. Professor Hart approved the findings of the Report and indicated that law and morality should be kept entirely separate. He felt that morality was a private issue that the state had no right to intervene in, and that it was wrong to punish people who may have done no harm to others. Lord Devlin, however, felt that the judges have a **residual** right to protect and preserve some sort of common morality. An obvious example of judges exercising this right was in *Shaw v DPP* (1961) where the House of Lords invented a crime of conspiracy to corrupt public morality in respect of a 'contact magazine'.

The jargon

The action for '*wrongful life*' is one where the claimant is arguing that he has been denied the right to be aborted by a doctor's negligent failure to advise of abortion as an option.

Checkpoint 3

How can the cases of *Brown* and *Wilson* be distinguished? Where do you think is the proper point at which to say consent is not available as a defence?

Checkpoint 4

Do you know what the issue was in the *Gillick* case?

The jargon

Residual simply means what is left when other things are taken out.

Don't forget

For the synoptic study paper you will need to illustrate your answers with the law that you have studied in units 4 and 5.

Examiner's secrets

In question 1 you should use examples of where this has been argued as well as arguing your own point of view.

Exam questions   answers: page 182

1   Consider whether there are areas of morality in which it is not the business of the law to intervene. (45 min)

2   Explain the distinction between legal rules and moral rules. (20 min)

Natural law and justice

Justice is something that we all want from a law and believe should be an integral part of any legal system. However, there are numerous examples from history of societies creating unjust laws, and in modern times there are many examples of miscarriages of justice occurring even in a legal system we consider to be fair. Aristotle, the Greek philosopher, was one of the earliest to put forward the view that all law should promote justice. There are many varied theories on the relationship between law and justice.

Theories of natural law

Natural law is a strange concept. It is based on the idea that there is a divine source of law which is superior and based on moral rules, and that law and morality should therefore absolutely reflect each other. The logical extension of this view is that the legal rules of a country can be broken if they do not conform to moral laws, a view that was favoured by St Thomas Aquinas. Professor L. L. Fuller is a modern follower of the idea of natural law. His work *The Morality of Law* focuses on an 'inner morality' which he says should be followed. Lord Devlin, as we have seen, believed that law is based on morality, and that judges are justified in interfering in moral issues.

Positivism

Natural lawyers conflict with *positivist* thinkers who believe that if the law is made according to correct procedure then it should be followed however much it conflicts with morality. Positivists like Kelsen argue that law and morality are entirely separate concepts and that even law that is immoral should be followed and that justice is too vague a concept to be defined. Professor Hart also considers that law and morality are separate concepts. He believed that law should be based on logical ideas that produce correct decisions from the rules. Durkheim took the view that society is held together by social structures and that the law is an integral part of making those structures work.

Utilitarianism

Utilitarianism is a theory that moves away from the basic principles of natural law while still concentrating on the conflict between legal rules and divine law. Jeremy Bentham, the originator of this school of thought, considered that the purpose of law was to achieve the greatest happiness for the greatest number. The obvious defect in this view is that the interests of the individual are ignored, only the majority is considered. John Stuart Mill also developed the theme. It was his view that legal intervention should be minimal and that the only justification for interfering with a person's basic freedom was where that person was causing harm to someone else and thus interfering with their freedom.

Checkpoint 1

Can you think of a major event of the 20th century involving a society creating unjust laws?

Checkpoint 2

An example of a person breaking a law that conflicted with his moral principles was *Ponting*. Can you say in what way his case is an example of this point?

The jargon

Positivism merely refers to a separation of law and morals, with law being based on logic that must then be followed positively, with justice being a mere preference of values.

Action point

Can you write down some examples of laws that are for the good of the majority but which tend to ignore individual rights?

Economic views of law and justice ●●●

Karl Marx argued simply that in any *capitalist* society all law is essentially unjust since it represents the means by which one class oppresses the class or classes below it. Marxist views of justice, therefore, are based on the redistribution of wealth.

Robert Nozick, on the other hand, argues that a just society is one where the state has the least possible power to interfere with the rights of the individual. His theories are based on the ownership of property and the manner in which it has been gained. If it has been gained fairly then the state has no right to interfere. Redistribution of wealth is unfair because it interferes with basic individual rights.

The problem of balancing out economic considerations and justice is that what may be just for society as a whole may be very unjust to a particular individual. A classic case of this was that of Jaymee Bowen where there was controversy over the refusal by a health authority to fund treatment for her leukaemia. Another example of how justice can be affected by economic considerations is the decision in *R v Gloucestershire County Council ex parte Barry* (1997) allowing a local authority to avoid its statutory duty to provide services based on an assessment of their available resources.

Problems of ensuring justice in law ●●●

The law does not always provide justice although ensuring justice should be an aim of any legal system. Justice can be difficult to define and may mean different things to different people. If we take the examples of Marx and Nozick above, the first would see it as unjust that one person should enjoy greater wealth and power than another, the second would see it as unjust to interfere with a person's property rights to achieve a redistribution of wealth. Clearly justice may depend on:

→ treating like situations alike, e.g. imposing the same sentences for the same crime, or giving the same remedy for the same loss
→ having discretion to concentrate on the justice of an individual situation rather than being bound by hard and fast rules

But of course the two of these are mutually exclusive. An example of injustice created by ignoring the individual situation would be the inability of battered women like *Ahluwalia* (1992) to use the law of provocation in defence of murdering their abusive husbands. As convicted murderers they in effect carry the same stigma as the Moors Murderers and there is no discretionary sentencing in murder.

The jargon

A *'capitalist'* society is one like our own based on individual ownership of capital rather than state or collective ownership.

Checkpoint 3

What is the justification for the decision in this case and how can it be criticized as it was in the dissenting judgment of Lord Lloyd?

Checkpoint 4

Why was Kiranjit Ahluwalia unable to use the defence of provocation despite her husband's abusive behaviour?

Links

See pages 66–9.

Examiner's secrets

For the synoptic paper you may wish to give examples of unjust laws or unjust outcomes to illustrate your answer to question 1.

Exam questions   answers: pages 182–3

1   To what extent are law and justice the same thing? (45 min)

2   Explain the differences between natural law and positivism. (20 min)

Balancing of interests and concepts of fault

We are all keen to ensure that our interests are protected and the law achieves this with specific sets of rules. Interests can also be classed as rights and the law protects rights by imposing a corresponding duty on another person not to interfere with our rights. The interests of the individual and the interest of the majority may sometimes be in conflict. *Fault* is a concept that is commonly applied in determining whether in fact a person has interfered wrongly with another person's interests.

The jargon

Fault is described in the dictionary as responsibility for something done wrongly.

The nature of rights or interests

Interests or rights are not that easy to define. It may seem easy to point to a particular thing and say that you own it. However, in demonstrating your right or interest in the property you would often be arguing over an abstract concept of ownership in a court of law with the court demanding concrete proof or evidence of your ownership. Our ability to prove a legal right or interest is then demonstrated by our being able to enforce it. An obvious example is in a contract where we have an interest in the property to be passed. If the contract is not performed we may sometimes be able to enforce performance but most often we have a right to compensation for the loss of the bargain that we made.

Checkpoint 1

What is the difference between ownership of property and mere possession of property?

Links

See page 112.

Rights and duties

Each right generally has a corresponding duty attached to it, e.g.:

→ in criminal law our right not to be robbed or burgled or assaulted imposes on others the duty not to rob, burgle or assault
→ in tort our right not to be injured, e.g. by the careless driving of another, imposes on other drivers the obligation to drive safely
→ in contract our rights to receive the goods or services under the contract are based on the duty of the other party to deliver them
→ in marriage our right to an uninterrupted union is based on the duty of our partners not to commit adultery, or to act intolerably, or to desert us or live apart from us

We may also owe a duty in order to gain the right, e.g. paying National Insurance contributions entitles us to claim contributory benefits. Often our rights involve both power and choice. We may for instance have the power to sell our property, but we may also choose not to do so. We may have the power to sue but choose not to do so.

Checkpoint 2

Can you think of some other obvious right and duty situations involving areas of law besides those identified here?

Balancing rights and interests

Very often it is impossible to exercise a right or interest without it infringing another person's right or interest. A common example is the law of nuisance where neighbouring landowners may complain about indirect interferences. Often a landowner may be unable to enforce the right to quiet enjoyment of the land, e.g. because the locality is one where the nuisance is allowed as stated in *obiter* in *St Helens Smelting v Tipping*, or it is not in the public interest as in *Miller v Jackson*, or

Checkpoint 3

Why is nuisance sometimes referred to as the law of give and take? How is that relevant here?

Links

See pages 146–7.

because the interference was not continuous as in *Bolton v Stone*. Another example is in contract law where a person may be prevented from enforcing his rights under the contract because the contract has been made following an innocent misrepresentation as in *Esso v Marden*. Sometimes an individual's rights or interests are sacrificed for the greater public good. Examples include the defence of statutory authority in tort, strict liability where there is no requirement to prove fault, the defences of absolute privilege and fair comment in defamation actions, the changes to the right to remain silent after caution by a police officer, etc.

The concept of fault ●●●

Fault as a concept is very close to the idea of blame and the effect of finding fault is certainly also to find responsibility.

→ Fault is a concept relevant to the law of torts and negligence in particular. In negligence a defendant will not be liable unless the claimant can also show fault. This is done by demonstrating that the defendant owed the claimant a duty which he has breached by falling below the standard of care appropriate to the specific duty. It is tested according to the 'reasonable man' test, so the defendant must act so as to avoid foreseeable harm, *Donoghue v Stevenson*. Professionals, however, are measured according to their own standards, *Bolam v Friern Hospital Management Committee*.

→ Fault also appears in family law in some of the facts that can be used to prove an irretrievable breakdown of the marriage in a divorce petition such as adultery or behaviour.

→ Fault also surfaces in contract law when a party breaches a contract. One of the tests for deciding if damages are available is whether the loss was 'within the contemplation of the other party when the contract was made'. Also in fraudulent misrepresentation a party is liable who knowingly or deliberately makes false statements.

→ *Mens rea* in crime also concerns fault in that a defendant who has criminal intent and commits the act is guilty. Intention can be willing an event or foreseeing that a particular consequence will result, or even taking an unjustifiable risk which is therefore reckless conduct. It may even involve owing a duty and falling so far below the required conduct that it amounts to more than mere compensatable negligence but is gross negligence and a crime.

Test yourself

See if you can remember the facts of any of the important cases in this section.

Links

See pages 136–9.

Checkpoint 4

Can you say why the defendant was at fault in *Donoghue v Stevenson* but the defendant in *Bolam* was not?

Test yourself

See if you can say how fault is relevant to other vitiating factors in contract law.

Action point

Fault is not an issue in strict liability. Write down some crimes and torts whose liability is strict.

Examiner's secrets

For the synoptic study remember how fault is expressed in the area of law that you have studied.

Examiner's secrets

You can also consider defences in tort when discussing the effects of fault.

Exam questions   answers: page 183

1   Briefly consider situations in which a person will be unable to protect an interest in law. (20 min)

2   Discuss how the concept of fault can unfairly affect the victims of accidents that are beyond their own control. (20 min)

179

The OCR synoptic unit

The OCR synoptic unit brings together elements from the AS and elements from the options on substantive law. Material is given out in advance in a special study booklet. The present theme for the AS is judicial precedent, the theme for the criminal law option is duress, duress of circumstances and necessity, the theme for the contract law option is consideration and the theme for the tort option is nervous shock in negligence. These will be the themes for the 2004 exams and also for the January 2005 session. There will be new themes for June 2005 onwards, but the exam will be the same style. The pre-released special study material for June 2005 to January 2007 should be available from September 2004.

The pre-released materials

Schools, colleges and any other exam centres which have registered with OCR that they have candidates for law are provided with copies of the special study material. It is important that you have this source material to prepare for the exam. It can be obtained from OCR and may also be available on their website.

You cannot take your original copy into the exam but you will be given a clean copy in the exam room so that you can refer to the material. The booklet contains extracts from judgments of important cases on the theme, extracts from articles in legal journals and quality textbooks. The questions will be based on the topics in the source material.

The English Legal System theme

The special study material always contains at least one source on the theme to be examined. For June 2003 to January 2005 this source is adapted from *The Discipline of Law* by Lord Denning and contains many points about judicial precedent.

Key points on precedent in it include:

→ the doctrine of *stare decisis*
→ the need for justice
→ the development of law
→ the use of the Practice Statement
→ the position of the Court of Appeal

But for top grades you must also be prepared to go wider than the source. Learn as much as you can about precedent. You will need to know cases such as *Herrington v British Railways Board*, *R v Shivpuri*, *Davis v Johnson*, *Miliangos* etc, even though they may not be from your A2 option subject.

Don't forget

Make sure that you have the current special study material. You can get it from OCR. (Website www.ocr.org.uk)

Links

The knowledge you need on judicial precedent is given on pages 4–7.

Don't forget

The questions are all linked to the source material in the special study booklet. You need to know this material really well.

Action point

Make a list of all cases which are mentioned in the special study material for your substantive law option. Make sure that you know the facts and the point of law in each of them.

The first question on the synoptic exam paper for 2004 and January 2005 will be about precedent. As well as good knowledge of precedent you will be expected to be more critical in your comments than at AS and must make links to the substantive law you have been studying for A2.

Case studies ●●●

The second question on the paper will be about one of the cases in the special study material. It will require a discussion of the case in the light of the overall theme. While the theme is precedent this could be an understanding of how the case changed or developed the law, whether the case has restricted the law, whether the case remedies or produces injustice etc. It is the discussion that is important. The majority of marks are for analysis and evaluation.

Discussion of substantive law ●●●

The third question will be an essay question on a major point from your substantive law option. It will always be linked to the special study material and may well involve a quote from one of the sources. The source material will be relevant and should be referred to in the answer, but for top grades you must go wider and show good understanding of the topic. The discussion element is important. Merely reciting facts will not get good grades.

Application of substantive law ●●●

The final question will be a scenario style question in which it is necessary to apply the law. The question may contain one large scenario or it may be broken down into three smaller scenarios. Again the law involved will be from the theme of the special study material for your option. In this question the examiner wants you to show your understanding of the law through applying it to the scenario. The important points to cover in this style of question can be summed up as having an IDEA:

→ **I**dentify the issue(s)
→ **D**efine the main principle of law involved
→ **E**xpand that point of law with cases
→ **A**pply the law to the facts in the scenario

Using the source material ●●●

As the questions draw on the source material, you should refer to the sources in your answers where relevant. When referring to a source there is no need to write out long quotations, just use the source number and the line references. For example, 'In source 6 at lines 4 to 7, the judgment (or the article) shows that . . .'.

Links

The themes for criminal law until January 2005 are dealt with on pages 78–9. The themes for contract law until January 2005 are dealt with on pages 92–3. The themes for tort until January 2005 are dealt with on pages 138–9.

Action point

Try re-writing some of the shorter sources in your own words to make sure you really understand them.

Don't forget

You need to go wider than the source material. Read up on the theme for your option and make a list of extra cases which you could link to the cases in the source material.

Examiner's secrets

On this paper if you have used information in an earlier question which you want to use in question 4, the examiner is quite happy for you to merely refer back to your earlier answer, e.g. saying 'see answer to question 2 for full details on this case'. This saves you time in the exam.

Answers
The OCR synoptic unit

Rules and morals

Checkpoints

1 'Euthanasia' is killing a sufferer of an incurable disease. 'Vivisection' is dissection of live animals for research purposes.
2 There are probably only three and two are of doubtful relevance now. Killing in self-defence, which is a complete defence to a murder or manslaughter charge; a lawful execution, which is unlikely now; and killing of an enemy alien in time of war.
3 Consent to the sadomasochism in Brown was said to be against the public interest. The branding in Wilson was said to be a domestic occurrence beyond the interference of the courts. The Law Commission suggests consent should not be available for wounding offences, only assault.
4 DHSS guidelines on giving contraceptive advice and support to girls under 16. Mrs Gillick felt that this was ignoring the rights of the parents to be informed.

Exam questions

1 This is a discussion of a quite complicated area and there is much room for argument on both sides.

First of all both law and morality need defining. Law is easily defined in Salmond's words as 'the body of principles recognized and applied by the state in the administration of justice'. Morals on the other hand are more difficult to define. They involve belief about what is acceptable behaviour but they can involve individual as well as shared or cultural viewpoints. Durkheim might be cited here as suggesting that it is impossible to find a moral code that is universally acceptable. It can also be identified that much 'morality' is based on religious beliefs or doctrine. Common areas of morality such as killing can also be discussed.

Much of this area inevitably focuses on the Hart/Devlin debate, on the extent to which the state should be able to intervene through law in areas of what we may consider private concern. Devlin felt the judges have a duty to act for our moral protection and this justifies cases such as Shaw v DPP. Hart feels law and morality should be separate. A lot of the debate here will inevitably focus on areas such as abortion, sexual preferences, justifications for killing such as euthanasia, and any other relevant examples.

2 This is only part of a broader question and focuses on a mere comparison between law and morals.
   - Rules can be defined as 'norms guiding conduct'.
   - Differences between legal rules and morals can be explored including: laws are enforceable, morals are not; legal rules are developed according to procedural requirements, morals develop haphazardly over time; a moral code is followed because of belief in the code, laws are kept because of risk of a penalty if broken; laws apply to the whole country, but communities or cultures may have different morals.

Natural law and justice

Checkpoints

1 The extermination of Jews in Nazi Germany by first denying them citizenship was carried out according to the 'Nuremberg laws'. A more recent example of unjust laws involved 'apartheid' in South Africa.
2 Because he felt that Parliament was being denied access to the truth and so broke the Official Secrets Act to give vital information on the sinking of an enemy ship to an opposition MP.
3 The Council must be able to take its own financial position into account before allocating services even though it has a duty to provide them. Lord Lloyd says that if an Act imposes a duty to provide services then the Government should make proper funds available.
4 Because of the 'cooling off period' before she killed.

Exam questions

1 This is a difficult discussion requiring an understanding of what both law and justice mean.

Law can be defined using Salmond's definition 'the body of principles recognized and applied by the state in the administration of justice'.

Justice is a difficult concept. Kelsen feels that it is too vague a concept to be defined adequately. The law is more concerned with seeing that society is orderly rather than worrying whether there is individual injustice or not.

Our own sense of justice probably depends on our moral sense of right and wrong. We know that there is a link between morality and law but that the one does not automatically depend on the other.

The law tries to ensure justice. Examples are the creation of equitable remedies like injunctions; providing different sentences for different types of crime and grading sentences according to other factors; the higher standard of proof in criminal cases as loss of liberty may be involved; the rules of evidence; the rules of natural justice in Judicial Review; the availability of an appeals system to ensure that mistakes are rectified.

Of course there are also many examples of the law operating unjustly or unfairly. These include erosion of the right to silence in criminal practice; the failure to protect the dead from destruction of their reputation; the limitations on the availability of state-funded legal provision meaning many people are denied access to justice; imbalances in the remedies available to employees in comparison with the power enjoyed over them by employers; imposing vicarious liability on people who are not the actual tortfeasor; the lack of an available action without proof of fault in many personal injuries;

the many miscarriages of justice in the criminal law, e.g. Birmingham six, Bridgewater three, Guildford four, etc.

Any suitable examples can be used to develop the argument either way.

2 This is a straightforward comparison between two theories of law and is a short question.

Natural law should be defined as being to do with a higher moral order, probably to do with religious beliefs that should be seen as superior to any secular law developed by society. It can be credited to theorists like Fuller. The fact that the superiority of such laws may justify breaking the actual law might also be explored and credited to St Thomas Aquinas.

Positivism, on the other hand, views law and morality as entirely separate issues. In this way law is based on logic and morals on emotion. The view expressed by positivists like Kelsen is that law should be followed even if it is immoral.

Examiner's secrets

Remember that for the synoptic study as well as showing a good understanding of the theory you must use illustrations from the law that you have learned in units 4 and 5.

Balancing of interests and concepts of fault

Checkpoints

1 Ownership involves holding 'title' to the property. An owner can legally dispose of the property. Someone who is merely in possession cannot, and holds the property only subject to the owner's superior rights.

2 An employer's right to receive work from the employee is based on the duty to pay for it. Our rights to do what we want with our land are tempered by our duty to avoid harming others. The state's right to punish is balanced by its duty to offer a fair and impartial trial.

3 Because it involves the court in trying to balance out competing rights and interests which is exactly what this section is about.

4 Stevenson had fallen below the standards expected of a manufacturer in avoiding harm to consumers.

The doctor in *Bolam* had carried out a procedure accepted by a competent body of medical opinion, so was faultless although the patient was harmed.

Exam questions

1 This is a broad-based short question which requires an understanding that even though people may appear to have obvious rights there are many limitations imposed on enforcing those rights. Any sensible approach could be rewarded but a number of points stand out:

- Limitation periods – usually six years, but three years from the date of knowledge in personal injury.
- Defences – the general defences in tort are an obvious example here, particularly those which seem to deliberately allow wrongdoing such as statutory authority, *Allen v Gulf Oil*, and public policy, *Miller v Jackson*, but specific defences also can have an effect, e.g. privilege in defamation.
- Remoteness of damage – and this can be an issue in both tort, *The Wagon Mound*, and contract, *Hadley v Baxendale*.
- Rules of evidence – even though the person claiming an interference with their right may appear to have a case the evidence that would support it may be inadmissible.
- Capacity – the person may lack the capacity to enforce the right in some way. An obvious example is an unborn child. Another is a dead person who has been defamed but whose right of action dies with him. A party may also be unable to enforce a contract with a company that acted *ultra vires* (beyond its powers) in entering into the contract.

2 This question specifically deals with fault. It is a short question and needs an explanation of the concept of fault and also some illustrations of the effect not being able to prove fault can have on an accident victim's claim.

- First define fault as legal responsibility and put it in the context of accidents.
- Next explain that fault is an essential element of a claim in most torts. Even in strict liability faults like *Rylands v Fletcher* (with the requirement since *Cambridge Water v Eastern Counties Leather* to show that damage is foreseeable in this tort) it is almost like having to show fault.
- Give sensible examples of the requirement of fault preventing what appears to be a justifiable claim, e.g. medical cases such as *Sidaway v Governors of Bethlem Royal Hospital*.

This chapter focuses on the learning process and answering techniques rather than on areas of law or of the legal system. Nevertheless it is important to take note of the points made here because it should help you to plan and to organize yourself during your course; to prepare effectively at the time of revision; and also to be well equipped to answer the different types of questions that appear in exams by being more familiar with what they are demanding of you.

You will benefit if you try to develop skills from the beginning of your course. Modern A-level exams are not tests of your recall of text books or teachers' notes. Examiners who set and mark the papers are guided by assessment objectives which include skills as well as knowledge. You will be given advice on revising and answering questions. Remember to practise the skills.

Exam board specifications

In order to organize your notes and revision you will need a copy of your exam board's syllabus specification. You can obtain a copy by writing to the board or by downloading the syllabus from the board's website.

AQA (Assessment and Qualifications Alliance)
Publications Department, Stag Hill House, Guildford, Surrey
GU2 5XJ – www.aqa.org.uk

OCR (Oxford, Cambridge and Royal Society of Arts)
1 Hills Road, Cambridge CB2 1GG – www.ocr.org.uk

WJEC (Welsh Joint Education Committee)
245 Western Avenue, Cardiff CF5 2YX – www.wjec.co.uk

Making notes and learning

For most of you, your A-level course will be the first time that you have studied law. One difference you may have found from other subjects is the amount of information that you are expected to remember. Also there will be many new terms and expressions that you have not come across before. For these reasons it is important that you have a good set of notes that are easily understandable and can form the basis of your revision.

The purpose of note-taking

You have a number of resources available to you to help you to learn and indeed to help you when you come to revision. Your teacher or lecturer may have given you prepared handouts but your own notes are best because you will understand them. You can take notes in class and when you read text books. Getting into the habit of reading and note-taking will ensure that you are building up information to help your learning. The more you do it the more familiar you become with the information and the more you get used to writing about law so that you feel comfortable doing so in the exam. It is active and aids memorizing.

Sensible reading

Reading when you are studying a subject is not like reading generally. You do not have the time to read the book from cover to cover, and it is unnecessary to do so. What you need to do is to read those things that are relevant to you at the time. So you need to build up some familiarity with your text books and knowledge of where you can find the areas of law or the legal system in them that you need to study at the time, e.g. you may wish to read on juries in three different books because they all have something slightly different to say. You need to be able to get to the appropriate sections quickly, and using the index effectively may be important here. It is a good idea to learn to scan-read so that you can look through books quickly to locate appropriate information. You can do this by learning to focus on key words as you scan down the page. When you are reading to try to understand something that you are not clear on then you will need to read more slowly and comprehensively, and at these times in particular you should then make notes on what you have read.

When to take notes

There are four different times when you are likely to need to take notes:

→ during lessons, either from books or from what the teacher is saying or writing on the board or from discussion or even from watching videos
→ when you are following up information given by your teacher
→ when you have been asked to prepare for a discussion
→ when you are preparing the outline for your homework

Watch out!

After writing notes try to make sure that the first time you look at them again is not when you begin revising.

Action point

If your teacher gives you handouts you can see how they are structured and possibly use the structure for your own notes.

Test yourself

Read a section in a text book, try to identify the main points then write them down from memory.

Watch out!

Listen to your teachers. Sometimes they will tell you when to take a note and when not to or they will slow down when they expect you to take notes.

How to take notes

The most important thing about your notes is that they should mean something to you and you should be able to use them easily and effectively. This is particularly important when you are preparing for your exams. But there are also some basic points about taking notes that you should try to follow:

→ Try to make clear, concise notes. If you copy down everything that your teacher says then you will have a lot of irrelevant detail in them (particularly the jokes) and copying everything from a book is a waste of time – you might as well just read the book. Also use abbreviations *consistently*, e.g. D = defendant, V = victim.
→ Make use of bullet points, numbered sections, headings and sub-headings. This makes your notes organized and makes recall easier.
→ Try to leave some spaces and not cram everything in as extended prose. This will allow you to make amendments and add information that you have found from other sources.
→ Add diagrams, flow charts and other visual aids to your notes where possible. We remember most easily from these. Often I draw cartoons of cases on the board to help students remember them.
→ Try always to link your points of law to cases or statutory sources that support them and critical comments to quotes or arguments that you have read. Statistical information can also be useful.
→ Read through your notes soon after you have made them to see if you understand them.

You might use the following headings and subheadings on the jury:

1 Eligibility for service:
   (a) basic requirements
   (b) disqualified people
   (c) ineligible people
   (d) excused people
   (e) criticisms of the selection process
2 Empanelling and selecting a jury.
3 Civil juries:
   (a) use of
   (b) reasons for decline
4 Criminal juries:
   (a) challenges
   (b) reaching verdicts and majority verdicts
5 Advantages, disadvantages, possible alternatives to the jury.

In your notes on precedent you might have a diagram identifying the highest court in the system down to the lowest.

How to use your notes

Your notes can be the central core of your learning. They represent the information that you have gathered from your lessons and from text books, articles and other sources that supplement and add extra detail to your class notes. If your notes are effective they can be used not only to help with your homework but also when you want to make reduced notes or key cards during revision.

Watch out!

Try not to spend all of the time in class just copying down what the teacher is saying. If you do, you are not listening.

Test yourself

Pick any topic and make a list of the important aspects of the topic. Then see if this compares to the headings and subheadings in your handouts or in text books.

Watch out!

It is particularly important in your substantive law areas to support your points with cases, and in areas like crime you will need to refer to sections of Acts to work out the answers.

Take note

Try producing a flow chart for a substantive law area, e.g. for manslaughter and murder or a diagram to illustrate the difference between offer and invitation to treat.

Revision techniques

Revision is the last stage in the process before you actually sit your exam, although it may actually start a long time before the exam. Revision should not be the start of your learning but a way of making what you already know and understand available to you in the exam. Revision can take up a lot of your time and for the best use of that time should be organized and make use of effective techniques.

Starting early ●●●

Revision is very much like training is to an athlete. If the athlete is not warmed up before the event then he is unlikely to perform well because the muscles will be sluggish. Similarly if you have not exercised your brain sufficiently before the exam it may let you down. Just like training, the earlier you start your programme the fitter and more finely tuned your mind will be. A long span of short sessions is much more useful than 'burning the midnight oil' at the last minute.

Watch out!

Remember leaving everything to the last minute not only gives you little chance of doing it effectively but it will add to your anxiety.

Gathering the necessary material together ●●●

Your revision time is precious to you so you do not want to waste it by spending your time going to the library, looking for information, or borrowing your friends' notes on topics you missed when you were ill. *Before* starting revision try to ensure that you do the following:

→ read necessary sections or chapters of textbooks and make notes if you need to do so
→ get all of your lecture notes up to date and in order
→ if you intend to use essays you have completed in your revision make sure you have amended them to include any comments made by your teachers and have corrected any errors in them

Action point

Ask your teacher for replacements of important handouts you have missed or lost. It may make you look inefficient but it is better than being without important information.

Organizing your time ●●●

This is one of the most important aspects of revision. Simply sitting in front of your book or notes and randomly selecting topics to read is likely to leave you unprepared for the exam, or at least you will have no idea how well or how poorly prepared you are. Prepare a *Revision Programme* for yourself and work to it. If you can start your revision four to six weeks before the exam then you have time to break it down into manageable sessions rather than wearing yourself out at the end. You can begin by identifying the harder areas you need to learn because you will probably need to spend more time on these.

You can make a *chart* like a calendar with all the dates until your exam on it. If you make it big enough you can also break the days down into time slots or you could have separate charts for each day.

→ Divide the time up and write on the chart what topic you are going to revise on what date and at what time.
→ Make a daily note of your progress if only by a tick.
→ Leave some spaces clear so that you can go back to areas you still feel unsure about.

Action point

You can prepare a revision programme a long time in advance and then you can make a note as you go along about how much time you need to give individual areas.

Preparing revision aids

During your course you will have learnt and hopefully understood a lot of detailed information on the law. Often your source material will not have broken this information down into manageable proportions, e.g. a lot of textbooks contain lengthy sections of prose. Your revision needs to help your memory filter through all of your knowledge for the relevant parts from the small bits of information that you are given in the question in the exam. One of your first jobs during revision, then, is to go through all your notes, and possibly the texts, and prepare condensed versions of the important key points. Many students make *key cards* and as their revision progresses they can use the cards to test themselves. In law, a great number of students have difficulty remembering case names. Sometimes for my students I prepare very brief topic lists including the point of law, the case name, and a very short summary of fact (ideally all that on one line) e.g.:

Literal rule
Use plain ordinary words – *Fisher v Bell* – offer for sale of flick-knives
Causes injustice – *LNER v Berriman* – killed on railway not 'repairing'
Absurd results – *Whiteley v Chappell* – used dead man's vote

Golden rule
May use if literal rule leads to absurdity – Lord Wensleydale
Narrow application, avoid ambiguity – *Adler v George* – in vicinity/in
Broad application, avoid result – *Re Sigsworth* – son murdering mum

Whatever works for you is acceptable as long as it provides key points to jog your memory.

> **Action point**
>
> You can prepare a series of key cards on individual cases with the point of law and summary of facts and then later have cards with groups of cases.

> **Test yourself**
>
> Select an area and make up a list like this and see if it works for you.

Taking time off

Your rest and getting away from revision is as important as the revision itself. If you become too tired you will not revise effectively. When you prepare your *Revision Timetable* you can ensure that you avoid this by building in breaks as follows:

Session 1   6.00–6.30 revise precedent
6.30–6.45 break
Session 2   6.45–7.15 test yourself on precedent key cards
7.15–7.30 break
Session 3   7.30–8.00 revise statutory interpretation

> **Watch out!**
>
> As well as breaks between revision sessions you should also try to relax by doing something different at least once a week.

Final preparations

→ In the last couple of weeks make sure you are still on schedule.
→ You should be testing yourself more often at this stage.
→ With a couple of days to go make sure you are eating and resting properly and do not have too many stimulants such as coffee.
→ On the day before the exam make sure you have got together everything you need to take into the exam such as pens, ink, spares.
→ On the day of the exam make sure you leave home in plenty of time.

> **Watch out!**
>
> Make sure you also know where the exam is taking place well in advance.

Essay writing

In exams, essay questions often seem to be the easiest to answer. This is generally because you are being told the exact topic area that the examiner wants you to write about. This of course does not necessarily mean that the question is an easy one. The area may be one that you know well but the actual question may be a very difficult one, so it is important that you read the question carefully and that you answer the question that has been set.

Reading the question ●●●

Before putting pen to paper you must first read the paper carefully.

First of all you must read the **rubric**. If you have to answer four questions out of eight on the paper then you are losing marks if you only answer three and you are wasting time if you answer five. I have seen papers where the candidate has attempted all eight.

Secondly you must read each question carefully. It is the question that is telling you what the examiner wants you to do in the exam.

Answering the question set ●●●

Examiners will generally ask questions on specific parts of individual areas, so you only need to write on those specific areas. It is unlikely that you will ever see the following essay titles:

→ Write all you know about statutory interpretation.
→ Repeat your lecture notes on lay magistrates as closely as you can.

However, most examiners will have marked such essays at some time. You are more likely to see essay titles such as:

→ Discuss the use of intrinsic and extrinsic aids in statutory interpretation.
→ Discuss the role played by laymen in the administration of justice.

In the first, therefore, you would not need to write about language rules and presumptions. Also while you might show how extrinsic aids are more likely to be used by judges favouring a purposive approach you would not need to recount every case you know on the three rules. In the second you would need to consider juries and members of tribunals as well as the magistrates.

Having a structure ●●●

In any form of writing you need a structure. This not only means that the reader can follow more easily what is written but that you will not forget anything important when you are writing. A simple structure can be completed in a few minutes before you start answering the question and can start as a simple brainstorming session. Then you need to put your list of important points in some sort of order.

The jargon

The *rubric* is the written instructions on the exam paper telling you what you must do.

Watch out!

Try to think of a list of headings and subheadings that you would need for these questions, and imagine how long it would take you to do everything.

Action point

Select a topic and make a list of past exam questions on it to see what differences or similarities there are.

Watch out!

When making an essay plan use the type of plan you are most comfortable with to avoid any anxiety.

A simple structure for the lay people in justice question might be:

Para 1: introduction, explaining what lay people are

Para 2: role of juries

Para 3: advantages/disadvantages of jury system

Para 4: role of magistrates

Para 5: advantages/disadvantages of using magistrates

Para 6: lay people in tribunals, arbitration and mediation

Para 7: conclusions – where you might say how much is covered by lay people and consider whether there are any alternatives

Using only relevant law

This also applies to substantive law. If the question is on involuntary manslaughter there is no point including cases on voluntary manslaughter.

Using quotations

The examiner will be impressed if you use quotes or cite a person as authority for a point that you are making, so do it wherever you can. In statutory interpretation, for instance, you may remember that the literal rule means giving the words their plain, ordinary and literal meaning even if it leads to a manifest absurdity. If you remember also that it was Lord Esher (in *R v Judge of the City of London Court*) that said this then show the examiner how much you have learnt by saying so.

Using cases and statutes in illustration

As with lawyers generally, your points are made far more effectively if you have the necessary authority for making them, e.g. in statutory interpretation if you want to say that the literal rule can lead to injustice you may discuss how injustice occurred in *LNER v Berriman*. You do not always need to refer to the facts. For instance, when you are considering when Hansard may be used in statutory interpretation you would identify the general conditions in *Pepper v Hart*. In your substantive law you may need to be able not only to cite cases but also sections of Acts to explain the law. For example if you are discussing Occupiers' Liability in tort you may need to refer to section 2(2) Occupiers' Liability Act 1957 to identify the scope of the duty the occupier owes.

Do not answer last year's question

One final important reminder. Teachers and lecturers will often prepare their candidates by showing them how a question from a previous paper should be answered, and indeed you may have practised last year's question for homework or in a mock. It will be different to this year's question and 'discussing the range of aids available to a judge in statutory interpretation' will not get you the best marks on an essay entitled 'discuss the literal/purposive debate in statutory interpretation'.

Action point

Try to prepare a structure for the statutory interpretation question on intrinsic and extrinsic aids.

Test yourself

Write down some quotes that you know and try to remember the important parts.

Watch out!

Try not to spend too much time repeating all the facts of a case, a brief outline will usually do.

Watch out!

Try not to predict what this year's question will be. Answer the question that appears on the paper.

Answering source questions

Source-based questions are relatively new in A-level law exams and not every exam board uses them but they are common in GCSE law papers. However, you will almost certainly have experienced source-based questions, or 'data response' questions as they are sometimes called, in some form in your GCSEs. The main advantage of such questions is that the source material gives you big clues to the answers and also useful information to use in your answers.

Reading the source material

As with both essay questions and problems it is vital to read the source material properly. Usually you will have far more to read in a source-based question than even in a problem, but there is generally time built into the exam for this purpose. The big advantage of the source material is that it can lead you to what the questions are about and what information you need to answer them. For instance if the source is the Practice Statement 1966 then you might in reading it identify the key elements as follows (it would be useful here for you to refer back to a copy of the Practice Statement in a textbook):

→ The first paragraph refers to the importance of certainty in the law and the second refers to the possibility of rigid adherence to precedent leading to injustice or lack of development in the law – so there is a good chance one question will be on whether precedent achieves one or the other.

→ It also refers to the judges being able to depart from past precedent 'when it is right to do so' – so again there is a chance that one question will be asking you to discuss when it will be right to do so.

→ Finally it says that it will only apply to the House of Lords – this is the opportunity for the examiner to ask you if it should apply to other courts, in which case you can use Lord Denning's arguments in *Davis v Johnson*.

You will then go on to read the questions and will probably find that all of these examples or some of them are there.

Using the source material in your answers

There is nothing wrong with using the source material provided in your answers, the trick is to use it effectively. For instance, say the source material was an extract from *Pepper v Hart* (1992) including Lord Browne-Wilkinson's statement, *'In many cases references to parliamentary materials will not throw any light on the matter. But in a few cases it may emerge that the very question was considered by Parliament in passing the legislation.'* If one question then asked 'what justifications are there for referring to Hansard' you would not get many marks for just repeating this quote. But if you were to add to and explain the quote and give examples, such as explaining the limited conditions in which the court accepted a reference to Hansard was possible, then you should gain marks.

What questions can the examiner ask you? ●●●

A source-based question is not a particular type of question as such;
it is a way of giving you extra information on which to base your
answers. So the examiner can ask you different types of question
on the same source material.

→ You might be asked questions that purely test your knowledge of
  the area, e.g. in the statutory interpretation exercise on *Pepper v
  Hart* on page 192 you may be asked to outline the main extrinsic
  aids available. You have been given one, Hansard, but you need to
  explain others such as dictionaries, Law Commission Reports, etc.
→ You may be asked to comment on parts of the source, e.g. to
  discuss the advantages and disadvantages of using Hansard.
→ You may be set a problem or have to apply the source, e.g. in the
  Pepper v Hart exercise you might be given different sets of facts, an
  Act, and asked to say whether reference to Hansard could be made.

Being asked to complete a number of different types of question on
the same paper may seem harsh. In fact it helps you as it directs you
towards the particular skill needed for the answer, and you have the
chance to use those that you are good at as well as those you are not.

Making use of your own knowledge ●●●

The source material is not there to give you all the answers and
some of the information you need will not be in the source. In any case,
as with any exam, the highest marks come from bringing your own
understanding into your answer and selectively illustrating with the
best examples from your knowledge. So in the question on extrinsic
aids you would want to impress the examiner with your knowledge
of the full range, even to *travaux preparatoire* in the case of EC law
provisions. Similarly, in the question on the Practice Statement 1966 on
page 192 as to whether it should be restricted to the House of Lords
you should be prepared to explain and illustrate the sorts of arguments
put by Lord Denning in cases such as *Davis v Johnson* (1978), *Schorsch
Meier v Hennin* (1975), *Miliangos v George Frank Textiles* (1976).

Preparing a structure to your answers ●●●

In preparing structures for the various parts of the question on a
source, the same rules apply as for questions of that type anyway.
So if you are asked to 'discuss' then you should structure your answer
so that there is an introduction to the area, an argument supported by
appropriate law, etc. and finally some conclusions. If you are asked to
apply elements of the source to different situations then you should be
careful to separate the different situations and answer methodically,
remembering to support your points from the source and/or appropriate law. One final point to remember, if the question is in separate
parts, answer each part separately rather than in one lengthy jumble.
Also, if you find that you are writing the same answer to several
questions, you've got it wrong.

Watch out!

Remember that reading the questions is
just as important as reading the source
material.

Action point

Find a past source-based paper with
some application on it and write answers
to that part being careful to add in law,
etc. rather than just repeating the source.

Test yourself

Write a list of all of the important
information for an answer and mark down
next to each which came from the source
and which you introduced.

Watch out!

Sometimes marks for information are not
transferable between parts of questions.

Answering problem questions

Problem questions often seem the most frightening to answer but in fact with good technique you can probably score higher marks than you would on essays. This is because having been told the area of law you are to write on in an essay, the danger is that you repeat everything that you remember from your lecture notes rather than focusing on the question. In a problem, however, you are more likely to concentrate only on what is relevant.

Watch out!

As in essay questions, problems will probably not involve all of the law in the area the problem concerns.

Reading the problem ●●●

→ First of all you must always read the rubric because if it says that you must answer two problems and two essay questions you must do just that and not answer three of one and one of the other.
→ Secondly you must read the problem through very carefully because, usually, as well as giving a solution to the problem you will first of all have to identify what it is all about.

Action point

Check out past exam papers, particularly the most recent, and make sure, if there are different sections, that you know how many to do on each.

It is a good idea with problem questions to underline important words or to write down as you go along a brief note next to individual parts on what law the fact seems to be suggesting. Also write down cases the scenario reminds you of, then you can form a structure from this. Generally you need to write less for problems so the time spent preparing an answer is vital.

Identifying what the problem is about ●●●

You might not always see what a problem is about at first glance. What you should remember is that the examiner is trying to build up a set of facts in a problem that will make you think of existing cases or areas of law. There are a lot of 'buzz words' in problems that should lead you to the area of law the examiner wants you to answer on, e.g.:

The jargon

Buzz words simply means that some things appear in the problem that make the relevant law instantly recognizable.

→ In a criminal paper, if somebody has been killed it is obviously a homicide offence of some kind; if there is some medical negligence then causation may be an issue; if the killer suffered uncontrollable rages then diminished responsibility may be an issue.
→ In contract, if a party has entered a contract after being given false information there is a good chance the area is misrepresentation.
→ In tort, if a van driver has given a hitchhiker a lift against company rules and injured him while driving carelessly then vicarious liability is likely to be involved.

Test yourself

Spend some time looking through past papers just to identify what the problems are about.

The more practice you have of doing problems before the exam the easier it is to recognize what a problem is about, and answering past problem questions is a very good way of building up your understanding of the law and getting used to these types of scenarios.

Preparing a structure

However you write your answer, all problem questions involve going through the same basic process:

→ identifying key facts upon which resolution of the problem depends
→ identifying the appropriate law that is relevant to the facts
→ applying that law to the facts in the problem
→ reaching conclusions

Identifying the key facts in the problem

In interviewing a client in a solicitor's office, you might hear many irrelevant facts. Usually in exam problems all of the facts are relevant as the examiner is trying to point you in the right direction. It can still be important to organize the facts into some order, particularly if there are many different aspects to the problem. It is best to deal with each incident separately so that you do not forget anything.

Using only the appropriate law

It is very important to use only relevant law. There are three very important reasons for this:

1   using irrelevant law will gain you no marks and you will lose time that you could have spent writing things that would
2   if you bring irrelevant law into your answer it may confuse you when you are trying to apply the law to the facts
3   the examiner may think that you are just putting down everything that you know on the area in the hope that some of it is relevant

So, if the Occupiers' Liability problem concerns an electrician but no children then there is no point in using the cases you know on children. If the criminal law problem concerns a woman suffering from depression who has also suffered beatings from her husband and she kills him, then you know that it probably involves voluntary manslaughter and there is no need to write on involuntary manslaughter. Similarly if the contract problem on offer and acceptance does not involve any written communications then there is no point in treating the examiner to your extensive knowledge of the postal rule.

Applying the law to the facts

Here, you must analyse the situation in the problem and see how the law you have introduced fits the facts in order to reach a solution. Very often the facts in the problem will push you towards particular cases that you know or to sections of Acts.

Reaching conclusions

If the question says 'discuss the legal consequences', you do not have to reach a firm conclusion. If you are asked to 'advise', you must be prepared to say whether the party you are advising should sue or defend in a civil claim, or what their plea should be in a criminal trial.

Action point

Write a simple plan for a problem question and see whether it achieves all of these four points. There is no set order in which they should appear in your answer.

Examiner's secrets

Usually if there are many parts to a problem then the individual parts are simple to answer, so break the problem down into its parts to answer it.

Test yourself

Find a problem on a past paper. First identify the area of law, then practise using only relevant law by picking out the important facts one by one and then putting the relevant cases or sections of Acts next to them.

Watch out!

Make sure that you always do give advice in your conclusions if that is what you are asked to do.

Glossary of terms used in the book

Actus reus	In crime the 'guilty act' – can involve the conduct of the accused, the circumstances in which it occurs and also the consequences of the act
ADR	Alternative dispute resolution – including conciliation, mediation, and arbitration
Condition	In contract law a term of the contract that is essential and the breach of which then allows both repudiation and/or damages as a remedy
Conveyancing	The legal process for the transfer of land
Court of Chancery	The former court in which equity was used
Delegated legislation	Legislation that is not made by Parliament but by a subordinate body given the power to legislate by Parliament
Direct applicability	In EC law a measure that is directly applicable automatically becomes law in member states without need for enactment
Direct effect	In EC law a doctrine devised by the European Court of Justice that allows citizens of member states to enforce EC law in national courts
Disease of the mind	In the defence of insanity the cause of the defect of reason
Ejusdem generis	In statutory interpretation where a list of specific words is followed by general words the general words must be interpreted in the light of the list
Fiduciary	A special relationship depending on trust – examples include trustees and beneficiaries, solicitors and their clients
Expressio unius est exclusio alterius	In statutory interpretation a rule that where there is a list of specific words then words that are not mentioned are expressly excluded
Gross negligence	In manslaughter where a defendant owed the victim a duty of care and in causing the victim's death fell so far below the standard expected that it went beyond mere compensation and amounted to a crime
Innominate terms	In contract law where the court determines the remedy available for breach of a term by looking at the consequences of the breach rather than the classification of the term
Inter absentes	In contract law in unilateral mistake this is where the parties are contracting at a distance
Inter presentes	In contract law in unilateral mistake this is where the parties are in a face to face dealing
Invitation to treat	In contract law not an offer but an invitation for the other party to make an offer
Jellicoe procedure	A procedure introduced to speed up the passage of Law Commission proposals through Parliament
Malice aforethought	The mental element in murder – the intention to kill or to cause serious harm
Nervous shock	In tort an action to recover for psychiatric injury caused by a single traumatic event
Noscitur a sociis	A rule of statutory interpretation that a word should be interpreted by the words surrounding it
Obiter dicta	In a judgment legal comments made by the judge
Paralegal	A person working in law without professional qualifications
Per incuriam	In precedent means a case has been decided without reference to all the proper authorities
Per se	Means simply without having to prove damage
Probate	The process by which wills are proved
Promissory estoppel	In contract law where a party is prevented from going back on a promise made to another party to waive rights under an existing contract
Pure economic loss	In tort an action where the loss is purely financial, i.e. a loss of profit or loss of value – not generally accepted because tort usually provides recovery only for physical damage or injury
Quantum meruit	In contract law a payment for the part actually completed in a contract where there is less than full performance
Ratio decidendi	In a judgment this is the point of law that decides the case in the light of the material facts – so it is the reason for the decision
Res extincta	In contract law a common mistake that is based on the existence of subject matter of the contract which in fact, unknown to the contracting parties, does not exist
Res ipsa loquitur	In tort a way of reversing the burden of proof in negligence – it means the thing speaks for itself
Res sua	In contract law a common mistake as to the actual ownership of the property which is the subject matter of the contract
Restitutio in integrum	In contract law where parties want to return to their pre-contractual position this is only allowed if it is factually possible

Stare decisis	The Latin name for the doctrine of precedent – means let what is decided stand
Strict liability	In crime this is where liability can be proved without need to show *mens rea* and in tort it is where liability can be shown without need to prove fault
Ultra vires	This means beyond the powers – so it is usually an act by a body that has no authority for that particular act
Vicarious liability	This is liability for someone else's wrongs (most commonly of an employer for the wrongful acts of his employee)
Void contracts	In contract law a vitiating factor may mean that the contract was in effect never made
Voidable contracts	In contract law a vitiating factor may mean that one party may choose to avoid his obligations under the contract
Volenti non fit injuria	In tort a defence which means voluntary assumption of risk – to succeed the other party must have been aware of and accepted the actual risk
Warranty	In contract law a descriptive term of a contract for breach of which only damages is available

Sources of further reading

English legal system

Charman, Vanstone and Sherratt: *AS Law*. 3rd edn. Willan Publishing.
Derbyshire, P. (2002) *Eddy on the English Legal System*. 7th edn. Sweet & Maxwell.
Elliott and Quinn (2002) *English Legal System*. 4th edn. Longman.
Ingman, T. (2000) *The English Legal Process*. 8th edn. Oxford University Press.
Martin, J. (2001) *Key Facts: The English Legal System*. Hodder & Stoughton.
Martin, J. (2002) *The English Legal System*. 3rd edn. Hodder & Stoughton.
Martin, J. (2003) *Looking at the English Legal System*. Hodder & Stoughton.
Slapper, G. and Kelly, D. (2002) *Principles of the English Legal System*. 5th edn. Butterworths.

Criminal law

Allen, M. (2001) *Criminal Law*. 6th edn. Oxford University Press.
Bloy, D. (2000) *Principles of Criminal Law*. 4th edn. Cavendish Publishing.
Clarkson, C. and Keating, H. *Criminal Law: Text and Materials*. 5th edn. Sweet & Maxwell.
Jefferson, M. (2000) *Criminal Law*. 4th edn. Pearson.
Martin, J. (2001) *Key Facts: Criminal Law*. Hodder & Stoughton.
Roe, D. (2002) *Criminal Law*. 2nd edn. Hodder & Stoughton.
Smith, J. and Hogan, B. (2002) *Criminal Law*. Butterworths.
Storey, A. and Lidbury, A. (2002) *Criminal Law*. 2nd edn. Willan Publishing.
Turner, C. (2003) *Looking at Criminal Law*. Hodder & Stoughton.

Law of contract

Beale, Bishop and Furmston (2001) *Contract: Cases & Materials*. 4th edn. Butterworths.
Charman, M. (2002) *Contract Law*. 2nd edn. Willan Publishing.
Elliott and Quinn (2001) *Contract Law*. 3rd edn. Longman.
Furmston, M.P. (2001) *Cheshire & Fifoot's Law of Contract*. 14th edn. Butterworths.
Richards, P. (2002) *Law of Contract*. 5th edn. Longman.
Stone, R. (2000) *Principles of Contract Law*. 4th edn. Cavendish Publishing.
Turner, C. (2001) *Key Facts: Contract Law*. Hodder & Stoughton.
Turner, C. (2003) *Contract Law*. Hodder & Stoughton.

Law of tort

Cooke, J. (2001) *Law of Tort*. 5th edn. Longman.
Elliott and Quinn, (2001) *Tort Law*. 3rd edn. Longman.
Harpwood, V. (2000) *Principles of Law of Tort*. 4th edn. Cavendish Publishing.
Hodge, S. (2002) *Tort Law*. 2nd edn. Willan Publishing.
Kidner, R. (2002) *Casebook on Torts*. 7th edn. Oxford University Press.
Rogers, W. (2002) *Winfield & Jolowizc on Tort*. 16th edn. Sweet & Maxwell.
Turner, C. (2001) *Key Facts: Tort*. Hodder & Stoughton.
Turner, C. (2003) *Tort Law*. Hodder & Stoughton.

Index

absolute liability   62
acceptance   90, 91
acquittal, appeal against   30
Act of God   150
action plan order   37
Acts of Parliament   8, 9
actual bodily harm   70
actus reus   58–9
ADR   26
adult offender   36
advice agencies   46
agreement   112
Alternative Dispute
    Resolution   26
animals and liability in tort   143
appropriation   72
arbitration   26
arrestable offence   32
arson   75
assault   70
assault causing actual bodily
    harm   70
assault in tort   146, 147
attempts   65
automatism   77

bail   28
Bar Vocational Course   44
barristers   44
basis of assessment   114
battery   70
battery in tort   146, 147
Bills (Public Bills and Private
    Member's Bills)   8
binding precedent   5
breach   112
breach of duty of care   134
burglary   73
'but for test'   135
by-laws   9

Caldwell recklessness   61
capacity   96, 97
case law   4
case stated appeal   30
causation (criminal law)   59
certiorari   167
challenging a juror   52
citizen's powers of arrest   32,
    40–1
civil appeals   25
civil claims   24
civil courts   24
civil liberties   160, 164–5
civil remedies   36
codification   17
collective bargaining   95
commercial agreements   94, 95

committal proceedings   28
common assault   70
common law   4
common mistake   106
Common Professional
    Examination   44
Community Legal Service   46
Community Legal Service
    Fund   46
community service order   35, 37
conciliation   26
conditional fees   47
conditions   99
consent (criminal law)   71
consideration   92–3
consolidation of statutes   17
constructive manslaughter   68
consumer contract   125
consumer protection   128–9
contract law   89–122
Contracts (Rights of Third Parties)
    Act 1999   103
contributory negligence   151
control test   140
conveyancing   45
Council of Ministers of the EC   12
Council on Tribunals   27
County Court   24
Court of Appeal (Civil
    Division)   25
Court of Appeal (Criminal
    Division)   30
criminal appeals   30
Criminal Cases Review
    Commission   30, 31
criminal damage   75
Criminal Defence Service   47
Crown Court   29
Crown Court, appeals to   30
Crown Prosecution Service   29
Cunningham recklessness   61
curfew order   37

damages   36, 114
deception offences   74–5
Decisions   13
defamation actions   164
delegated legislation   9
denunciation   34
detention at a police station   33
deterrence   34
diminished responsibility   67
direct applicability of EC law   13,
    15
direct effect of EC law   15
Directives   13, 15
Director-General of Fair
    Trading   129

discharge of a contract   112–13
discharges (criminal law)   36
dishonesty   72
disposable capital   46, 54
disposable income   46, 54
dissenting judgments   5, 18
distinguishing   5
drunkenness as a defence to
    crime   80, 81
duress and undue influence
    108–9
duress as a defence to a
    crime   78
duress (in forming a contract)
    108
duress of circumstances   78
Durkheim   168, 170
duty of care   134
duty solicitor   47

early administrative hearings   28,
    51
economic duress   108
economic reality (multiple)
    test   140
electronic tagging   37
enabling Acts   9
equitable remedies   36, 42, 115
EU institutions   12, 13
European Commission   12
European Commission of
    Human Rights   161
European Court of Human
    Rights   160, 161, 163, 167
European Court of Justice   13, 25
European Parliament   12
evading a liability   74
ex turpi causa (illegality)   150
exemption clauses   100, 101
existing duty   93
extrinsic aids   11

false imprisonment   147
fast track cases   25
fault liability   133, 173
fingerprints   33
fitness for purpose   124
foresight of consequences   60
freedoms
    from discrimination   165
    of assembly   165
    of association   165
    of expression   164
    of movement   164
frustration   113
funding criteria   47

General Council of the Bar   44
golden rule   10

gross negligence manslaughter 69

Hart/Devlin debate 169
hierarchy of courts 6
hire of goods 126
honourable pledge clause 95, 117
House of Lords, appeal to 25, 31
House of Lords, judges in 48
human rights 162
Human Rights Act 1998 162

illegality in a contract 110
incitement 164
incorporation of terms 98
independence of the judiciary 49
indictable offence 28
inevitable accident 150
injunctions 36
innominate terms 99
Inns of Court 44
insane automatism 77
insanity 76
integration (organization) test 140
intention to create legal relations 94, 95
interests of justice test 47
interviews at police station 33
intimate sample 33
intoxication as a defence to a crime 80
intrinsic aids 11
invitation to treat 90
involuntary intoxication 80
involuntary manslaughter 68–9

judicial immunity 49
judicial review 166–7
Judicial Studies Board 48
jury
    in civil cases 53
    in criminal cases 53
    qualifications 52
    role 53
    trial by 29
just deserts 34
justice and law 171

language rules 11
Law Centres 46
Law Commission 17
Law Reform (Frustrated Contracts) Act 1943 113
Law Society 45
lay magistrates 50–1
legal executives 45
legal intent 94, 95
Legal Services Commission 46

Legal Services Ombudsman 45
legislative function 49
legitimate interest 110
literal rule 10
Lord Chancellor 45, 49

magistrates 50–1
magistrates' clerk 51
Magistrates' Court 28
making off without payment 75
malicious wounding 70
Mandamus 167
manslaughter 68–9
Marxist views on justice 171
mediation 26
mens rea 60–1
minimum sentences 34, 41
minors 96, 97
Minors' Contracts Act 1987 97
miscarriages of justice 31
mischief rule 10
misfeasance 137
misrepresentation 104, 105
Misrepresentation Act 1967 105
mistake (contract law) 106–7
mistake (criminal law) 81
mistake over documents 107
M'Naghten Rules 76
Montesquieu 49
morals 168–9
multi-track cases 25
murder 66–7
mutual mistake 107

natural law 170
necessaries 96
necessity as a defence to a crime 79
necessity as a defence to a tort 150
negligent misstatement 137
negotiation 26
'neighbour principle' 134
nervous shock 136
non-feasance 137
non-insane automatism 77
'non-natural use of land' 142
novus actus interveniens 151

obiter dicta 4, 5
objective recklessness 61
Obtaining property by deception 74
obtaining services by deception 74
Occupiers' Liability Act 1957 138, 139
Occupiers' Liability Act 1984 139

occupiers liability
    and children 138, 139
    and independent contractors 139
    and people carrying out a trade 139
offer 90
omissions and liability in negligence 137
omissions as *actus reus* 58
Orders in Council 9
overruling 5

PACE 32
Package Holiday Regulations 125
paralegals 44–5
part payment of a debt 93
participation 64–5
passing of property in goods 125
per incuriam 7
performance 112
personal injury cases 24
persuasive precedent 5
Plea and Directions Hearing 29
police powers 32–3
positivism 170
postal rule 91
powers of arrest 32
Practice Statement 1966 7
presumptions 11
previous convictions 35
primary victims 136
Prime Minister 49
prison sentences 36–7
private nuisance 144–5
privity 102–3
producer 128
prohibition 167
promissory estoppel 93
protection of society 34
provocation 67
public nuisance 145
Public Order Act 1986 165
public policy 134
pupillage 44
pure economic loss 137

Queen's Bench Division 6, 38
Queen's Bench Divisional Court 27, 30

ratio decidendi 4, 5
'reasonable man test' 134
recklessness 61
reformation 35
Regulations (EC) 13, 15
rehabilitation 35
remedies 36, 114–15

remedies in tort
  damages 151
  injunctions 151
remoteness of damage 115, 135
reoffending 34
reparation 35
rescission 36, 105
res ipsa loquitur 135
res sua 106
restitution 35
restraint of trade 110
retribution 34
reversing 5
rights
  and duties 172
  and interests 172–3
robbery 73
Royal Assent 8
rules 168
Rylands v Fletcher 142–3

sale by sample 125
Sale of Goods Act 1979 98,
  124–5
  acceptance of goods under 125
  implied terms 124
Sale and Supply of Goods
  Act 1994 98
satisfactory quality 124
Scott v Avery clauses 26
searching premises 32
secondary parties 64
secondary victims 136
self-defence in crime 79
self-defence in tort 151
self-induced automatism 77

sentencing aims 34
sentencing and Government
  policy 35
separation of powers 49
silence and
  misrepresentation 104
small claims cases 25
social and domestic
  arrangements 94
solicitors 44–5
specific intention 60
specific performance 36
stare decisis 4
state of the art defence 129
statutory authority 150
Statutory Instruments 9
stop and search 32
strict liability offences 62–3
subjective recklessness 61
sufficiency of consideration 92
summary offences 28
supervision order 37
supply of goods and services
  126–7
supranationalism 14
supremacy of EC law 14
sureties 28

tariff sentences 34
termination of an offer 90
terms and representations 98
terms of a contract 98, 99
theft 72–3
trade description 129
Training Contract 45
transferred malice 61

trespass to goods 148
trespass to land 148–9, 165
trespassers 138–9
triable either way offences 28
trial by jury 29
tribunals 27

undue influence 111
Unfair Contract Terms
  Act 1977 100–1
Unfair Terms in Consumer
  Contracts Regulations 1994
  101, 127
unilateral mistake 107
unreasonable use of land 144
unsolicited goods 127
utilitarianism 170
Utilitarian theories of sentencing
  34

vetting of jurors 52
volenti non fit injuria (consent)
  147, 150
voluntary intoxication 80
voluntary manslaughter 66–7

warranties 99
Wednesbury unreasonableness
  167
Woolf reforms 24, 45
wound 71
wounding with intent 71

young offenders 37
youth courts 28, 51
Youth panel 50